Contents

Zionism and the Quest for Justice in the Holy Land

Zionism and the Quest for Justice in the Holy Land

Edited by
Donald E. Wagner
and Walter T. Davis

Foreword by
Walter Brueggemann

PICKWICK *Publications* · Eugene, Oregon

ZIONISM AND THE QUEST FOR JUSTICE IN THE HOLY LAND

Copyright © 2014 Wipf and Stock Publishers. All rights reserved. Except for brief quotations in critical publications or reviews, no part of this book may be reproduced in any manner without prior written permission from the publisher. Write: Permissions. Wipf and Stock Publishers, 199 W. 8th Ave., Suite 3, Eugene, OR 97401.

Pickwick Publications
An Imprint of Wipf and Stock Publishers
199 W. 8th Ave., Suite 3
Eugene, OR 97401

www.wipfandstock.com

ISBN 13: 978-1-62564-406-0

Cataloguing-in-Publication Data

Zionism and the quest for justice in the Holy Land / edited by Donald E. Wagner and Walter T. Davis, with a foreword by Walter Brueggemann

xxiv + 250 p. ; 23 cm. Includes bibliographical references.

ISBN 13: 978-1-62564-406-0

1. Arab-Israeli conflict. 2. Jewish-Arab relations—Religious aspects—Christianity. 3. Christians—Middle East. 4. Christian Zionism—Controversial literature. 5. Middle East—Religion—20th century. I. Wagner, Donald E. II. Davis, Walter T. III. Brueggemann, Walter. IV. Title.

BT93.6 W34 2014

Manufactured in the U.S.A.

Acknowledgments

ANY PUBLICATION OF THIS scope takes a community to envision the task and bring it to print. As editors, we look back on this project with gratitude for the remarkably committed and talented team we were privileged to work with this past year.

The initial vision for this volume emerged through a series of conversations between the two of us that was gradually enlarged to involve our organizations: the Friends of Sabeel—North America (FOSNA) and the Israel Palestine Mission Network of the Presbyterian Church (USA) (IPMN). Once we drew up a concept paper and shared it with a few colleagues, the Board of Directors of FOSNA voted unanimously to support the project with a modest grant, and it was housed in our new Theology Committee. The Committee consisted of Dr. Walt Davis, Dr. Pauline Coffman, and Noushin Framke, all from IPMN, as well as Dr. Rosemary Radford Ruether (Claremont School of Theology and FOSNA) and Rev. Don Wagner (FOSNA's National Program Director). Within a relatively short period of time, we launched Phase I of a four-phase project by selecting eleven authors with expertise in the area of their chapter assignment.

The authors represent a remarkable diversity of scholarship, expertise, and experience in their particular area of research. They include Walt Davis, Pauline Coffman, Rabbi Brant Rosen, Carole Monica Burnett, Rosemary and Herman Ruether, Don Wagner, Gary Burge, Mustafa Abu Sway, Naim Ateek, and Mark Braverman. All were gracious and timely in delivering their chapters, and we deeply appreciate the time and commitment they brought to this project. We would add our appreciation to the respected theologian Walter Brueggemann, whose foreword is a welcomed addition.

Phase One of the project included a theology seminar in early April 2013 at Fuller Theological Seminary (Pasadena, CA), where the authors presented the initial drafts of their chapters to a group of twelve responders, who offered suggestions for content changes. Here we must thank the late

Prof. Glen Stassen and his assistant Abigail Cook for their hospitality and arrangements at Fuller, and the responders, who included FOSNA Board Chair John Erickson, Barbara Erickson, Jonathan Kuttab, Dr. Glen Stassen, Rev. Dr. Tony Wolfe, Jonathan Cook (Fuller), Rev. Katherine Cunningham (Moderator of IPMN), Noushin Framke (IPMN), Dr. Santiago Slabodsky (Claremont School of Theology), Rev. Darrel Meyers (FOSNA), theologian Ched Myers, Rev. Robert Assaly (Canadian Friends of Sabeel, or CFOS), Dr. Herman Ruether (Claremont).

Following the seminar, Phase II began. The authors were given sixty days to make revisions based on the suggestions offered at Fuller Seminary. In addition, each author had one or two content editors assigned to developing the second draft. They included Ched Myers, Rev. Tony Wolfe, and Rev. Robert Assaly, plus FOSNA friends Dr. Joy Lapp and Rev. Arnie Voigt. Once their editorial work was completed, Phase III began with three highly skilled, professional copy editors, who worked closely with the authors for nearly three months. Here we extend our profound gratitude to Barbara Erickson, Maurine Tobin, and Carole Monica Burnett for the long hours, careful work, and highly professional approach to this phase, which extended into four months.

By the end of October 2013, our team was ready to submit the manuscript to the publisher, Wipf and Stock, and Phase IV would commence, which would include the final editing and printing of the volume. We are indebted to Christian Amondson for his encouragement and guidance throughout the project as well as to Dave Belcher for his astute editorial advice. From the early stages of conceptualizing the volume to its completion, we have been touched by the passionate commitment of the authors, the responders, and the copy and content editors. As we present this volume to potential readers, we find ourselves indebted to all of those mentioned above and only hope that the final project will begin a critical conversation that will stimulate a long overdue debate on a subject often viewed as taboo in academic, church, and even political circles. We hope that our readers will be moved toward a more critical, compassionate, and realistic assessment of the "things that make for peace" and justice in the land of Jesus and the Prophets.

Walt Davis and Don Wagner
June 2014

Contributors

Mustafa Abu Sway holds the Integral Chair for the Study of Imam Ghazali's Work at Al-Masjid Al-Aqsa and at Al-Quds University in Jerusalem, Palestine. Prof. Abu Sway earned his B.A. at Bethlehem University (1984) and both his M.A. (1985) and Ph.D. (1993) at Boston College in Massachusetts. He has taught at the International Islamic University in Malaysia and at Bard College in New York; in addition, he was a visiting Fulbright Scholar-in-Residence at the Wilkes Honors College at Florida Atlantic University. Among his published works are two books: *Islamic Epistemology: The Case of Al-Ghazali* (Dewan Bahasa dan Pustaka, 1995), and *Fatawa Al-Ghazali* (ISTAC, 1996).

Gary M. Burge is Professor of New Testament at Wheaton College and Graduate School, an evangelical institution in Chicago. Among numerous other publications, he is the author of *Whose Land? Whose Promise? What Christians Are Not Being Told About Israel and the Palestinians* (Pilgrim Press, 2003, 2013) and *Jesus and the Land: The New Testament Challenge to "Holy Land" Theology* (Baker Academic/SPCK, 2010).

Carole Monica Burnett is the editor of, as well as a contributor to, the recent book *Zionism through Christian Lenses: Ecumenical Perspectives on the Promised Land* (Wipf and Stock, 2013). A member of the Antiochian Orthodox Church, she holds the Ph.D. degree in Early Christian Studies. She is employed as Editor of the Fathers of the Church series, published by the Catholic University of America Press, and as adjunct faculty member at the Ecumenical Institute of Theology and St. Mary's Seminary, both in Baltimore.

Pauline Coffman is a professor and director (retired) of the School of Adult Learning, North Park University, Chicago. She is a member of the Israel

Palestine Mission Network of the Presbyterian Church (USA), the Middle East Task Force of the Chicago Presbytery, and the Chicago Faith Coalition on Middle East Policy. Pauline attends First United Church of Oak Park, Illinois, formed by a union of PCUSA and United Church of Christ (UCC), and is a regular leader of traveling seminars to Israel/Palestine and other parts of the Middle East. Pauline serves on the Board of Directors of Kairos USA.

Walter T. Davis is a Presbyterian minister and professor emeritus of the Sociology of Religion at San Francisco Theological Seminary. He holds the M.Div. degree in theology from Union Theological Seminary and a Ph.D. in Social Ethics from Boston University. He is one of the founders of Keep Hope Alive, the annual olive tree planting and harvesting mission project of the San Francisco Bay Area Presbyteries in partnership with the YMCA of East Jerusalem and the YWCA of Palestine. Since 2008 he has been co-chair of the education committee of the Israel Palestine Mission Network of the Presbyterian Church (USA).

Brant Rosen is a congregational rabbi in Evanston, Illinois, the co-founder/co-chair of the Jewish Voice for Peace Rabbinical Council, and the author of *Wrestling in the Daylight: A Rabbi's Path to Palestinian Solidarity*, published in 2012 by Just World Books. The ideas expressed in his essay are his own and do not reflect the opinions or platforms of his congregation or any organization with which he is affiliated.

Rosemary and Herman Ruether are a team of spouses whose concerns and insights regarding Palestine and Israel have been discussed in their book *The Wrath of Jonah: The Crisis of Religious Nationalism in the Israeli-Palestinian Conflict* (Fortress Press, 1989, 2002). Herman J. Ruether, a political scientist with a special interest in Asian Studies, has served as acting director of the Palestinian Human Rights Campaign. Rosemary Radford Ruether, a theologian, has taught at the School of Religion of Howard University, at Garrett-Evangelical Theological Seminary, at the Pacific School of Religion, and at the Claremont Graduate School. She has published books and articles on feminism, ecology, and religion.

Donald E. Wagner is an ordained Presbyterian minister (PCUSA) and the National Program Director of Friends of Sabeel–North America. He was a Professor of Middle Eastern Studies and Director of the Center for Middle Eastern Studies at North Park University from 1995 to 2010, and National Director of the Palestine Human Rights Campaign from 1980 to 1989. He is the author of four books on the Israeli-Palestinian conflict, including *Anxious for Armageddon* (Herald Press, 1995) and *Dying in the Land of Promise: Palestine and Palestinian Christianity from Pentecost to 2000* (Milesende, 2003).

Foreword

Walter Brueggemann

The Rev. Dr. Walter Brueggemann, a scholar of the Old Testament and Professor Emeritus at Columbia Theological Seminary in Decatur, Georgia, has published a vast number of books and articles. These include The Prophetic Imagination *(Second Edition, Fortress Press, 2001) and* Theology of the Old Testament: Testimony, Dispute, Advocacy *(Fortress Press, 2012).*

THIS IMPORTANT COLLECTION OF essays is situated amid the most vexatious, dangerous geo-political crisis in the world. The seemingly intractable conflict in the Holy Land that concerns the State of Israel as well as the status and future of the Palestinians turns out to be the pivot point for much of the violent anger that leads to destabilization and threatens all parties to the dispute. The focal point of the many different angles in this collection is insistently justice as a precondition of peace in the Holy Land. Thus all "peace negotiations" are futile if a way is not found to assure justice of a political and economic variety. Such justice requires, perforce, a radical rethinking of practices and policies that continue to sustain and to legitimate political injustice and economic inequity. The writers in this collection are agreed that Zionism, in its intransigent politics and its military aggressiveness, is at the center of the crisis. Readers who have followed this long-standing issue closely will be further informed with important historical perspective. Readers who come to the issue with some lack of orientation will find this collection to be a reliable benchmark in the discussion concerning justice and equity in the Holy Land and an urgent summons to new thought and new policy formation.

Benedict Anderson, in his important but not-much-noticed book *Imagined Communities*, has shown the way in which nation-states are fundamentally practices of sustained imagination.[1] That imagination is an angle of vision prior to the facts that shapes and positions the facts to serve an interest that requires obedience and resists criticism. Thus "nationalism" in all of its variety is not primarily a matter of hardware or even of paper agreements. Rather, it is an outcome of rhetoric that characteristically reflects passion, eloquence, and courage along with some historical requirement. It is clear that the State of Israel is an act of compelling imagination that appeals to the biblical tradition and to the data of historical crisis. Insofar as Palestinian nationalism is given voice, it also is an act of imagination. So we deal with competing acts of imagination. Of course, the imagination that constitutes the State of Israel is much informed and legitimated in our eyes by an imagined U.S. constituted by Christian foundations that suggest a ready affinity with the State of Israel.

The historical lessons offered in this volume are an invitation to rework such acts of imagination. Thus the chapter on Orthodoxy focuses on the ways in which contemporary Orthodoxy has given courageous voice to human rights. The tracing of Catholic and especially Vatican sensibility evidences the ways in which the Vatican has moved, ever so slowly, to an awareness that is beyond a singular acknowledgment to the State of Israel. The Protestant analysis, in two chapters, deals with evangelical viewpoints and explores the ways in which mainline theologians Paul Tillich, Reinhold Niebuhr, and Krister Stendahl gave important support to the State of Israel when the post-war crisis of Jews after the German Holocaust was front and center in our awareness; they did not, however, voice any critique of or restraint about the State of Israel in its subsequent development. Another stimulating feature of this book is its inclusion of a Jewish and a Muslim perspective, each in a chapter of its own.

The volume is a powerful witness to the fact that 2015 cannot be a replay of 1940 or 1948 or 1950. While national imagination always takes some liberties with facts, such imagination must be to some extent informed by geopolitical realities. At the founding of the State of Israel, the danger to Jewish identity and existence was a defining preoccupation, but to continue to imagine the State of Israel in 2015 as we imagined it in the post-war period is an act of irresponsibility. Now the shoe of vulnerability is on the other foot, the foot of the Palestinians, and critical attention must be paid to that decisive alteration of political, economic, and military reality. Many of us—including a roster of leading Christians—are summoned by this volume to update national and international imagination to have some

---

1. Benedict Anderson, *Imagined Communities: Reflections on the Origin and Spread of Nationalism*, rev. ed. (New York: Verso, 2006).

informed contact with the facts on the ground. And the facts on the ground include the enormous economic and military power of the State of Israel, its control of institutions and finance, and a seemingly unrestrained practice of abuse, exploitation, and ruthless assaults on the vulnerable, so that a viable social life for Palestinians is placed in acute jeopardy.

While this matter is of great importance to Orthodox, Catholic, and Protestant communities, as is made clear in these essays, the matter is especially urgent for evangelicals. With too much airtime given to "Pastor Hagee" (he being such an easy target), it is clear that all the talk about "dispensationalism" and pre- and post-millennial faith needs to be demystified and exposed, as it is a gross misrepresentation of the gospel. My friend Bart Campolo, in our conversations on this matter, has reduced it to a simple calculus:

- Presently the State of Israel operates with a free pass in the international community.

- That free pass is made possible by U.S. policy, and Israel will not be restrained in its oppressive, aggressive policies and practices toward the Palestinians until U.S. policy is altered.

- U.S. policy cannot and will not be altered as long as evangelical Christians in the U.S. are singularly and without reserve committed to whatever policy Israel chooses to adopt.

For that reason, a reconsideration of such a policy is most urgent among evangelicals, so that what passes for theological thought of a simplistic kind can be tempered by historical reality as well as by a more sober reading of the theological tradition.

There is now an extensive literature, including the work of Mark Braverman, that shows how Christians are held in hock by accusations of anti-Semitism if they criticize Israel, or by a fear of such accusations that might come. It is clear now, as it could not have been clear in the 40s and 50s, that a critical stance toward the State of Israel is now an important matter, not only for the sake of the Palestinians, but for the sake of justice and security in the region. It will not do to re-perform the courage of Niebuhr and Tillich or any of the others who had such courage in support of Israel in those bygone days. There is, of course, great pressure simply to repeat that old stance. But such support only endorses and legitimates violent state policy that produces injustice and therefore precludes and prevents peace. Of course the matter is complex, but for a beginning, imagination must catch up with the realities on the ground.

The pressure against any new imagination is immense. I know only a little of it but enough of it. When I urged in print that Braverman's book merits positive attention, I received a thirty-minute scolding and reprimand from a friend, a highly respected professional advocate for Jewish-Christian relations. This little experience is not important. It is enough, however, to permit me to sense how important this reconsideration is, and how much is now required to bring our imagination into critical contact with new historical reality.

We may be grateful to the editors and the contributors to this volume for their clear, disciplined thought that summons to fresh work. New occasions do teach new duties! This volume makes clear that one such "new duty" is to recognize that issues of justice and peace pertain in powerful ways to the Holy Land (just as Deuteronomy insists). This is a summons to those of us who cherish Jewish tradition and Jewish friends and who are zealously committed to the security of the State of Israel to recognize that, in the long run, security depends on justice. (The same is true for the U.S., a truth we have yet to take seriously in our own national imagination.) In the short run, easy mantras and self-congratulatory shibboleths prevail. But we know better. This volume is one place from which to begin afresh.

Walter Brueggemann
Columbia Theological Seminary
October 7, 2013

Introduction

A Call for a New Conversation on Justice and Peace in Palestine and Israel

Donald E. Wagner and Walter T. Davis

BETHLEHEM PALESTINIAN PASTOR AND theologian the Rev. Dr. Mitri Raheb has summarized the influence of the Zionist narrative in the media, in political discourse, and in most churches and synagogues across Europe and North America as "mythistory."[1] While the term "mythistory" may be new to most of us, it has been discussed in academic circles at least since the Greek historian Herodotus. The central issue is how historians, theologians, politicians, and perhaps all of us distinguish between myth and actual historical events. How do the founding mythologies of a people shape history and the decisions of future political leaders? Whether we are discussing the Crusades, the conflicts in the Balkans, or the recent U.S. war in Iraq based on non-existent "weapons of mass destruction," how do politicians urge or even manipulate their people to adopt certain political decisions based on invented myths, and what are the actual facts that may be displaced or eclipsed in that process?

One of the most hotly debated cases of the collision of myth and history arises in the Israeli-Palestinian conflict. Raheb references the work of Israeli historian Shlomo Sand[2] for the application of "mythistory" to the history of Zionism and the Israeli-Palestinian conflict. Long before the issuance of the Balfour Declaration (1917), Zionists, both Christian and Jewish, had adopted the compelling public relations phrase "a land without a people for a people without a land." While the phrase had a convincing ring, the

---

1. Raheb, *Invention of History*, 13.
2. Sand, *The Invention of the Jewish People*.

facts on the ground pointed to a different reality. The actual population of Palestine in 1897 was 94 percent Palestinian Christian and Muslim whereas the Jewish population was approximately 5 percent and the remainder was mostly Western businessmen and missionaries.[3] Some historians have noted that the source of the "land without a people" myth may have been the British evangelical Christian writer and lobbyist Lord Shaftesbury, who in an article published in the *Quarterly Review* in 1839 called for England to support a Jewish state in Palestine and used the phrase "a country without a nation for a nation without a country."[4] Whether Shaftesbury invented the phrase or Zionist leaders generated it is beside the point. The mythistory of Palestine being a "land without a people" was successfully marketed and branded. The mythistory became a political program when the British Parliament adopted the Balfour Declaration (November 1917), and the Palestinian majority became invisible in the eyes of the Western powers, which readily embraced the Zionist narrative.

The goal of this volume is to call for a new conversation about the "mythistory" surrounding the Israeli-Palestinian conflict, a "mythistory" that has become the foundation of political Zionism and various forms of Christian Zionism. This narrative not only has shaped the theological discourse in the churches and synagogues in the West but also has dominated the ways in which the conflict has been analyzed and discussed in literature, in film, in most academic discourse, and most clearly in the formulation of foreign policy regarding Israel and Palestine by European and American governments.

While this discussion may seem "heady" or esoteric to some, it is the daily life and blood of Israelis and Palestinians as their conflict plays out on the land that the State of Israel has come to control. However, in recent years a new spirit of critical debate has emerged and is raising awareness of the crisis in the Holy Land on university campuses, in churches, synagogues, and mosques, and certainly in the halls of Congress and the media. With this new interest in a more critical conversation about Israel and Palestine, we believe the moment has arrived for the book we have written.

There are a number of unique features about the essays you will be reading. We have chosen to write these chapters in a journalistic style in order to make them more accessible and hopefully more readable for the layperson and casual reader. Each author writes from his or her particular religious or theological tradition, and, as a result, each brings a particular

3. These figures are based on quotations cited in two sources: Farsoun and Aruri, *Palestine and the Palestinians*, 43–44, and Rubenberg, *Israel and the American National Interest*, 26.

4. Sokolow, *History of Zionism*, 1:127.

perspective to the topic. The authors represent an average of twenty-five years of research, writing, reflection, and lived history with the Israeli-Palestinian conflict. They recognize the urgency of this conversation, and some have paid a significant price in terms of threats to their livelihood and reputation as they have lived out the responsibility to speak the truth of prophetic justice on this issue. Obviously, those resident in the United States have several protections that Palestinians living under the Israeli occupation do not have.

We have arranged the chapters with the history of Zionism at the beginning to set the stage for the theological and religious chapters that follow. We encourage readers to purchase the study guide that accompanies the book as it will take them deeper into the major issues.[5] We also urge readers to form a study group in their religious or academic communities or simply in their homes. Chapters One and Two trace the history of the Zionist movement, beginning with its roots in nineteenth-century European nationalism and in reaction to the powerful forces of anti-Semitism. They then follow the steps by which Zionism began as a marginalized movement among European and North American Jews, accumulated power and influence in the British Parliament with the issuance of the Balfour Declaration, and finally gained access to a succession of U.S. Presidents and Members of Congress who embraced the Zionist narrative.

Chapter Three by Rabbi Brant Rosen, a congregational rabbi in Evanston, Illinois, author, and chair of the Rabbinical Council of Jewish Voice for Peace, presents a lucid and passionate essay, "Rising to the Challenge: A Jewish Theology of Liberation." Rabbi Rosen calls for a recovery of the universal vision of justice and peace that is found in the Torah, the Hebrew prophets, and the early rabbinic tradition, yet is tragically absent in the current debate over the conflict in Israel-Palestine. Rosen warns that contemporary Zionism is becoming the "state religion" of most synagogues and within the organized and powerful Jewish establishment. He calls for a Jewish theology of liberation that uses different theological sources but finds common ground with Palestinian Christian (and perhaps Muslim) liberation theology and may provide a way forward that can bring the three Abrahamic religions together to reshape the discourse and even influence political formulations in the future.

Chapter Four begins the Christian theological section, starting with an ancient Christian ecclesiastical tradition, that of the Eastern Orthodox churches. Members of what is often called "the Mother Church," Orthodox Christians trace their origins in Palestine to the day of Pentecost. Their

---

5. Israel Palestine Mission Network, *Zionism Unsettled.*

theological formulations about Palestine and Palestinian Christianity are still shaped by the early church fathers, many of whom lived in Palestine and neighboring regions in the early centuries of Christianity. Dr. Carole Monica Burnett traces this theological and spiritual trajectory forward from the patristic literature and explains the ways in which that literature reflects the universal message of Jesus and the early church concerning such issues as land, people, the Kingdom of God, and the divine presence within the Church. Eastern Orthodox theology generally rejects both Jewish and Christian Zionist tendencies to reduce a theological interpretation of the land to a divine land grant for a particular ethnic group or nation, a view that can lead to a form of idolatry.

In Chapter Five Rosemary and Herman Ruether trace the responses of another ancient Christian tradition, Roman Catholicism, to Zionism and the growth of the State of Israel. Influenced by the centuries-old notion that the Jews had been relegated to perpetual homelessness by divine decree, the Vatican's initial statements in the late nineteenth and early twentieth centuries rejected the possibility that Jews might ever have control over the Holy Land. Their disbelief in the divinity of Christ allegedly disqualified them. After World War II and the establishment of the State of Israel, however, the Vatican came to focus on alleviating the sufferings of the Palestinian people, both Christian and Muslim. Moreover, the Second Vatican Council, with its statements of tolerance toward non-Christian religions, made obsolete the earlier theological concerns about a Jewish state. For these reasons the concern for social justice is now the primary aspect of the Vatican's approach to the current situation in the Holy Land.

Next in order is Chapter Six, "The Mainline Protestant Churches and the Holy Land," which describes the influence of the Zionist narrative as having acquired dominance in the media, in political discourse, and in the Protestant churches. The chapter begins with a brief review of the idea that eventually came to be known as "manifest destiny" and the way in which most European settlers carried with them the Christian understanding that they were on a "divine mission" as the new Israel and were entitled to settle and dominate a land that was already home to the native American populations. In what seems to have been an unfortunate but natural political progression, successive U.S. presidents and Christian leaders embraced the Zionist narratives and translated them into a pro-Zionist foreign policy, beginning with President Wilson's embrace of the Balfour Declaration. The chapter notes the overwhelming impact of the Nazi Holocaust on both presidents and theologians, leaving justice for the Palestinian people lost amidst the understandable urge to establish a home for the Jewish refugees of Europe. The chapter looks at three case studies of mainline Protestant

Christian Zionism in the theology of Reinhold Niebuhr, Paul Tillich, and Krister Stendahl, all theological giants in their time. The chapter concludes with the emergence of new movements within most Protestant denominations that work for justice for Palestinians and Israelis alike, although the jury is still out concerning their impact on the theological and political debate concerning the destiny of the Holy Land.

Chapter Seven by Gary Burge, Professor of New Testament at Wheaton College in Illinois, the flagship evangelical Christian college, examines the evangelical or fundamentalist Christian Zionist tradition. Dr. Burge summarizes and critiques the theology called "premillennial dispensationalism" and the ways it provides an interpretation of the Bible that lends itself to the privileging of the modern State of Israel not only as a fulfillment of biblical prophecy but also as a political movement. He reviews the rise of the Rev. John Hagee, pastor of the Cornerstone Baptist Church in San Antonio, Texas, who is president of the newly influential organization, Christians United For Israel (CUFI). Hagee has become the public face of evangelical/fundamentalist Christian Zionism, which now has representatives in every state in the United States and works closely with the powerful pro-Israel Jewish political lobby, the American Israel Public Affairs Committee (AIPAC). Burge focuses on various ways in which the CUFI program and the theology that drives it contradict basic biblical principles concerning a reformed evangelical understanding of the land, biblical prophecy, and biblical justice.

Chapter Eight comes to us from Jerusalem, where Professor Mustafa Abu Sway is a Professor at Al-Quds University. Dr. Abu Sway presents a compelling Muslim theological statement that is punctuated by his personal experiences as a Palestinian Muslim who has lived most of his life under Zionism and Israeli military occupation, with its daily humiliation and losses. He draws upon the Qur'anic vision that clearly states that all people are created as equal before God, and he finds common ground with the theology of prophetic justice that calls us to be Allah's emissaries of love, justice, and peace where there is no peace. His moving personal stories and analysis present a compelling call for a new conversation that is not confined to Christian-Jewish dialogue and action but must include the large Palestinian Muslim community if there is to be a truly just and durable peace in Palestine-Israel.

The final chapter, "A Concluding Theological Postscript," which also comes from Jerusalem, has been written by the "father" of Palestinian liberation theology, the Rev. Dr. Naim Ateek of the Sabeel Ecumenical Liberation Theology Center in Jerusalem. The Rev. Ateek summarizes the underlying thesis of the present volume:

> Zionism *is* the problem. Zionism is a doctrine that provides the
> State of Israel with a firm—even dogmatic—religio-national
> identity justified by an appeal to God's will, to historical mem-
> ory, and to mythical racial ancestry. It provides many Jews in
> Israel and worldwide with a deep-seated, emotionally powerful,
> personal and social identity. As such, Zionism is a theologically
> infused ideology of Jewish identity that has changed the course
> of Jewish life in the twentieth and twenty-first centuries. . . . Zi-
> onism with its creation of "A New Jew" has a dark side that has
> resulted in almost a century of Palestinian humiliation, dispos-
> session, and death.[6]

Ateek argues that Zionism is a false theology as it is the ideology that drives the daily humiliation, disenfranchisement, and dispossession of the Palestinians from their farms, homes, jobs, and future. As Zionist ideology is translated into evangelical, mainline Protestant, or Roman Catholic theology and church policy, it not only becomes an accomplice with the churches but the churches become Zionism's instruments. Ateek calls us to embrace the theological document *Kairos Palestine*, published in December 2009, which declares the Israeli occupation "a sin against God and human-ity" and calls us to redress the theological and political distortions that are bringing death and destruction to the Palestinian community.[7] He reminds us that the message of *Kairos Palestine* echoes the cry of the South African Christians struggling to end apartheid, who declared Christian support for apartheid a heresy and a sin against God and humanity. The challenge that the Palestine question brings is not an isolated issue in the Middle East or a problem only for the West, but it is a global challenge, and one that weighs heavily on the Christian and Jewish communities that bear much of the responsibility for creating this injustice.

When the highly regarded biblical theologian Walter Brueggemann reissued his important volume *The Prophetic Imagination* in 2013,[8] he noted in the new preface that the contemporary political, cultural, and religious context has shifted dramatically since the original was published in 1977. He points to the urgent need for courageous and principled lay people and leaders who can address our present political and social ills and articulate the prophetic tasks today. He names as the central issue of the twenty-first century the culture of consumerism that seduces Christian and other clergy,

6. Ateek. See pp. 218–19 of the present volume.

7. *Kairos Palestine*, section 2.5. The document is reprinted as an appendix to this book. It is also available at http://www.kairospalestine.ps/sites/default/Documents/English.pdf.

8. Brueggeman, *Prophetic Imagination*.

social critics, politicians, and nearly every sector of society and distracts them from addressing the most pressing injustices in today's world. The challenge before us is to return to the prophetic theology of the Hebrew prophets, Jesus, the prophet Muhammad, and other great leaders such as Mahatma Gandhi, Dietrich Bonhoeffer, Nelson Mandela, and Martin Luther King.

We believe the "mythistory" promulgated by political and Christian Zionism and accepted as historical fact by many of our political and religious leaders has been a major obstacle to genuine understanding of the Palestine question. The conversation and the actions that we are suggesting in this volume call for an honest, sometimes controversial, but necessary journey toward that which is true, just, and liberating for all—Palestinian and Israeli, Christian, Muslim, Jew, or secular—whoever we are and wherever we find ourselves in this issue. We hope and pray that the God of justice will lead us into a new future where the healing of the nations is truly possible, even in the land we call "Holy."

Bibliography

Brueggemann, Walter. *The Prophetic Imagination*. Revised edition. Minneapolis: Augsburg Fortress, 2001.

Farsoun, Samih K., and Naseer H. Aruri. *Palestine and the Palestinians*. 2nd ed. Boulder, CO: Westview, 2006.

Israel Palestine Mission Network of the Presbyterian Church (U.S.A). *Zionism Unsettled: A Congregational Study Guide*. Presbyterian Distribution Service (http://store.pcusa.org). 2014.

Kairos Palestine: A Moment of Truth: A Word of Faith, Hope, and Love from the Heart of Palestinian Suffering. 2009. www.kairospalestine.ps. Reprinted in an appendix in the present volume.

Raheb, Mitri. *The Invention of History: A Century of Interplay between Theology and Politics in Palestine*. Bethlehem, Palestine: Diyar, 2009.

Rubenberg, Cheryl A. *Israel and the American National Interest*. Urbana: University of Illinois Press, 1986.

Sand, Shlomo. *The Invention of the Jewish People*. Translated by Yael Lotan. London: Verso, 2009.

Sokolow, Nahum. *History of Zionism (1600–1918)*. Vol. 1. A facsimile reprint of the 1919 edition by Longmans, Green and Company of London. Chestnut Hill, MA: Adamant Media, 2001.

Introduction to Chapters One and Two

Walter T. Davis and Pauline Coffman

FOR ISRAEL AND THE organized American Jewish community, Zionism is one of the most influential ideologies of our times. Although the tenets of political Zionism have shifted over the years, the impact of Zionism continues unabated, shaping the identity of many Jews worldwide as well as the geopolitics of the Middle East, North America, and Europe. Our experience and research have led us to believe that over the years political Zionism has, in the words of Simcha Flapam, "hardened into this impenetrable, and dangerous, ideological shield."[1] This explains in part why a just peace in Israel-Palestine has been so elusive over the past sixty-five years. Our Jewish peacemaking partners, often called "Jews of conscience," have reminded us of God's command in the Torah, "Thou shalt not stand idly by."[2] This study is our attempt to engage individuals and congregations in a serious discussion of both that ideological shield and our theological and ethical responsibility as Christian peacemakers to help bring an end to Israel's military occupation of Palestine and to encourage justice, peace, and reconciliation between the two peoples. We have sought to provide a sympathetic yet critical overview of political Zionism. We also ask ourselves, and our churches, "What must we do to avoid standing idly by?"

The adherents of Christian Zionism accept a fairly common, unchanging doctrinal formulation derived in part from biblical texts. This is not the case

---

1. Flapam, *The Birth of Israel*, 8.

2. See Landau, *Thou Shalt Not Stand Idly By*. This phrase is the translation of Lev 19:16 used in the *Sifra*, the Halakic midrash to Leviticus. See "Sifra," *Jewish Encyclopedia*, at http://www.jewishencyclopedia.com/articles/13646-sifra. Holocaust survivor and Nobel Peace Prize winner Elie Wiesel claims this text as his mantra; for him it is the greatest of the commandments. See "Elie Wiesel to Wes: 'Thou Not Stand Idly By,'" at http://wesleying.org/2010/10/27/elie-wiesel-to-wesleyan-thou-shalt-not-stand-idly-by/, and Paulson, "Commencement 2011."

with the Jewish adherents of political Zionism, who have provided multiple interpretations of Zionism as historical circumstances have changed. We have found that the best way to understand Jewish Zionism today is to review the historical context as well as the ideas and the practices of a few of its major spokespersons from the late nineteenth century to the present. These include Theodore Herzl, the founder of organized political Zionism; three "cultural" Zionists (Ahad Ha'am, Judah Leon Magnes, and Martin Buber) who opposed Herzl's political vision; Vladimir Jabotinsky, the founder of Revisionist Zionism; David Ben-Gurion, leader of left-wing Labor Zionism and architect of the institutions that would shape the eventual State of Israel, as well as the first prime minister of Israel; Menachem Begin, the first prime minister from the right-wing Likud party; and Binyamin Netanyahu, the current Likud prime minister, who has presided over a steady hardening of right-wing Zionism.

The writers wish to express appreciation to the following people for their contributions to the editing of these two chapters: Robert Assaly, Mark Braverman, Carole Monica Burnett, Katherine Cunningham, Jeffrey DeYoe, Barbara Erickson, Noushin Framke, Donald and Nahida Gordon, Jonathan Kuttab, Joy Lapp, Brant Rosen, Maurine Tobin, Arnie Voigt, and Donald Wagner. The writers, not the editors, bear responsibility for the accuracy and the interpretation of this history.

The bibliographical information for this introduction appears at the end of Chapter Two.

Chapter One

Political Zionism from Herzl (1890s) to Ben-Gurion (1960s)

Walter T. Davis and Pauline Coffman

Historical Context

Political Zionism as Jewish Nationalism

IN EUROPE DURING THE second half of the nineteenth century, the Age of Nationalism and the Age of Imperialism converged. Building on ideas of the Enlightenment and the French Revolution, which promised equal rights for all, nationalist movements based on blood and soil arose all over Europe while their countries competed with each other to expand their colonial empires overseas. Political Zionism was one of these national-colonial movements, but Zionism faced obstacles that the other nationalist movements did not have: Jews were dispersed throughout Europe, had no common national identity, and possessed no common territory. Moreover, many had turned away from Jewish religious practices and become secular. In Western Europe this shift took the form of assimilation into the bourgeois culture of their host countries. In Eastern Europe, especially, many joined revolutionary socialist movements. Both forms of assimilation threatened Jewish identity.

Moving out of the sphere of religion, political Zionism sought to create a common secular ethnic identity among these diverse groups and to establish a homeland for all Jews in Palestine. Traditional Judaism had always taught that only God could redeem them and bring them back to Zion;

3

political Zionism replaced the hope of divine redemption with the dream of national redemption and the creation of a "new Jew" through human agency, to remove the scars of humiliation and oppression inflicted by centuries of Christian anti-Semitism and state oppression.

Max Nordau, a leading Zionist at the turn of the twentieth century, explained two major forces that gave rise to this kind of Zionism—racial pride and anti-Semitism:

> The new Zionism has grown only in part out of the inner impulses of Judaism itself, . . . out of an awakened pride in their racial qualities, out of ambition to save the ancient people for a long future and to add new great deeds of posterity to those of their ancestors.
>
> . . . The Jewish nationalist . . . must make tireless efforts to render the name Jew a title of honor. . . . He knows what terrible harm centuries of slavery or disability have done to his originally proud and upright character and he seeks to cure himself by means of intense self-discipline.
>
> . . . Only the return to their own country can save the Jewish nation, which is everywhere hated, persecuted, and oppressed, from physical and intellectual destruction.[1]

Nordau, like other Zionists before him, was fully aware of the depth of humiliation and shame of the past and the herculean tasks that the Zionist dream required:[2]

> The Zionists know that they have undertaken a work of unparalleled difficulty. Never before has the effort been made to transport several million people peacefully and in a short space of time, from various countries; never has the attempt been made to transform millions of physically degenerate proletarians, without trade or profession, into farmers and herdsmen; to bring town-bred hucksters and tradesmen, clerks and men of sedentary occupation, into contact again with the plough and with mother earth.[3]

---

1. Nordau, "1905 Survey of Zionism," *Jewish Virtual Library*, at http://www.jewishvirtuallibrary.org/jsource/Zionism/Nordau_Zionism_Survey.html, excerpted in Hertzberg, *The Zionist Idea*, 242–43. *The Zionist Idea* is a classic anthology of Zionist writings from 1843 to 1944, which includes excerpts from thirty-seven major Zionist thinkers.

2. For an examination of this humiliation and shame, see Goldberg, *The Divided Self*.

3. Nordau, "1905 Survey," excerpted in Hertzberg, *The Zionist Idea*, 144. See note 1.

Toward Emancipation in Western Europe

In the early nineteenth century, after the French Revolution and the introduction of the Napoleonic Code, Jews in Western Europe gained equal rights and began an apparent process of assimilation. Although they quickly ascended to prominent positions in finance, education, science, government, business, and the arts, full equality and social acceptance by non-Jews eluded them. Like a simmering volcano, the millennia-old prejudice and discrimination against them were ready to erupt at any time. This gave rise to the "Jewish Question."

The Question took a different form for Jews and for non-Jews. Non-Jews asked: "Can Jews be assimilated into our national culture without changing the nature of that culture?"[4] Jews wondered: "Even if we assimilate, will we ever be accepted as equals, free of anti-Semitism? Can we fully assimilate into France or Germany or Britain and remain Jews?"

Ongoing Oppression in Eastern Europe

The situation of Jews in Eastern Europe and the Russian Empire was markedly different from that of Jews in Western Europe, who suffered discrimination from Gentile social rejection and government failure to implement laws granting equal rights to all. In the East official legal discrimination and periodic pogroms had traumatized and pauperized the masses of Jewish residents. Shortly after the widespread pogroms of 1881, Russian Jews under the leadership of Leo Pinsker created a political movement named *Hibbat Zion* (Love of Zion), the purpose of which was to urge persecuted Jews to resettle in Palestine and create a national life of their own. In response, between 1882 and 1903, over thirty-five thousand Jews emigrated to Palestine and established agricultural settlements or created Jewish communities in Arab towns.[5] These agricultural settlements were capitalist, not

4. In our time the Senate of France struggled with a similar question regarding Muslims; in September 2010 it banned wearing in public a *burqa* or any veil that covers the face. So at a deeper level the "Jewish Question," and now the "Muslim Question" in France, involve a clash of exclusivities, each with its own claim to special status either by virtue of ethnic origin, divine election, or both. Christianity and Islam claim to be universal religions, but they dare not cast stones at the ethnic separatism of Jews, because Christianity and Islam also make claims that often sound to outsiders like imperialistic dogmas of exclusivity and superiority.

5. A greater number of Jews immigrated to the United States during this period and in most other periods of intense emigration from Europe, indicating that the Zionist negation of life in the *Galut* (exile from Palestine) was not acceptable to the majority of Jews.

socialist-communal, as would be the case in the following decades with the establishment of the collectivist kibbutzim. This wave of immigration is known as the First *Aliyah*.[6] Because of illness, Arab resistance, and other hardships, almost half of these new arrivals left the country.[7]

At the same time, contact with the modernizing trends of their host societies in Eastern Europe and Russia had begun to dissolve the unifying fabric of Jewish religious life. "The eastern form of the spiritual problem is absolutely different from the western," wrote Ahad Ha'am in 1897 shortly after the First Zionist Congress:

> In the West it is the problem of Jews; in the East the *problem of Judaism*. The first weighs on the individual; the second, on the nation. The one is felt by Jews who have had a European education; the other by Jews whose education has been Jewish. . . .
>
> It is not only the Jews who have come out of the ghetto; Judaism has come out, too. . . . of its own accord, wherever it has come into contact with modern culture. . . .
>
> In exile, Judaism cannot, therefore, develop its individuality in its own way. When it leaves the ghetto walls, it is in danger of losing its essential being, or—at very least—its national unity; it is in danger of being split up into as many kinds of Judaism, each with a different character and life, as there are countries of the dispersion.[8]

The debate about the value of diversity among Jews continues today. It is documented in the 2011 film by Alan Snitow and Deborah Kaufman entitled *Between Two Worlds*, which the liberal Zionist author Peter Beinart calls "one of the best films I've ever seen about the contradictions of American Jewish life."[9] Fear that internal diversity of opinion among Jews may weaken Jewish commitment to Zionism and consequently undermine U.S. support for Israel may be a dominant factor in the effort of major Jewish

---

6. *Aliyah* means "ascent." Departure from Palestine is called *yerida*. These terms are derived from two sections of the Psalter known as the Psalms of *Aliyah*. Both groupings recall the arduous return from exile to Jerusalem in the sixth century BCE. Psalms 107–119 culminate with the triumph of the rebuilding of the Temple, and Psalms 120–134 with the building of the city walls. Ascent connotes both spiritual "return" and the physical climb, with Mount Zion rising four thousand feet above the Dead Sea.

7. "The First Aliyah," *Jewish Virtual Library*, http://www.jewishvirtuallibrary.org/jsource/Immigration/First_Aliyah.html.

8. Ha'am, *The Jewish State and the Jewish Problem*, excerpted in Hertzberg, *The Zionist Idea*, 266–67.

9. *Between Two Worlds*; see http://btwthemovie.org/.

organizations in the United States to maintain control over the public discussion about Israel-Palestine.

Major Contributors to the Development of Political Zionism

Theodor Herzl (1860–1904), Founder

Theodor Herzl is generally regarded as the father of *organized* political Zionism. During the last half of the nineteenth century, prior to Herzl's conversion to Zionism, numerous proposals were made by Jews and non-Jews alike for a national homeland for Jews. The pogroms that terrorized Jewish communities in the Russian Empire from 1881 to 1884 and in 1903 and 1905 precipitated the immigration of millions of Jews to America and Western Europe and of thousands to Palestine, demonstrating the need for a Jewish homeland. It was Herzl's writings, organizing, and tireless diplomacy that, at the end of the nineteenth century, created an international Zionist movement with *institutional structures*.

Herzl was a thoroughly secular Austro-Hungarian Jew bent on assimilating into Gentile culture until the Dreyfus Affair in France, where he was living as a journalist during the mid-1890s. His desire for assimilation died with the Dreyfus Affair. Captain Alfred Dreyfus, a Jew and a member of the French General Staff, was falsely accused of treason for allegedly giving French military secrets to the Germans. Herzl covered the trial and the ceremony during which Dreyfus was stripped of his captain's epaulets and publicly humiliated while a French mob cried, "Down with the Jews!" Anti-Semitic outbursts followed all over France.

As a result, in 1896 Herzl wrote *The Jewish State*, calling for the creation of a national homeland for all Jews. Certain ideas of Herzl gained widespread acceptance among many Zionists, although at the time Zionism was still a marginal ideology among most Jews. Taken together, Herzl's views formed a consistent and mutually reinforcing Zionist worldview that would gain in strength among Jewish immigrants in Palestine in the decades after Herzl's death. The central features of his Zionism were as follows: (1) anti-Semitism is a permanent, endemic, and ineradicable element of European cultures; (2) Jewish life and culture in the *Galut* (Exile) is distorted, producing passive, servile, and self-deprecating masses of people; (3) only a Jewish state can provide safety and well-being for Jews and reverse the negation of the *Galut* by creating a new Jew; and (4) therefore, once a Jewish state is created, Jews should eventually immigrate to their national homeland, thus bringing an end to anti-Semitism.[10]

Herzl's rhetoric was persuasive, and he produced many ringing passages calling for Jewish emancipation, such as the following on the status of Jews in the Diaspora:

> You are pariahs. You always have to worry about being deprived of your rights and your property. On the streets you are subject to ridicule, if not more. When poor, you doubly suffer. If you are rich, you have to hide your wealth. You are not tolerated in respectable professions, and if you deal in money, you are seven-fold endangered and humiliated. You are blamed for socialism, like everything else. This will not change, will not improve. . . . There is only one way out. To the promised land! . . . The promised land, in which we can have a crooked nose, a black beard, or a bent leg, without being shamed . . . so that the epithet "Jew!" will become a term of honor, like German, British, French.[11]

On the necessity for a Jewish state:

> The Jewish Question still exists. It would be foolish to deny it. It is a misplaced piece of medievalism which civilized nations do not even yet seem able to shake off, try as they will. They proved they had this high-minded desire when they emancipated us. The Jewish question persists wherever Jews live in appreciable numbers. Wherever it does not exist, it is brought in together with Jewish immigrants. We are naturally drawn into those places where we are not persecuted, and our presence there gives rise to persecution. . . . I consider the Jewish question neither a social nor a religious one, even though it sometimes takes these other forms. It is a national question, and to solve it we must first of all establish it as an international political problem to be discussed and settled by the civilized nations of the world in council. We are a people—*one* people. We have sincerely tried everywhere to merge with the national communities in which we live, seeking only to preserve the faith of our fathers. It is not permitted us. In vain are we loyal patriots.[12]

10. Some of these ideas have been disputed by both Zionists and non-Zionists. For example, Abba A. Solomon's 2011 monograph, *The Speech and Its Context*, recounts the attempt in 1950 of the American Jewish Committee to persuade Prime Minister David Ben-Gurion and other Israeli Zionists to repudiate their negative view of Jewish life in America and the call for Western youth to return "home" (to the state of Israel).

11. Beit-Hallahmi, *Original Sins*, 38.

12. Herzl, *The Jewish State: An Attempt at a Modern Solution of the Jewish Question*, excerpted in Hertzberg, *The Zionist Idea*, 208–9.

On creating a new breed of Jews:

> And what glory awaits the selfless fighters for the cause! There-
> fore I believe that a wondrous breed of Jews will spring up from
> the earth. The Maccabees will rise again. . . . We shall live at last
> as free men on our own soil, and in our own homes peacefully
> die. The world will be liberated by our freedom, enriched by our
> wealth, magnified by our greatness. And whatever we attempt
> there for our own benefit will redound mightily and beneficially
> to the good of all mankind.[13]

And on the choice before Jews, to emigrate or to be absorbed:

> Nowhere can there be a question of an [immediate] exodus of
> all Jews. Those who are able or who wish to be assimilated will
> remain behind and be absorbed. When . . . a systematic Jewish
> migration begins, it will last only so long in each country as that
> country desires to be rid of its Jews. How will the current be
> stopped? Simply by the gradual decrease and final cessation of
> anti-Semitism. Thus it is that we understand and anticipate the
> solution of the Jewish problem.[14]

In 1897 Herzl convened the First Zionist Congress in Basel, which in
turn established The Zionist Organization (later renamed The World Zionist Organization) to implement the stated goal of the congress: "Zionism
seeks to establish for the Jewish people a publicly recognized, legally secured, home in Palestine."[15] From then until his death in 1904 Herzl traveled
the world negotiating with the sultan of the Ottoman Empire, the German
kaiser, the king of Italy, the pope, and many other political leaders to gain
diplomatic support for his Zionist dream.

Cultural, Humanistic Zionists: Ahad Ha'am (1856–1927), Judah Leon Magnes (1877–1948), and Martin Buber (1887–1965)

Ahad Ha'am was born in Eastern Europe (the Russian Ukraine), where the
situation of Jews was considerably different from that in Western Europe.
He opposed the "political materialism" of Herzl's form of Zionism "which
sees the physical organism—the Jewish State—as the be-all and end-all of
Jewish life." Instead he insisted on an "uplifting of the body by the spirit,"

13. Ibid., 225–26.

14. Herzl, *Address to the First Zionist Congress*, excerpted in Hertzberg, *The Zionist Idea*, 230.

15. See http://www.jewishvirtuallibrary.org/jsource/Zionism/firstcong.html.

the gradual inner transformation of Jewish culture in Palestine by a cultural elite. This revived Jewish community would embrace the true spirit of Judaism, the ethical teaching of the Hebrew prophets; this spirit would then expand to transform Jewish life all over the world.

Ha'am's critique of Herzl's Zionism, from *The Jewish State and the Jewish Problem:*

> The spiritual problem appears in two differing forms, one in the West and one in the East. . . . The western Jew, having left the ghetto and having sought acceptance by the gentile majority, is unhappy because his hope of an open-armed welcome has been disappointed. . . . The pursuit alone [of a Jewish State] is sufficient to cure him of his spiritual disease, which is that of an inferiority complex. . . .
>
> [Judaism] does not need an independent State, but only the creation in its native land of conditions favorable to its development: a good-sized settlement of Jews working without hindrance in every branch of civilization. . . .
>
> Political Zionism cannot satisfy those Jews who care for Judaism. . . . A political ideal which is not grounded in our national culture is apt to seduce us from loyalty to our own inner spirit and to beget in us a tendency to find the path of glory in the attainment of material power and political domination, thus breaking the thread that unites us with the past and undermining our historical foundation.[16]

The American Reform Rabbi Judah Magnes (1877–1948), who helped found Hebrew University in Jerusalem, and the renowned social philosopher Martin Buber (1878–1965) were heirs of the cultural Zionism of Ahad Ha'am. In a 1930 pamphlet entitled "Like All the Nations?" Magnes took exception to political Zionism's negation of the Diaspora, declaring: "The dispersion of this people, the Diaspora, is a marvelous instrumentality for the fulfillment of [Judaism's] function as a teacher. The dispersion is an irrevocable, historical fact, and Palestine can be a means of making this fact into an even greater blessing. . . . The dispersion and Palestine are both required for the fullest development of the Jewish people."[17]

---

16. Ha'am, *The Jewish State and the Jewish Problem,* excerpted in Hertzberg, *The Zionist Idea,* 264–68.

17. Magnes, *Like all the Nations?* (pamphlet printed in Jerusalem, 1930), excerpted in Hertzberg, *The Zionist Idea,* 445, reproduced in *JTA* archive, at http://www.jta.org/1930/01/24/archive/full-text-of-dr-judah-l-magness-pamphlet-like-all-the-nations.

Magnes also favored a binational state of Jews and Arabs, warning against "ordinary nationalistic patriotism."[18] He was alert to the dangers of dependence on military force: "If as a minority we insist upon keeping the other man from achieving just aims, and if we keep him from this with aid of bayonets, we must not be surprised if we are attacked and, what is worse, if moral degeneration sets in among us." And he warned against the call for an exclusive state: "The slogan Jewish state or commonwealth is equivalent, in effect, to a declaration of war by the Jews on the Arabs."[19]

Martin Buber argued for cultural Zionism on biblical grounds of truth and righteousness. Israel must be something more than a state: "The prophets knew and predicted that in spite of all its veering and compromising Israel must perish if it intends to exist only as a political structure."[20] He held up righteousness as the true basis for Israel: "I am setting up Hebrew humanism in opposition to that Jewish nationalism which regards Israel as a nation like unto other nations and recognizes no task for Israel save that of preserving and asserting itself."[21] And he warned that Israel would be in peril without its spiritual mission: "There is no re-establishment of Israel, there is no security for it save one: It must assume the burden of its own uniqueness; it must assume the yoke of the Kingdom of God."[22]

Ze'ev (Vladimir) Jabotinsky (1880–1940): Founder of Revisionist Zionism[23]

Jabotinsky came to prominence in the Jewish community in Palestine (the *Yishuv*) in the 1920s and 1930s. While he agreed with other Zionist leaders that "the only rescue [for Jews] is general immigration to Palestine," Jabotinsky

18. Ibid., 447.

19. Magnes, "Opposition to the Biltmore Declaration," quoted in Goren, *Dissenter in Zion*, 46.

20. Buber, *The Jew in the World*, (address delivered in Frankfurt am Main, Germany, 1934), available at http://beth-torah.org/sites/www/uploads/adultlearning/13345MHL_072509_class.pdf, excerpted in Hertzberg, *The Zionist Idea*, 455.

21. Ibid., 459.

22. Ibid., 457.

23. Revisionist Zionism became the secular right-wing ideology of the Zionist movement in opposition to the more dominant labor Zionism, which was socialist during Jabotinsky's time. Revisionist Zionism's primary goal was the creation of a Jewish state in all of Mandatory Palestine (*Eretz Yisrael*) by military conquest. It consistently opposed all plans to partition Palestine into two states, one Jewish, the other Arab. The Likud party of current Israeli Prime Minister Benjamin Netanyahu is the heir of Jabotinsky's Revisionist Zionism. Shlaim, "The Likud in Power," 278–93.

rejected the idealistic view of human nature that he detected in Labor Zionism, which took over the leadership of the Palestinian Jewish community during the early twentieth century. At that time many socialist Jews from Russia immigrated to Palestine. He also rejected Labor's gradualist program. Instead, he adapted Herzl's idea of a "new breed of Jews," believing a state could come only through militant "selfless fighters for the cause." He was forthright about the need for a military conquest of the land, colonial settlement by Jews, and the expulsion of Arabs. In one of his earliest essays, written in 1910 and entitled "Man is a Wolf to Man," he wrote: "Worse than the wolf is man to man, and this will not change for many days to come. We will not change this through political reforms, nor through culture. . . . Stupid is the person who relies on justice. Justice exists only for those whose fists and stubbornness make it possible for them to realize it. . . . This is the only way of surviving in this wolfish battle of all against all."[24]

Jabotinsky was born in the cosmopolitan city of Odessa, where his father was a wealthy merchant. Although his family kept a kosher household and he began studying Hebrew as a boy, the gifted young Jabotinsky was thoroughly assimilated into the European culture of his time. He attended Russian, not Jewish, schools, and went on to study law in Switzerland and Italy. He mastered several languages, wrote articles in eight, and poetry in four. In time he became a journalist, orator, poet, essayist, and novelist.

In 1915 he helped form a Jewish Legion in Egypt to fight alongside the British and for a time commanded the paramilitary *Haganah* (Defense) forces of the Jewish community in Jerusalem. The heroic militarism of Garibaldi's Italian volunteers captured his imagination and served as a model for his version of Jewish nationalism. The Jewish history that inspired his pride was not that of the Diaspora but of the military accomplishments of the Maccabees.

In 1921 Jabotinsky was elected to the Zionist executive but resigned in 1923 over policy differences and founded a youth movement, *Betar*, whose name has two meanings: (1) an acronym for the Jewish settler Joseph Trumpeldor whose dying words while defending his settlement against an Arab revolt in 1920 were, "Never mind, it is good to die for our country,"[25] and (2) the place name of the last Jewish fort to fall to the Romans in 135 CE during the revolt led by Simon bar Kokhba. The message was clear: stand and fight, even if you sometimes lose. The anthem that he wrote for *Betar* envisions a new race of Jews who transform themselves from degradation

---

24. Avineri, *The Making of Modern Zionism*, 164.
25. Yadid, "Word of the Day/Tov lamut be'ad artzeinu."

by dint of "blood and sweat" into a people who are "proud, generous, and cruel."[26]

Jabotinsky's most influential essay, "The Iron Wall," was written in 1923, long before the attempted Nazi genocide would provide Zionists with the ultimate rationale for establishing a nation-state in Palestine as a haven for the Jewish people, regardless of the impact on an existing population and culture. No colonization can succeed by ignoring the "iron law" of armed force, Jabotinsky believed. "That is morality for you," he asserted. "Zionism is a colonizing adventure, and therefore it stands or falls by the question of armed force. It is important to build, it is important to speak Hebrew, but unfortunately, it is even more important to be able to shoot. . . ."[27] Israeli scholar Benjamin Beit-Hallahmi summarizes Jabotinsky's position:

> The Labor Zionist attitude towards the natives and their predic-
> ament was one of denial. The right-wing approach, developed
> by Jabotinsky, stated bluntly that the conflict was real, that dis-
> possession was real and inevitable, but it was justified to fulfill
> Zionist plans. . . . The right-wing Zionist attitude was one of
> defiance and confidence. The natives would have to accept their
> fate—namely an historical defeat. Right-wing Zionism has been
> quite open, even proud, about the colonialist role of Zionism
> and about its inherent violence vis-à-vis the natives of Palestine.
>   Jabotinsky . . . did not play games nor mince his words.
> He called a spade a spade and Zionism armed colonialism.
> Jabotinsky never denied the conflict between Zionism and the
> Palestinians. On the contrary, he made it into one of the basic
> assumptions of his political program.[28]

In 1925 Jabotinsky organized his own Zionist party, the Revisionists. A decade later he broke with the World Zionist Organization and founded the New Zionist Organization. In 1937 hardliners in the *Haganah* defense forces split off to form the underground militia *Irgun*, adopting the militant ideology of the Revisionists. The *Irgun* carried out violent attacks on their British rulers until Israeli statehood in 1948, and on Palestinian villages during the same time period. Their most notable acts of terrorism were the bombing of the King David Hotel, which housed the British Mandate head-quarters, in Jerusalem on July 22, 1946, and the massacre of Palestinians in the village of Deir Yassin on April 9, 1948.

---

26. See the website Hebrewsongs.com, "The Betar Song," at http://www.hebrews-ongs.com/song-shirbetar.htm.

27. Beit-Hallahmi, *Original Sins,* 103.

28. Ibid.

The *Irgun* emblem captures the heart of Jabotinsky's doctrine: the establishment of a Jewish state in all of Palestine by military force. Superimposed on a map of the British Mandate of Palestine, including Trans-Jordan, is a hand-held rifle. Underneath the map are the words, "Only Thus."

The current website of The Zionist Youth Movement, *Betar* USA, contains pictures of Jabotinsky and the *Irgun* emblem with the words *Eretz Yisrael* ("The Land of Israel") written across the map. Although Ben-Gurion and other Labor Zionists managed to modulate and even neutralize Jabotinsky's influence in the 1920s and 1930s, his fundamental doctrine of the essential necessity of military force is firmly embedded today not only in the Israeli Defense Force, the Likud party, and other parties on the right, but in other more centrist parties as well.

David Ben-Gurion (1886–1973): Labor Zionism Prior to Statehood in 1948

Major figures in the development of Labor Zionism include Moses Hess, Ber Borochov, and A. D. Gordon.[29] In his 1862 work *Rome and Jerusalem,* Hess, a former colleague of Karl Marx who had broken with materialistic determinism in favor of an ethical socialism, called for a Jewish state in which Jews would engage in agricultural labor for the "redemption of the soil" and cease being merely an intermediary non-productive class of merchants.[30]

Almost half a century later, the Russian Marxist Borochov did a class analysis of the economic forces that produced "the inverted pyramid" of European Jewish society, with a preponderance of professionals and a paucity of workers and peasants. The pyramid could be righted, he thought, only by proletarian Zionism in a Jewish state in Palestine.

Arthur Hertzberg claims that A. D. Gordon is Labor Zionism's secular mystic and saint. Gordon left his family in Russia and immigrated to Palestine in 1904 to devote his life to "the religion of labor." Hertzberg states, "The

29. Hertzberg, *The Zionist Idea,* 117–39; 353–86.
30. Hess, *Rome and Jerusalem.*

redemption of man as a whole, and of the Jew in particular, could come, he believed, only through physical labor."[31] Gordon and Borochov inspired the establishment of the first kibbutz, Degania, near the Sea of Galilee in 1909.

Ben-Gurion, who is regarded as the founding father of the State of Israel, was undoubtedly deeply influenced by these pioneers of Labor Zionism. He was born in Plonsk, Poland, as David Grün, became a Zionist during his youth, and at age seventeen helped create the *Poale Zion* (Workers of Zion) political party in Poland. He also helped organize Jewish self-defense following the Kishinev (Russia) pogrom in 1903, which left nearly fifty dead and seven hundred houses destroyed.

In 1906 he left Poland for Palestine to join the growing number of immigrant Zionist farm workers, gained membership in the *Poale Zion* party of Palestine, and swore never to speak Yiddish again. Later, like other early Zionist pioneers, he would drop his European family name, Grün, in favor of a Hebrew name, Ben-Gurion ("Son of Lions"). In his memoirs Ben-Gurion describes how his motivation for going to Palestine differed from the rationale provided by Herzl and other Western European Zionists:

> For many of us, anti-Semitic feeling had little to do with our dedication [to Zionism]. I personally never suffered anti-Semitic persecution. Plonsk was remarkably free of it . . . Nevertheless, and I think this very significant, it was Plonsk that sent the highest proportion of Jews to *Eretz Israel* from any town in Poland of comparable size. We emigrated not for negative reasons of escape but for the positive purpose of rebuilding a homeland . . .[32]

Ben-Gurion quickly rose in the ranks of Zionists, becoming a delegate to the Eleventh World Zionist Congress in 1913. In 1915 he was exiled by the Turkish rulers of Palestine and spent three years in New York organizing American Labor Zionism. Then in 1918 he persuaded a large group of Russian Jews in the United States to join him in Palestine to serve in the British military under the command of General Edmund Allenby. This put him in the good graces of the British, who would soon replace the Turkish rulers of Palestine as World War I came to an end.

31. Ibid., 369–70.
32. Ben Gurion, *Memoirs*, 36.

The Balfour Declaration: Diplomatic Recognition of a Future Jewish State

It was a propitious time for the up-and-coming Ben-Gurion, because the Zionists had recently achieved their most significant victory to date, namely, the formal international diplomatic endorsement of Jewish claims to a homeland in Palestine. After intense diplomatic lobbying in London by Chaim Weizmann and other Zionist leaders, this approval came in the form of the Balfour Declaration, a brief letter by Lord Balfour, the British foreign secretary, to Lord Rothschild, one of the preeminent British Zionists. The declaration reads:

> Foreign Office,
>
> November 2nd, 1917
>
> Dear Lord Rothschild,
>
> I have much pleasure in conveying to you, on behalf of His Majesty's Government, the following declaration of sympathy with Jewish Zionist aspirations which has been submitted to, and approved by, the Cabinet.
>
> His Majesty's Government view with favour the establishment in Palestine of a national home for the Jewish people, and will use their best endeavours to facilitate the achievement of this object, it being clearly understood that nothing shall be done which may prejudice the civil and religious rights of existing non-Jewish communities in Palestine, or the rights and political status enjoyed by Jews in any other country.
>
> I should be grateful if you would bring this declaration to the knowledge of the Zionist Federation.
>
> Yours,
>
> Arthur James Balfour[33]

For reasons particular to each country, the United States, France, Italy, Holland, Greece, Serbia, China, Siam, and Japan quickly endorsed the Balfour Declaration. In December 1920, the League of Nations mandated Britain to rule over Palestine and included the terms of the Balfour Declaration in the official mandate. These were heady times for Zionism, for the most challenging goal of Herzl's dream—formal international support for a national homeland for Jews—had been achieved, albeit through a declaration made a world away, without the input of the indigenous people. Ben-Gurion

---

33. See http://www.jewishvirtuallibrary.org/jsource/History/balfour.html.

and his colleagues could now direct all of their attention to the other half of the dream—the actual creation of a Jewish state.

Creating the Institutions of a Future State

The tireless, charismatic Ben-Gurion now became a central player in the Jewish community in Palestine. In 1920 he helped found the *Histadrut* (General Federation of Hebrew Workers), which became the dominant organization for collectivized land settlement and cultivation. Ben-Gurion served as its general secretary from 1921–1935, turning the federation into a welfare organization for all Hebrew workers and creating a holding company for the investment of workers funds. The federation would become the heart of the developing socialist Jewish economy.

The *Haganah* (Hebrew Defense Organization) was founded in 1920 and put under the control of the *Histadrut* labor federation, giving Ben-Gurion a dominant role in military affairs in addition to his influence on the economy and the political life of the Jewish community. After statehood in 1948, the *Haganah* would become the core of the Israeli military.

In 1922 the League of Nations authorized the establishment of "an appropriate Jewish Agency. . . as a public body for the purpose of advising and co-operating with the [British] Administration of Palestine in such economic, social and other matters as may affect the establishment of the Jewish National Home and the interests of the Jewish population of Palestine. . . ."[34] Seven years later the Sixteenth Zionist Congress officially created the Jewish Agency for Palestine, a virtual Jewish government-in-formation. Ben-Gurion headed this agency from 1935 to 1948, serving as the de facto head of the Jewish community. When the state was established on May 14, 1948, the Jewish Agency of Palestine became the provisional government of Israel, with Ben-Gurion as its first prime minister. With the exception of two years during the 1950s, he served as both prime minister and minister of defense until his retirement in 1963.

Labor Zionist Ideology

From the time of his early years in Palestine until the end of World War II, Ben-Gurion repeatedly gave voice to the dominant ideology of Labor Zionism—the revolutionary task of creating a new Jew in a new Jewish state,

---

34. "League of Nations: The Mandate for Palestine," *Modern History Sourcebook*, at http://www.fordham.edu/halsall/mod/1922mandate.html.

where pioneer Zionists would honor labor, conquer the land, restore Jewish dignity, be free from fear generated in Gentile nations, and have opportunity for individual creativity. It would be a socialist, collectivist, egalitarian, Hebrew-speaking society.

The dream was utopian and persuasive. Speaking to Zionist youth in Haifa in 1944 in an address entitled "The Imperatives of the Jewish Revolution," Ben-Gurion repeated themes of earlier political Zionists but gave them a socialist twist:

> No parallel exists in the history of any nation to the unique fate of the Jews, . . . an inspired people that believed in its pioneering mission to all men, in the mission that had been preached by the prophets of Israel. . . . This people was the first . . . to see the vision of a new human society. . . .
>
> After two thousand years of exile our numbers would not be so small were it not for two factors: extermination and conversion. These have plagued us since the beginning of the *Galut* [Exile]. Many Jews could not bear the ever-present contempt, persecutions, and expulsions; they could not withstand the fear that was forever threatening. . . . Yes, individuals may have surrendered and left our ranks—*but the nation as a whole neither surrendered nor lost heart!* . . . In the *Galut* the Jewish people knew the courage of *non-surrender*. . . . [But] resisting fate is not enough. *We must master our fate; we must take our destiny into our own hands!*
>
> *Galut* means dependence—material, political, spiritual, cultural, and intellectual dependence . . . . Our independence will be shaped . . . by the conquest of labor and the land . . . self-government and self-defense . . . the ingathering of the exiles . . . self-reliance . . . *the unity of its protagonists* . . . the development of the Hebrew language and culture, freedom for the individual and the nation, co-operation and social responsibility . . . and the welding together of the arrivals from the various Diasporas into a nation.
>
> *The goal of our revolution . . . is the complete ingathering of the exiles into a socialist Jewish state.*[35]

At the time, Ben-Gurion knew that World War II was winding down. He also knew that their next great challenge would be the fight for independence and the struggle for official recognition by the European powers. This may account for Ben-Gurion's strong condemnation of factionalism in the

35. Ben-Gurion, "The Imperatives of the Jewish Revolution," excerpted in Hertzberg, *The Zionist Idea*, 607–18.

labor unions, kibbutz movement, and *Mapai* (the socialist labor party that he helped found in 1930):

> Unity is the imperative of our mission and our destiny. Nevertheless, of all the values in our movement it is the one that is perhaps most honored in theory and least respected in practice. . . . The habits of disunity and anarchy which grew wild among us in the course of hundreds of years of exile and subservience cannot easily be corrected. . . . Only together, in one *Hehalutz*[36] and in one Socialist-Zionist party, in a united Jewish community and an undivided World Zionist Organization, can we assure Jewish immigration (by whatever means), redeem and rebuild the land, and fight our way through to victory.[37]

Ben-Gurion and company would win the struggle for a Jewish state in Palestine, but he would not be able to maintain the socialist dream of Labor Zionism long after independence.

The Elephant in the Room

Missing from Ben-Gurion's speech is any mention of the elephant in the room—the presence of over 1.3 million Palestinian Arabs who comprised over two-thirds of the population of British Mandate Palestine and who for decades had been resisting Jewish settlement, sometimes violently. This reticence to mention the "Arab Problem" in public was characteristic from the inception of Zionism, although most, including Herzl himself, recognized that a Jewish state would require the forceful removal of Palestinians. In a diary entry of 1895, Herzl had written: "We must expropriate gently the private property on the state assigned to us. We shall try to spirit the penniless population across the border by procuring employment for it in the transit countries, while denying it employment in our country."[38] As early as 1914, Chaim Weizmann, who would play a major role in lobbying British leaders on behalf of Zionism and would become Israel's first president, spoke of a marriage between a people that "has no country" and "a country without a people," a myth later transformed into propaganda as "a land without a people for a people without a land."[39]

36. The *Hehalutz* (Pioneer) Movement, was a world Zionist association that prepared young Jews to settle in Palestine and engage in a life of labor there, principally on kibbutzim.

37. Ben-Gurion, excerpted in Hertzberg, *The Zionist Idea*, 614. See note 35.

38. Morris, *Righteous Victims*, quoted in Alam, *Israeli Exceptionalism*, 76.

39. Masalha, *Expulsion of the Palestinians: The Concept of "Transfer" in Zionist*

Although the 1917 Balfour Declaration had called for the protection of Palestinian rights, and later, in 1948, the Israeli Declaration of Independence would assure "complete equality of social and political rights to all its inhabitants irrespective of religion, race or sex,"[40] there is little evidence that these promises were anything more than window dressing.

During the 1920s and 1930s, Jabotinsky and the Revisionists would have no truck with a denial of "The Arab Problem." They had been forthright in declaring that Jewish conquest of the land would require the removal of all the Palestinian Arabs by force. At the time, although Ben-Gurion was committed to the control of the whole country and to the political domination of Palestinian Arabs by obtaining a Jewish majority through massive immigration, he feared that use of force or even the rhetoric of force would alienate the international community. After the Palestinian riots of August 1929, he had objected to the proposal to organize an army and seize power:

> The world will not permit the Jewish people to seize the state as a spoil, by force. . . . We would then be unable to awaken the necessary forces for building the country among thousands of young people. We would not be able to secure necessary means from the Jewish people, and the moral and the political sustenance of the enlightened world. . . . Our conscience must be clean . . . and so we must endorse the premise in relation to the Arabs: The Arabs have full rights as citizens of the country, but they do not have the right of ownership over it.[41]

Between 1930 and 1936 the Jewish population in Palestine doubled, exacerbating Palestinian fears of dispossession and Jewish dominance and leading to the Arab revolt of 1936 to 1939. At the same time, Jewish fears were stoked by the increasing anti-Semitism of Nazi Germany. Events like *Kristallnacht* (the November 9, 1938, "night of broken glass"), when gangs of Nazi storm troopers destroyed seven thousand Jewish businesses and burned over nine hundred synagogues in cities all over Germany, reinforced the fundamental premise of Zionism: as the revisionists argued, Jews must take charge of their own destiny and provide a homeland for all Jews, irrespective of resistance from Palestinian Arabs or anyone else.

By this time, in the late 1930s, Ben-Gurion had come to recognize the irreconcilable differences between the national aspirations of most Zionists and the response of the indigenous Palestinians: "There is fundamental conflict. We and they want the same thing: We both want Palestine. And that

---

Political Thought, 1882–1948, quoted in Alam, *Israeli Exceptionalism,* 77.

40. See http://www.jewishvirtuallibrary.org/jsource/History/Dec_of_Indep.html.

41. Teveth, *Ben-Gurion and the Palestinian Arabs,* 97.

is the fundamental conflict. . . . I now say something which contradicts the theory which I once had on this question. At one time, I thought an agreement [with Palestinians] was possible."[42] In 1937, at the height of the Arab Revolt, he asked Elimelech Avnir, the *Haganah* paramilitary commander in Tel Aviv, to draw up guidelines for the complete takeover of Palestine should the British relinquish their governing role. At a meeting of Jewish Agency Executive in June 1938, Ben-Gurion declared, "I am for compulsory transfer; I do not see anything immoral in it."[43]

Later, Ben-Gurion would be more explicit about the problem that Zionist settler colonialism had created. In an interview in 1956 with Nahum Goldmann, President of the World Jewish Congress, Ben-Gurion described the elephant in the room as Jewish versus Palestinian survival:

> If I was an Arab leader, I would never make terms with Israel. That is natural; we have taken their country. Sure, God promised it to us, but what does that matter to them? Our God is not theirs. We come from Israel, it's true, but that was two thousand years ago, and what is that to them? There has been anti-Semitism, the Nazis, Hitler, Auschwitz, but was that their fault? They only see one thing: we have come and stolen their country. Why should they accept that? They may perhaps forget in one or two generations' time, but for the moment there is no chance. So, it's simple: we have to stay strong and maintain a powerful army. Our whole policy is there. Otherwise the Arabs will wipe us out.[44]

A major factor in desensitizing the Zionists to Palestinian concerns during World War II was the growing awareness, after the Nazi annihilation of the Warsaw Ghetto in April 1943, of the enormity of Hitler's "final solution." Nothing else could have so reinforced a major premise of Zionism, that Jews would never be safe in Gentile societies. With the survival of millions of Jews at stake, Palestinians became even more invisible and dispensable to the Zionist leadership.

Implementation of Plans for Ethnic Cleansing

The opportunity to begin systematic transfer, today commonly called "ethnic cleansing," came in December 1947 when, in response to the United

---

42. Ibid., 171.

43. Pappé, *The Ethnic Cleansing of Palestine*, xi.

44. Goldmann, *The Jewish Paradox*, 99–100.

Nations resolution on partition, Palestinians vandalized Jewish buses and shopping centers. Thus began retaliatory Jewish attacks on Palestinian villages and urban neighborhoods. In March 1948, Ben-Gurion and his advisors adopted the *Haganah's Plan Dalet*, which called for the systematic and total expulsion of Palestinians from their homeland.[45] From December 1947 until the armistice between Israel and its Arab neighbors in 1949, this strategy of ethnic cleansing would remove all the inhabitants from over five hundred Palestinian villages, totally destroy over four hundred Palestinian villages, create 750,000 Palestinian refugees, and kill most who resisted dispossession of lands and homes.

The new State of Israel that came into being on May 14, 1948, would justify this policy as a necessary defense against the invading Arab armies of Egypt, Jordan, Lebanon, and Syria. However, Palestinian and Israeli historians point out that before the arrival of the Arab armies on May 15, 1948, Jewish militia had already committed large-scale massacres of Palestinians and "cleansed" the land of over 250,000 Palestinians. They also note that the Arab armies never attacked Israel proper (that is, the area allotted by the UN for a Jewish state) but restricted their military activities to the defense of that portion of Palestine that the UN had allocated for an Arab state.[46]

In sum, Ben-Gurion and company were so preoccupied with Jewish nationalism as the answer to the Jewish Question and a solution to the plight of European Jews, that the needs of the Palestinians were either denied or dismissed. Because they were seen as a backward people with no moral claim to the land since they had not developed it as the Zionists would, their rights were regarded by Zionists and the Western world as of little consequence. In 1919 British Foreign Secretary Lord Balfour had given unapologetic expression to colonial racism, which Zionists shared with the Western world, when he declared: "In Palestine we do not propose to go through the form of consulting the wishes of the present inhabitants. . . . The four great powers are committed to Zionism, and Zionism, be it right or wrong, good or bad, is rooted in age-long tradition, in present needs, in future hopes, of far profounder import than the desires and prejudices of the seven hundred thousand Arabs who now inhabit that ancient land."[47] Although Ben-Gurion was more tactful than Jabotinsky, and more sensitive to international opinion, in 1947 and 1948 his policies mirrored those of the Revisionists: grab as much land as we can and drive the Palestinians off it by military force. This represents a compromise of

45. Pappé, *Ethnic Cleansing*, 28.

46. Ibid., 129–30.

47. Edward Said, *The Question of Palestine*, quoted in *Only a Northern Song*, "Review of Edward Said's 'The Question of Palestine,'" at http://northernsong.wordpress.com/2011/02/25/review-of-edward-saids-the-question-of-palestine/.

the idealism of Ben-Gurion's earlier years. After the state was founded, Ben-Gurion would have to make even more compromises, radically altering his original socialist-Zionist dream.

Ben-Gurion the Pragmatist—Compromises and Contradictions: 1948–1963

If new occasions teach new duties, they sometimes demand uncomfortable compromises and even contradictions. After independence Ben-Gurion engineered a number of compromises that would radically alter the dream of the Labor Party and prepare the way for its replacement by its nemesis, a new incarnation of Revisionism.

A Parliament Without a Bill of Rights for All Citizens

When the armistice took effect in 1949, a constituent assembly was elected to write a constitution. Ben-Gurion realized that the assembly was too diverse to agree upon the basic principles of a constitution, so he persuaded a majority to convert the constituent assembly into a parliament (the Knesset), who would rule with a set of "basic laws" rather than a constitution. This arrangement provided several advantages. For the religious parties, the absence of a constitution with a bill of rights meant the Orthodox Rabbinate did not have to relinquish its control over marriage, divorce, burial, Sabbath observance, and other matters. For all parties, it meant that the pledge in the Declaration of Independence of equal rights for all citizens would not be enshrined in national law. This opened the door for what in time would become a Jim Crow system of laws, discriminating in favor of Jewish Israelis and necessarily against Palestinian Israelis who comprised one fifth of the population.[48]

New Demographics: From Centralized Socialism to a Market Economy

In the first decade of the new state, the Jewish population almost doubled. Holocaust survivors poured in from Europe; hundreds of thousands of Sephardic and Mizrahi[49] Jews from Morocco, Algeria, Tunisia, Egypt, Syria,

---

48. Adalah, the Legal Center for Arab Minority Rights in Israel, maintains an updated report of all of the discriminatory laws in Israel. See http://www.adalah.org/eng/Articles/1771/Discriminatory-Laws.

49. Sephardic Jews are those descended from Spanish and Portuguese Jews. Today

Iraq, and other Middle Eastern countries flooded Israel to escape the actual violent blowback or fear of blowback over the partition of Palestine, the creation of a Jewish state, the ethnic cleansing of Palestinians in 1947 and 1948, and the Sinai War of 1956.

By 1961 Jews from North Africa and Arab countries comprised 45 percent of the Israeli population and formed what has been called "Second Israel," a lower class of clerks, small retailers, car mechanics, taxi drivers, vegetable peddlers, and agricultural workers employed by the kibbutzim. The culture clash with the majority of Ashkenazi (European) Jews was intense. The Jews of "Second Israel" were religious rather than secular, modest in dress, opposed to gender equality, unaccustomed to collective living and child raising, and market-oriented rather than socialist.

Some of the Mizrahi (Arab Jews) were well-known poets and writers who joined with Palestinian poets to form a union of Arabic writers. In March 1955 Palestinian and Jewish poets held a conference of Arabic poetry in Nazareth attended by over five hundred people.[50] However, this bond between Palestinians and Arab Jews would not last, as many Mizrahi realized that "self de-Arabization was the key factor that would ensure their full integration into the more veteran Israeli Jewish society...."[51]

As early as 1951 Ben-Gurion realized that to provide housing and jobs for all anticipated immigrant refugees and to cover Israel's trade deficits, he would need foreign investment and aid grants. At the risk of subverting the planned economy of the all-powerful *Histadrut* (federation of labor unions), he launched the Israel Bonds Campaign and encouraged Jews in the Diaspora to start up private companies in Israel. He also recognized the need for a unifying institution other than the socialist *Histadrut* to initiate a process of cultural assimilation so that the diverse cultures of world Jewry could begin to form a new national identity. The unifying institution he chose was the military with its spirit of national pride, discipline, obedience, courage, and sacrifice. He called the new pragmatism "statism" and began creating a state cult or civil religion of patriotic nationalism to mobilize the diverse population. The intention was to make room for the rich diversity of economic, political, religious, and cultural differences without undermining national unity.

Many Labor Zionists were furious at the gradual marginalization of socialist institutions and influence and their replacement with capitalist

the term is often used to refer to almost any Jew who is not Ashkenazi (from Europe). This includes the Mizrahim (Jews from Arab countries) as well as Jews from North Africa and elsewhere.

50. Pappé, *The Forgotten Palestinians*, 78.

51. Ibid., 119.

institutions. In 1981, four years after the right-wing Likud party had taken the reins of government, Shlomo Avineri, professor of political science at Hebrew University and prominent leader of the Labor Party, ended his book *The Making of Modern Zionism* with these words:

> Laissez-faire economics—so well attuned, as Milton Friedman pointed out, to Jewish existence in the West—cannot be squared with the ethos of social responsibility necessary for nation-building in Israel, and the attempt to erect such an economy in Israel will always have catastrophic results for the social cohesion of its society. Laissez-faire in an Israeli context means bringing Exile back to Israel.[52]

In late 1953, just before Ben-Gurion took a two-year break from public life, he appointed the hard-nosed, charismatic Moshe Dayan as chief of staff of the Israeli Defense Force. Dayan epitomized the new ideal of Israeli manhood, rivaling if not eclipsing the image of the pioneer farmer-fighters with a hoe in one hand and a gun in the other. Although Ben-Gurion was back in office in 1956, when Israel went to war with Egypt in the Sinai, it was Dayan who emerged as the warrior-hero of the new generation. (In a 2005 poll of the general public, held by the Israeli news website *Ynet* to determine the two hundred greatest Israelis, Dayan would be voted the seventy-third greatest Israeli of all time.)

Ben-Gurion and the Bible

Ben-Gurion also introduced a major contradiction in Labor Zionism's commitment to a secular state by using the Bible as the foundation for Israeli nationalism. Although he too was a thoroughgoing secularist, Ben-Gurion saw the creation of a Jewish state in Palestine as a reflection of the biblical stories of exodus from exile in Egypt and the conquest of the land of Canaan. "Since I invoke Torah so often," he declared, "let me state that I don't personally believe in the God it postulates. . . . I am not religious, nor were the majority of the early builders of Israel believers. Yet their passion for this land stemmed from the Book of Books. . . . [The Bible is] the single most important book in my life."[53]

52. Avineri, *The Making of Modern Zionism*, 226–27.

53. Merkley, *American Presidents, Religion, and Israel*, quoted in "David Ben-Gurion on Belief in the Bible," *Jewish Virtual Library*, at http://www.jewishvirtuallibrary.org/jsource/Quote/bg6.html.

His reading of the Bible was buttressed by archeologists like W. F. Albright, whose literalist views of the biblical text helped Ben-Gurion achieve unity and messianic purpose for the new Jewish state. From the early 1950s until his retirement from public life in 1963, he conducted Bible studies every two weeks in his prime ministerial residence or his kibbutz in the Negev, lecturing to a wide range of political leaders and scholars.[54] In his memoirs Ben-Gurion noted the role of religious motivation in the recruitment of Jewish immigrants to Israel:

> Without a messianic, emotional, ideological impulse, without the vision of restoration and redemption, there is no earthly reason why even oppressed and underprivileged Jews . . . should wander off to Israel of all places. . . . The immigrants were seized with an immortal vision of redemption which became the principal motivation of their lives.[55]

Not surprisingly, his favorite book of the Bible was Joshua, which tells a story of the Israelite conquest of the land, the annihilation of the Canaanites, the settlement of the land by the twelve tribes of Israel, and a ceremony in which all the people promise to be faithful to their covenant with God.

In 1959 all the sessions were devoted to the book of Joshua. In one of those sessions Ben-Gurion compared the false consciousness of Diaspora Jews with the authentic consciousness of the builders of the new nation of Israel. Brushing aside rabbinical commentary on Joshua, he declared to the group of scholars present:

> Conquest, settlement, tribe, nation—I doubt if a scattered and dispersed people without a land and without independence is capable of knowing the true significance and full meaning of these words. They did not participate in conquests and did not know what is involved in conquest. And the same holds true for settlement. Only with the rebirth of Israel in our generation did these vague concepts take on flesh and we have become aware of their content and essence. Now that we are aware, we must delve anew into the stories of the Bible.[56]

In this manner the secular Ben-Gurion appropriated the biblical stories for a nationalistic civil religion that would buttress the expansionism

---

54. Ben-Gurion, *Ben-Gurion Looks at the Bible*, is a collection of Ben-Gurion's lectures to his Bible study groups.

55. Ben-Gurion, *Israel: A Personal History* quoted in Rose, *The Question of Zion*, 45.

56. Piterberg, *The Returns of Zionism*, 382.

of both religious and secular settlers after the Six-Day War in June 1967.[57] British scholar Jacqueline Rose, whose Christian Gaust Seminars at Princeton University were published in 2005 under the title *The Question of Zion,* comments on the effect of what she describes as Ben-Gurion's biblical messianism: "Slowly but surely the universalism of the socialist dream is absorbed back into the particularity of Jewish identity."[58]

The bibliographical information for this chapter appears at the end of Chapter Two.

57. In the preface to the German edition of *Fatal Embrace: Christians, Jews, and the Search for Peace in the Holy Land,* the Jewish American psychologist Mark Braverman observes that the civil religions of Nazi Germany and apartheid South Africa were both supported by state churches. Braverman expanded on this in an unpublished e-mail on April 3, 2013: "The civil religion of Zionism, which developed in the late nineteenth century, albeit non-theistic in origin, was ultimately embraced by the Orthodox Jewish establishment in Israel, and has now become a part of the religious identity and sensibility of Jews worldwide along a broad continuum of theology and practice, from progressive to conservative."

The discussion of civil religion in regard to Nazi Germany and apartheid South Africa is found in the preface to Braverman's *Verhängnisvolle Scham: Israels Politik und das Schweigen der Christen,* 11–24.

58. Rose, *The Question of Zion,* 47.

Chapter Two

From 1967 to the Present—The Triumph of Revisionist Zionism

Walter T. Davis and Pauline Coffman

IN CHAPTER ONE WE described several diverse forms of Zionism. These distinctions began to disappear after the June 1967 war, when they were eclipsed by Revisionist Zionism, a right-wing branch of political Zionism. Chapter Two describes the factors contributing to this phenomenon.

Zionism Turns to the Right: The Third Arab-Israeli War (June 5–10, 1967)

By the mid-1960s a long-standing pattern of belligerence between Israel and its Arab neighbors had been established. The pattern included an ongoing war of words, frequent cross-border attacks, and other mutual provocations that would eventually lead to another war. Each side would lick its wounds and then start the process again. In the spring of 1967 it appeared to both sides that the other was preparing for war. In May the Soviet Union informed Egypt that Israel was preparing for war against its ally, Syria. Nasser responded by ordering the removal of United Nations peacekeeping forces, which had been patrolling the Sinai since the end of the 1956 war.[1] Nasser also blocked the Straits of Tiran (between the Red Sea and the Gulf of Aqaba), thereby cutting off the Israeli port of Eilat. The Israeli govern-

1. The 1956 war, which was focused on the Suez Canal, involved Egypt, Israel, Britain, and France.

ment called this provocation an "act of war." Many Israelis, Europeans, and Americans feared another Holocaust. Would the Arabs finally achieve their threat to drive Israel into the sea? The General Staff of the Israeli Defense Force knew otherwise, and so did U.S. intelligence.

On June 2 the General Staff confronted the Israeli cabinet with the unanimous demand for an immediate preemptive strike against Egypt. General Matti Peled insisted that it would take a year and a half to two years for the Egyptian military to prepare for a full-scale war. General Ariel Sharon insisted on a preemptive strike "without delay." General Ezer Weizman threatened to resign as deputy chief of staff. When Prime Minister Levi Eskol and his cabinet insisted on waiting for diplomatic support, the army announced to the public, "The delay in attack is due to diplomatic considerations, but the existential threat remains imminent." Public pressure on the government mounted quickly. The U.S. government gave its blessing to a preemptive strike. The Israeli government then ordered the strike to begin on June 5.[2]

The ensuing Israeli victory was overwhelming. Israel destroyed the military capabilities of Egypt, Jordan, and Syria; took Gaza and the Sinai from Egypt; pushed Jordan out of East Jerusalem and the West Bank; and occupied the Syrian Golan Heights. A major goal of political Zionism had been achieved. All of Palestine was finally in the hands of the Jewish state. Never mind that the international community called these "occupied territories" and insisted that Israel respect UN resolutions, international law, and human rights covenants. The victory was celebrated in Israel and the Western media as the Six-Day Miracle, little David once again bringing down the mighty Goliath. Religious leaders in Israel and elsewhere declared that God was still alive (which many had doubted after the Holocaust) and had redeemed Israel. British author Geoffrey Wheatcroft captured the emotional catharsis of this military drama:

> Any ambiguous feelings Jews throughout the world may have had about Israel were dissolved; what had been suppressed broke out. . . . First the dread, horror and incipient shame as millions of Jews were once more seemingly threatened with

2. Scholars have provided differing accounts of the run-up to the Six-Day War. This account relies on Miko Peled's 2012 book, *The General's Son*, 42–49. Although one must take into consideration the possibility of bias coming from the proud son of a famous general, over the years he has had many conversations with the participants in these decisions. In addition, he had access to recently declassified military records not available to earlier researchers. To a lesser extent we have also drawn upon Louis and Shlaim, *The 1967 Arab-Israeli War: Origins and Consequences* and Wheatcroft, *The Controversy of Zion*.

extinction; then the exultation as the new race of Hebrews surged to their astonishing victory, more dramatic than either 1948 or 1956. Israel's triumph seemed a triumph for Jewry as a whole, everywhere enhancing their position. More than twenty years later Arthur Hertzberg [historian of Zionism] looked back on the mood which followed: "After the Six-Day War in 1967, Jews in America were freer, and more powerful, than Jews had ever been before in the Diaspora."[3]

On June 8, 1967, an editorial in the liberal Israeli newspaper *Haaretz* declared: "The glory of past ages no longer is to be seen at a distance but is, from now on, part of the new state." The following day, General Moshe Dayan, a self-declared secularist who led the capture of Jerusalem, could not repress the messianic sentiments which he shared with secular and religious Israelis: "We have returned to our holiest places, we have returned in order not to part from them ever again."[4]

Consequences of the 1967 War for Political Zionism

For our exploration of political Zionism, this war had three major consequences: (1) in Israel the Revisionist logic began to overwhelm Labor Zionism; (2) the messianic impulse within Jewish history reasserted itself, shaping government policy as well as public consciousness; and (3) in America anti-Zionism was silenced as the major Jewish organizations consolidated their control over what could be written or spoken in public about the laws, policies, and practices of the State of Israel, even within the Jewish community.

Revisionist Logic Takes Hold

After the Six-Day War, Israel annexed Palestinian East Jerusalem (6.4 square kilometers) and twenty-eight Palestinian villages (an additional sixty-four square kilometers) on land adjacent to East Jerusalem, in an action immediately condemned by the UN. In 1980 the Israeli Knesset passed the Jerusalem Basic Law, declaring Jerusalem to be Israel's "eternal and indivisible" capital. This action provoked UN Security Council Resolution 478, which declared Israel's annexation "null and void." Nevertheless, every Israeli

---

3. Wheatcroft, *The Controversy of Zion*, 274.
4. Louis and Shlaim, *The 1967 Arab-Israeli War*, 46.

prime minister since 1967 has declared that Greater Jerusalem will always remain a part of the State of Israel.

Palestinians have religious and emotional ties to East Jerusalem that rival those of Israel. As the heart of the Palestinian economy and hub of the remaining Palestinian geography, East Jerusalem would become the capital of any eventual Palestinian state. Moreover, Jerusalem holds special meaning for Islam and the world's 1.5 billion Muslims; it was the original direction toward which Muslims faced for prayer before Mecca took that distinction and is believed to be the place from which the prophet Moham-med ascended to heaven. For these reasons, the Israeli annexation casts a pall on hopes for a two-state solution. No nation recognizes Jerusalem as the capital of Israel.[5]

Since 1967 Israel has constructed in the West Bank and East Jerusalem a matrix of control[6] over most areas of Palestinian life. The matrix includes ethnic cleansing; land confiscation; massive home demolitions; the destruc-tion of hundreds of thousands of olive trees; the construction of illegal Israeli settlements housing a Jewish population of over half a million; the control of Palestinian water aquifers and diversion of about 85 percent of the Palestinian water supply to Jewish settlers and the State of Israel; indefi-nite imprisonment without trial of political prisoners; and the list goes on. Now the West Bank is divided into seventy isolated enclaves. Palestinians are separated from one another and the outside world by Israeli settlements; segregated Jewish-only highways in the West Bank; hundreds of military checkpoints; and a forbidding wall and fence, officially named the "separa-tion barrier," which expropriates 13 percent of Palestinian West Bank land. In January 2008 President George W. Bush called these isolated enclaves "Swiss cheese," adding: "To be viable, a future Palestinian state must have contiguous territory."[7]

The Reassertion of National Messianism

Jewish settlements in the occupied Palestinian territories became the means for merging political and religious Zionism. Israel has provided three

5. "Palestinian Territories: Positions on the Legal Status of Jerusalem," Konrad-Adenauer-Stiftung, at http://www.kas.de/palaestinensische-gebiete/en/pages/11509/.

6. "Matrix of control" is a term coined by Jeff Halper, co-founder and director of the Israeli Committee Against House Demolitions; see www.ICAHD.org/.

7. Williams, "I See Peace for Palestine," *Daily Mail*, January 11, 2008, at http://www.dailymail.co.uk/news/article-507328/Bush-I-peace-Palestine-year—Swiss-cheese-isnt-going-work.html.

ostensible reasons for the establishment of what the rest of the world calls illegal settlements within the occupied Palestinian territories: security, religion, and subsidized housing. Critics dismiss these as camouflage for Zionist national messianism bent on cleansing the land of Palestinians, where possible, and confining the rest to isolated cantons that resemble open-air prisons.

Security

In 1967 the Israeli government established settlements to ensure a Jewish majority in regions of the West Bank that it wanted to control, especially in the Jordan Valley.

Religion

Soon after the Six-Day War the religious idea of "Greater Israel" gained wide support. In 1967 the Labor government gave a boost to the religious Zionist movement by resurrecting biblical nomenclature, replacing the name "West Bank" with "Judea and Samaria." The education ministry issued to schools new maps of *Eretz Yisrael* that included "Judea and Samaria" without clear state boundaries and without the "Green Line" demarcation of the 1949 armistice. This had the effect of erasing Palestine not only from maps but also from the minds of Israelis. At the same time it demonstrated the de facto merger of political and religious Zionism by providing biblical justification for taking over Palestinian land.

In 1968 the Orthodox rabbi Moshe Levinger and a few of his followers occupied rooms in the Park Hotel in Hebron and refused to leave; the Israeli police and military, rather than evicting them, provided protection to them. The settlements multiplied and received official recognition from the Israeli government. These settlers believe that God redeemed Israel in the Six-Day War and commanded Jews to retake all the land of biblical Israel. Their abuse against Palestinians, combined with the passive or active participation of the police and the military, has turned the center of Hebron, formerly the hub of business and commerce in the southern West Bank, into a ghost town. An extremist group of Israeli settlers, protected by Israeli forces, calls the shots for the entire Palestinian population.

The nationalist religious settler movement took a leap forward in 1974 with the formation of *Gush Emunim* (Bloc of the Faithful), a messianic religious group committed to the establishment of Jewish religious settlements in the West Bank, Gaza, and the Golan Heights.[8] The new Zionism of Greater Israel gained official sponsorship when the Likud Party took power in 1977 under Prime Minister Menachem Begin, marking a rightward shift in Israeli politics that continues to the present. The government began to provide financial incentives for the establishment of religious settlements in non-strategic areas of the West Bank. The purpose was to solidify Jewish control of what they claimed to have been Israelite territory in biblical times and to prevent the establishment of a Palestinian state.

Subsidized Housing

Finally, the government began providing financial incentives for "economic" settlers, who were encouraged to buy cheap, subsidized housing close to their jobs in nearby Israeli cities and towns. These settlements also provide housing for immigrants and the growing national population. In the case of settlements in "Greater Jerusalem," they also serve Zionist goals by dividing the West Bank in half and making a viable, contiguous Palestine impossible. Ironically, these settlements also render a two-state solution most unlikely, thereby ratcheting up political tensions, strengthening the structure of apartheid, and further delegitimizing Israel in the eyes of the world.

In their recent book, *Chosen Peoples,* sociologist Todd Gitlin and journalist Liel Leibovitz ask, "Why the continuing support, encouragement, and tolerance for the [religious] settlements and their expansion by one Israeli government after another . . . ? Why the consistency with which secularists have yielded to religious, millenarian[9] settlers, even, at times, against strong opposition from the left?" And they respond:

> The answer must have something to do with the spiritual hold exercised by the settlers. . . . The existence of a Jewish state was not sufficient unto itself. . . . [It was] never the ultimate goal of Zionism. . . . Zionism has always been a messianic movement at heart. Even its secular leaders acknowledged, however vaguely, the mission articulated by Isaiah and other prophets: ushering in peace and justice for all. That is why the movement remains so popular with Jews the world over.[10]

8. Ed Snitkoff, "Gush Emunim: Settling all the land," *My Jewish Learning.com,* at http://www.myjewishlearning.com/israel/Jewish_Thought/Modern/Religious_Zionism/Gush_Emunim.shtml?p=3.

9. The term "millenarian" indicates adherence to beliefs regarding the "end times."

10. Gitlin and Leibovitz, *Chosen Peoples,* 54, 55, 57.

Gitlin and Leibovitz conclude that Israeli national messianism, whether in its overt religious form or in the form of a civil religion, reflects a conscious or unconscious recognition of divine election to be God's chosen people: "Zionism's inability to shake the messianic ideal became manifest in the hold that the West Bank settlers exercised on the conscience of the whole nation."[11] In other words, despite its secular birth, Zionism flourished because of the merger, especially after 1967, of its political and religious agenda.

The Consolidation of American Zionism

Jewish theologian Marc Ellis writes that before the Six-Day War, "Israel was not central to [American] Jewish identity. It only emerged as the central Jewish concern after the 1967 war."[12] This does not mean that Zionism was marginal to debates among leaders of Jewish religious and secular organizations before 1967. In 1885 the Central Conference of American Rabbis (CCAR) of the Reform movement rejected political Zionism, declaring, "We consider ourselves no longer a nation, but a religious community" and do not "expect . . . a return to Palestine."[13] In the mid-1930s, after Nazi Germany passed the anti-Semitic Nuremberg laws, Zionists mounted a campaign to alter the anti-Zionist position of Reform rabbis. In 1937 these Zionists prevailed; by a majority of one vote, the CCAR reversed its 1885 position, affirming "the obligation of all Jewry" to aid in the up-building in Palestine of "a Jewish homeland."[14]

Nevertheless, during the 1940s the American Jewish Committee (AJC), the most influential Jewish civic organization of the time, comprised largely of members of the Reform movement, remained anti-Zionist. In January 1948, the AJC committee on Palestine expressed grave concern that "the Zionists will now make an attempt to organize the community along Zionist lines and will try to capture the communal organizations."[15]

The Anti-Defamation League (ADL), which until then had been generally aligned with the AJC, switched sides quickly in the months leading

---

11. Ibid., 2.

12. Ellis, *Judaism Does Not Equal Israel*, 119.

13. From the *Pittsburgh Platform*, quoted in Ross, *Rabbi Outcast*, 10.

14. From *The Columbus Platform: Guiding Principles of Reform Judaism*, quoted in Ross, *Rabbi Outcast*, 32.

15. Solomon, *The Speech, and Its Context*, 127.

up to Israeli statehood. Since Israeli statehood, the ADL has equated anti-Zionism with anti-Semitism.[16]

In 1949, the *Reader's Digest* published two opposing articles, "The Case for Israel," by Rabbi Abba Hillel Silver, and "Israel's Flag is Not Mine," by Alfred M. Lilienthal. The public response within the Jewish community demonstrated the popularity of Zionism and the growing opposition to anti-Zionism. Lilienthal was widely denounced from rabbinical pulpits and by Jewish newspapers. The *Intermountain Jewish News* of Colorado called on the ADL to declare, "Jews can be anti-Semitic."[17] More recently the epithet "self-hating Jews" is used to defame and marginalize Jews who raise concerns about Israel's actions or profess opposition to Zionism.

Eventually the Zionists did capture the Jewish communal organizations. The Conference of Presidents of Major American Jewish Organizations is now comprised of fifty-one communal organizations that promote the Zionist cause.[18]

Menachem Begin (1913–1992): The First Likud Prime Minister

In 1977 Menachem Begin dealt Labor Zionism its first defeat at the polls, replacing the secular, elite Ashkenazi (Jews of European background) with a coalition representing the marginalized Sephardi, Mizrahi, and religious communities. Likud's victory also gave flesh to the spirit of the Greater Israel Zionism that emerged after the Six-Day War.

Begin was born in Brest-Litovsk, Poland, and raised in a religious home. His father was an ardent follower of Herzl's Zionism. The son received an Orthodox education and learned modern Hebrew. At age fifteen, he joined the local Zionist *Betar* group and came under the influence of Jabotinsky and his brand of militant Zionism.[19] "I was won over by his ideas: the willingness to fight for the liberation of the homeland, and the logical analysis of facts in political matters,"[20] said Begin.

The young Begin went on to become commander of *Betar* in Czechoslovakia and then in Poland before being arrested by the Soviet authorities

16. Ross, *Rabbi Outcast*, 89. See also the 2009 film *Defamation* by Israeli filmmaker Yoav Shamir.

17. Wheatcroft, *The Controversy of Zion*, 252.

18. See the website, Conference of Presidents of Major Jewish Organizations, at http://www.conferenceofpresidents.org/content.asp?id=55.

19. For *Betar*, see Chapter One, 12.

20. Avishai, *The Tragedy of Zionism*, 166.

in 1940 and imprisoned in the Gulag. He was released after Hitler attacked the Soviet Union, enlisted in the Free Poland Army in 1942, and went to Palestine for military training. By the end of 1943 he had resigned from the Polish military and become the commander of the *Irgun* paramilitary in Palestine. In this capacity he planned an armed revolt against the British, attacking British immigration offices in Jerusalem, Tel Aviv, and Haifa in early 1944. In his chronicle of the *Irgun*, which Ben-Gurion and others labeled a terrorist group, Begin glorified armed revolt: "Out of the blood and tears and ashes a new specimen of Jew was born, a specimen completely unknown to the world for over eighteen hundred years: 'the FIGHTING JEW' . . ."[21]

The tactics of the *Irgun* Gang, as they were known, had consequences. Fearing the loss of British diplomatic support, Ben-Gurion, the de facto leader of the *yishuv* (the pre-state Jewish community), responded by rounding up hundreds of *Irgun* members and declared: "If we want a Zionist political struggle we must . . . take action against terrorism and terrorist organizations."[22] In June 1948, a month after Israel gained statehood, Begin tried to bring a load of arms into Palestine on the ship *Altalena*. Ben-Gurion demanded that the Labor-backed *Haganah* take charge of the cargo. When Begin refused, declaring that most of the arms would go to the *Irgun*, Ben-Gurion ordered the forces of *Haganah* to sink the ship in the waters off Tel Aviv. Begin barely escaped with his life. As a result he developed a life-long disgust for Ben-Gurion and Labor Zionism. He quickly founded the right-wing *Herut* (Freedom Party) to oppose the Labor Party in Israel's first national elections.[23] (*Herut* made alliances with several other parties in 1965 and 1973 to become Likud ["The Consolidation"], Israel's major right-wing party.)

Begin had been a hard-liner from the beginning, planning *Irgun* attacks on the British from 1943 until 1948 and attacks on Palestinian towns and villages in 1947 and 1948. When the UN voted to partition Palestine in 1947, he rejected the plan in favor of a "war of liberation" for a single Jewish

---

21. Ibid., 167–68.

22. Ibid., 167.

23. In a December 2, 1948, letter to the editor of *The New York Times*, twenty-five prominent American Jewish leaders, including Hannah Arendt, Albert Einstein, and Sydney Hook, lambasted Begin and called *Herut* "a political party closely akin, in its organization, methods, political philosophy, and social appeal, to the Nazi and Fascist parties." They also berated American Zionist leaders for refusing to warn their constituents of the danger that Begin and "this latest manifestation of fascism" posed to Israel. Available at http://www.globalwebpost.com/farooqm/study_res/einstein/nyt_orig. html.

state.[24] In 1952 he vehemently opposed the reparations agreement that Ben-Gurion worked out with West Germany. He believed the agreement implied a pardon of Nazi crimes against the Jewish people. During the Six-Day War in June 1967, he and Yigal Allon urged the Minister of Defense, Moshe Dayan, to capture East Jerusalem without formal approval from the Israeli cabinet. In November 1967 the UN Security Council passed resolution 242 which condemned Israel's "acquisition of territory by war," leading Begin to call for outright annexation of the Palestinian territories that Israel had occupied since 1967. Using the resurrected biblical names in a modern political setting, Begin also threatened to withdraw from the governing coalition if it allowed resolution 242 to apply to "Judea and Samaria."[25]

In October 1973, during the Muslim holy month of Ramadan and on Yom Kippur, the holiest day in the Jewish calendar, Egypt and Syria launched a surprise attack on Israeli military positions in the occupied Sinai and Golan Heights that lasted almost three weeks. Israel was caught off guard and suffered over ten thousand casualties. Without the supply of U.S. military aid, Israel might have suffered a major defeat and been unable to reverse the early Arab successes. This war marked the downfall both of Israel's self-perception of invincibility and of Labor Zionism. During the next election in 1977, Begin became prime minister as Likud soundly defeated Labor and its allies. Now the Israeli settlement movement, which the international community had declared illegal, had an ardent champion as head of government. The number of settlements and settlers grew exponentially with government sponsorship and financing. By 1981, when Begin was elected for a second term, the consolidation of "Greater Israel" had become the number one priority of the Begin government.[26] This policy fed the zeal of nationalist religious settlers who have had great influence in the rightward trend of political Zionism since the Six-Day War in 1967.

Begin's "Greater Israel" policy so disturbed some American Jewish leaders that one of them, Laurence Tisch, in a 1978 interview with the Israeli daily *Haaretz*, accused Begin of undermining American support for Israel: "If Begin continues about the settlements, you will lose the war down to the last American. . . . For thirty years we have been building for Israel the image of a peace-loving country. Begin destroyed this image in three months."[27]

Begin's most significant foreign policy achievement as prime minister was the peace agreement with Egypt, which President Jimmy Carter

24. Avishai, *The Tragedy of Zionism*, 175.

25. Ibid., 252.

26. Ibid., 312.

27. Wheatcroft, *The Controversy of Zion*, 279.

brokered between Begin and Sadat in September 1978 at Camp David. Sadat had taken the initiative by his historic trip to Jerusalem in November 1977. Begin resisted Sadat's peace initiative until public pressure forced his hand. The Camp David Accords called for peace between Egypt and Israel, the return of the Sinai to Egypt (which Israel had controlled since 1967), and full Palestinian autonomy. When Begin returned from Camp David, the Knesset approved the accords, but members of his own party accused him of paving the way for a Palestinian state. He responded angrily by telling them that the only provision of the agreement on Palestinian autonomy that mattered was the one that gave Israel a veto on the progress of negotiations: "Don't teach me Jabotinsky's doctrine, and don't teach me love for the land of Israel."[28] Shortly after signing the peace accords in April 1979, Begin approved new settlements in Ramallah and Nablus. Even more insulting to Sadat and the peace agreement,[29] the prime minister's office prepared plans that would give Palestinians "autonomy over their persons but not over their resources."[30] Israel would maintain exclusive control over the West Bank water table, public land, roads, communications, immigration, and public order. Life without access to livelihood is the legacy Begin bequeathed to Palestinians.

That legacy includes Begin's refusal to meet even the most elementary conditions for peace with Palestinians, a position that has been followed by every Israeli administration since the early 1980s. The Likud Party Platform of the 1977 election, which Begin won, declared:

> The right of the Jewish people to the Land of Israel is eternal and indisputable and is linked with the right to security and peace. Therefore, Judea and Samaria will not be handed over to any foreign administration. Between the sea and the Jordan River there will be only Israeli sovereignty. Relinquishing parts of the Western Land of Israel undermines our right to the country, unavoidably leads to the establishment of a "Palestinian State," jeopardizes the security of the Jewish population, endangers the security of the State of Israel and frustrates any prospect of peace.[31]

Middle East historian and political analyst Rashid Khalidi cites a confidential CIA memo of August 24, 1982, which summarizes the Likud policy toward Palestinian statehood. The author (whose name has been redacted)

---

28. Avishai, *The Tragedy of Zionism*, 286.

29. Sadat refused to go to Oslo to receive the Nobel Peace Prize alongside Begin.

30. Avishai, *The Tragedy of Zionism*, 287.

31. Khalidi, *Brokers of Deceit*, 1.

states, "[Prime Minister Menachem] Begin asserts that the [Camp David Accords] rule out the emergence of a Palestinian state. . . . [and] guarantee that 'under no condition' can a Palestinian state be created." At best, Palestinian authority would be *"solely administrative . . .* leaving control of the territory and all key security issues with Israel. In sum, *autonomy is for people not territory.*"[32] From 1982 until now, the U.S. has accepted these unwavering Israeli conditions, in spite of all the rhetoric about peace talks.

Begin's fall from power would come quickly. The economy under his stewardship was in trouble, and the government was losing popular support. In June 1982 Begin authorized the invasion of Lebanon to root out the Palestinian Liberation Organization, which, under the leadership of Yasser Arafat, had been attacking Israeli communities in northern Israel. Israeli forces succeeded in ousting Arafat from Lebanon, but they got bogged down and could not extricate themselves quickly, thus suffering more casualties than had been expected. In addition, Israel suffered a major public relations setback when the Israeli military surrounded the Shatila refugee camp and the Sabra neighborhood of Beirut and allowed the Phalangists, their Lebanese Christian allies, to massacre hundreds if not thousands of Palestinians and Lebanese.[33] The official Israeli Kahan commission of inquiry found that Defense Minister Ariel Sharon was "personally responsible" and recommended that he resign. At first he refused to resign, claiming that all ministers of government were liable to prosecution for the crime of genocide if the government admitted prior knowledge of the massacre. According to Israeli documents released on February 21, 2013, at a cabinet meeting on February 10, 1983, Sharon declared:

> We all urged this, we all enabled it, by asking them [the Phalangist Christian militias] to enter the camps. We were present, we lit up the area and we evacuated casualties. It is common knowledge that we were in the area to keep the opposition away, and we did not isolate it from other areas. We kept forces in the area to ensure the mission was carried out, and in case they ran into trouble and needed help getting out.[34]

32. Ibid., 18–20.

33. See *Institute for Middle East Understanding,* "The Sabra and Shatila Massacre: 30 Years Later," http://imeu.net/news/article0023017.shtml, for various estimates of the number of victims.

34. "Sabra and Shatila documents revealed: Ariel Sharon feared indictment for genocide over Israel's role," *Middle East Monitor* at http://www.middleeastmonitor.com/news/middle-east/5301-sabra-and-shatila-documents-revealed-ariel-sharon-feared-indictment-for-genocide-over-israels-role.

This atrocity tarnished the reputation of the Begin government and weakened public support, much as did the war on Gaza in 2008 and 2009 and other Israeli military attacks on civilians.

Begin's wife died in late 1982, leaving him deeply depressed. The next year he resigned from office and withdrew from public life. In spite of his dubious economic and military policies, but perhaps because of his support for the new Zionism of Greater Israel, a poll conducted in 2005 by the Israeli news website *Ynet* named Begin the fourth most important Israeli of all time.

Benjamin Netanyahu (1949–): Toward a Single Jewish Apartheid State

The themes that run consistently through the leadership of the current prime minister of Israel, Benjamin "Bibi" Netanyahu, reflect a steady hardening to the right for political Zionism. Israeli politics are driven by actual and manipulated fear of annihilation (another Holocaust), the goal of radical separation from Arab Palestinians, and a policy of expanding settlements in the occupied territories to encircle Jerusalem and claim as much land as possible. It is hard to find evidence that recent Israeli governments have had any intention of negotiating a just peace with Palestinians.

Netanyahu's Background

With Netanyahu at the center of this move to the right, a look at his background is helpful. After Rabin, he is the second prime minister to be born in Israel (October 21, 1949). He is the son of Benzion Netanyahu (1910–2012), who was a professor of Jewish history at Cornell University, editor of *Encyclopaedia Hebraica*, and a senior aide to Ze'ev Jabotinsky, who has been called the ideological father of the Likud Party. When Jabotinsky died in 1940, Benzion Netanyahu succeeded him as leader of the Revisionist Zionists.[35]

Both Netanyahu's father and grandfather were leaders in the Zionist movement and served in the Israeli military. *The New York Times* reported that Benzion, born in Warsaw (then part of the Russian empire), was "relentlessly hawkish. Leaving no room for compromise, he argued that Jews

---

35. Gorenberg, "Benzion Netanyahu's Legacies," *Daily Beast,* at http://www.thedailybeast.com/articles/2012/05/01/benzion-netanyahu-s-legacies.html.

inevitably faced discrimination that was racial, not religious, and that compromising with Arabs was futile."[36]

A specialist in the history of Jews in Spain, Benzion thought that "Jewish history was a history of holocausts,"[37] and believed that Arabs would choose to exterminate Jews if they had the chance and would respond only to force. His study of the Spanish Inquisition had led him to believe that Jewish persecution was rooted in "pernicious racial enmity" toward those who possessed Jewish blood. In the *Jewish Journal*, David Myers writes:

> We might call this the Amalekite view of Jewish history, referring to the hated biblical foes of the Israelites whose existence—and even memory—should be blotted out. (Exodus 17:14). The historian's belief that the Jews have been subjected to constant genocidal threats did not lead him to a passive fatalism, as if there were nothing that the Jews could do in the face of Amalek. Rather, it inspired his own militant Zionism, which demanded a persistent willingness to wage war against one's enemies.[38]

Myers links Benjamin's "bellicose stance on Iran"[39] to Benzion's Amalekite worldview. Iran is not just a grave threat, in his view; Benjamin compares it to the most terrifying of Jewish persecutors.[40] In 2010, Benzion said in a televised interview, "We are very simply in danger of extermination today. Not just existential danger, but truly in danger of extermination. They think the extermination, the Holocaust, is over; it isn't, it goes on all the time."[41] Benjamin Netanyahu has said that the most important message he learned from his father is that ". . . whoever doesn't know his past, can't understand his present, and therefore can't plan for his future. [Benzion] predicted the

36. Martin, "Benzion Netanyahu Dies," *New York Times*, April 30, 2012.

37. Ibid.

38. Myers, "Benzion Netanyahu," *Jewish Journal*, at http://www.jewishjournal.com/opinion/article/benzion_netanyahu_in_life_and_death_2012051. The Amalekite view of Jewish history includes the mitzvah of genocide. As reflected in 1 Sam 15:3, it requires the elimination of the enemy, including men, women, children, and cattle. See note 40 for additional sources on the mitzvah (commandment) of genocide.

39. "Former Mossad chief backs Shin Bet counterpart over criticism of Netanyahu, Barak," *Haaretz*, April 29, 2012. http://www.haaretz.com/misc/iphone-article/former-mossad-chief-backs-shin-bet-counterpart-over-criticism-of-netanyahu-barak-1.427153.

40. Shmuly Yankowitz, "Genocide in the Torah: The existential threat of Amalek," *My Jewish Learning*, at http://www.myjewishlearning.com/beliefs/Issues/War_and_Peace/Combat_and_Conflict/Types_of_War/Genocide.shtml. This article provides a view of the Jewish debate on the Amalek issue.

41. Nir Hasson, Yossi Verter, and Barak Ravid, "Benzion Netanyahu, father of Prime Minister Benjamin Netanyahu, dies at 102," *Haaretz*, April 30, 2012.

attacks on the Twin Towers back in the early 1990s. He also predicted the threat of tyrannical Islamist regimes attempting to attain nuclear weapons."[42]

Benjamin was raised in a suburb of Philadelphia, Pennsylvania; studied architecture at the Massachusetts Institute of Technology; and from 1976 to 1978, worked at the Boston Consulting Group, a business management firm, where he was a colleague of Mitt Romney. In 1978, Netanyahu returned to Israel and ran the Jonathan Netanyahu Anti-Terror Institute, a non-governmental organization devoted to the study of terrorism and named for his brother who was killed in Uganda during Operation Entebbe in 1976.

Netanyahu served as Israeli ambassador to the United Nations from 1984 to 1988, when he joined the Likud party, the heir of Jabotinsky's Revisionist Zionism. In 1993 he was elected to lead the party, becoming standard-bearer for right-wing political Zionism. Three years later, in the first election in which Israelis elected their prime minister directly, he ran as Likud's candidate for prime minister and won, beating the favored Shimon Peres. A wave of suicide bombings that year helped spread his campaign message: "Netanyahu—making a safe peace." Labor, the centrist party, won the majority in the Knesset, however, and Netanyahu had to form a coalition with the ultra-Orthodox parties in order to govern.

First Term as Prime Minister: 1996–1999

Netanyahu made it clear from the start of his term as prime minister that he disagreed with the Oslo Accords, which had been signed in September 1993 by Yasser Arafat for the Palestinian Liberation Organization (PLO) and by Yitzhak Rabin for Israel. The accords gave limited autonomy in Jericho and Gaza to a newly created "Palestinian Authority." Netanyahu also emphasized a policy of "three no's": no withdrawal from the Golan Heights; no division of Jerusalem, which Israel had annexed in 1967;[43] and no negotiations under any preconditions.[44]

Netanyahu, however, signed further agreements, The Hebron Protocol and the Wye River Memorandum, to implement the Oslo accords. The

---

42. Ibid.

43. In July 1980, the Knesset passed the Jerusalem Law declaring that "Jerusalem, complete and united, is the capital of Israel." This law formalized Israel's unilateral annexation of Jerusalem. Resolution 478, which the United Nations Security Council adopted in August 1980, declared the Jerusalem Law to be "null and void."

44. "Benjamin Netanyahu," *Haaretz* at http://www.haaretz.com/misc/tags/Benjamin%20Netanyahu-1.476753.

United States and the international community had pushed for these agreements after a massacre of Muslim worshipers in Hebron in 1994[45] and the assassination of Prime Minister Yitzhak Rabin in 1995. The supplementary agreements brought limited self-rule to the cities of Hebron and Bethlehem and to other Palestinian population centers in the West Bank. In spite of the fact that these agreements eventually brought only minimal change, some of his Likud supporters felt betrayed. They had believed that Netanyahu, carrying the mantle of the Revisionist Zionists, "would never negotiate away rights of settlers in the ancient Jewish community of Hebron," or endorse "the Labor policy of trading 'land for peace.'"

These developments brought about a short-lived setback for the aggressive Zionism of Benjamin Netanyahu, who lost favor with the Israeli public after facing a series of scandals in his personal life, left-wing opposition to his conservative policies, and right-wing disillusionment over his concessions to Palestinians. He was defeated by Ehud Barak in the 1999 election for prime minister and temporarily retired from politics.

However, the significance of Netanyahu's opposition to the Oslo accords was noted two years later by Avi Shlaim, professor of international relations at St. Antony's College, Oxford University:

> The Oslo accords should not be adjudged a failure. They did not collapse under the weight of their own contradictions, as critics liked to argue; the process was subverted by Binyamin Netanyahu and his colleagues in the ultranationalist camp. By subverting the Oslo accords, Netanyahu inflicted serious damage not only on the Palestinians but on his own country and on the Middle East as a whole.[46]

The Oslo Accords included a timetable, which was to result in full implementation by 1999. Instead, the agreement transmuted into a process—"the peace process"—to renegotiate what already was agreed. Netanyahu ensured that the process would undermine prospective peace, becoming a cover for entrenching the military occupation with ever-increasing settlements, the separation wall, and other efforts to control the land while marginalizing the non-Jewish people. Fully twenty years later, the halting Oslo "process" is flogged back to life in the international rhetoric every couple of

45. The massacre was carried out by Baruch Goldstein, an Israeli-American settler, at the Ibrahimi Mosque, where Abraham and other patriarchs are said to be buried. Twenty-nine Palestinians died, another 125 were wounded, and thirty-five died in the riots that followed. The mosque is shared by both Muslims and Jews. Today the worship areas are divided and only one faith is admitted at a time. The area is heavily guarded by Israeli troops who protect the Israeli Jewish settlers.

46. Shlaim, *The Iron Wall*, 603.

years, with a new and doomed restart plan toward a nebulous goal, while the occupation becomes more brutal.

After the 2003 election, Prime Minister Ariel Sharon appointed Netanyahu to the post of finance minister. Meanwhile, in a surprise move in 2004, Sharon pulled the Israeli settlers out of Gaza, but rather than moving them to Israel proper, he re-settled them in the West Bank, adding to the settler numbers there and moving the Zionist expansion project forward. When Sharon evacuated all the Israeli settlements from Gaza, Netanyahu resigned in protest and moved politically to the right of Sharon. In 2008 Netanyahu opposed a ceasefire with Gaza, saying the end of hostilities did not result in any agreement and left Hamas in control of Gaza.

Netanyahu's Second and Third Terms as Prime Minister: 2009–2013

Netanyahu was appointed prime minister by Israeli president Shimon Peres to succeed Ehud Olmert in February 2009. Likud was able to control a majority of the seats in the Knesset by forming an alliance with Avigdor Lieberman's *Yisrael Beiteinu* ("Israel is Our Home"), the Russian immigrant party, which is further to the right than Likud and is associated with xenophobia.[47] Zionism, therefore, moved further to the right, in a continuing slide away from Diaspora Jews, especially those in the United States, who traditionally have been left-leaning Democrats.

That same year Netanyahu spoke at Bar-Ilan University and called for a Palestinian state but one with no military and no control of its airspace. He rejected the Palestinian right of return and said Jerusalem would be the undivided capital of a Jewish state. He also said that settlement expansion would have to continue to allow for natural growth.[48] His speech came after U.S. Secretary of State Hillary Clinton voiced support for a Palestinian state and only days after President Barack Obama had spoken in Cairo, saying, "The United States does not accept the legitimacy of continued Israeli settlements." Although Netanyahu's speech disappointed his right-wing supporters, who opposed any semblance of a Palestinian state, Saeb Erekat, the chief

---

47. "Disturbing Idea of Expelling Arabs from Israeli Territory Gains Ground," *Roger Hollander: News and Opinion* (blog), March 4, 2009, at http://rogerhollander.wordpress.com/tag/israel-xenophobia/. See also Filc, *The Political Right in Israel*, 103–23.

48. "Israel's Netanyahu Calls for Creation of Palestinian State for First Time," *FOXNews.com*, April 29, 2012, at http://www.foxnews.com/story/2009/06/15/israel-netanyahu-calls-for-creation-palestinian-state-for-first-time/.

Palestinian negotiator, said the speech had "closed the door to permanent status negotiations."[49]

Netanyahu's critics say he has also played up the alleged nuclear threat from Iran as another means of avoiding movement toward a just peace with Palestinians. In September 2009 he made a secret trip to Russia to persuade Russian officials not to sell anti-aircraft missile systems to Iran.[50] At the United Nations General Assembly in 2012 he declared Iran a threat to the peace of the world and called on the world body to prevent the Islamic republic from obtaining nuclear weapons. These demands have been described by many as building up the fear of annihilation and manufacturing an "existential threat" in order to justify an atmosphere of crisis and to thwart the movement toward a two-state solution.

Moreover, in spite of his stated support for a demilitarized Palestinian state, Netanyahu has continued to allow new Jewish-only settlement building in response to settler demands. When President Obama pressured both sides to resume peace talks, Netanyahu, in November 2009, announced a ten-month "partial freeze" on settlement building. Nevertheless, he allowed recently approved construction to go ahead in both the West Bank and East Jerusalem, angering the Palestinians. The partial freeze came to an end ten months later, and settlement growth has continued until the present.

In early 2012 Netanyahu appointed a three-member committee of jurists to study the legality of settlements, and in July the committee—in keeping with the Zionist vision of controlling all of *Eretz Yisrael*—published a report saying Israel's presence in the West Bank was not occupation and recommending that the state approve scores of unauthorized Jewish settlement outposts there. The commission, led by Edmund Levy, a retired Israeli Supreme Court justice, confirmed a position long held by Israel: that the territories are not occupied because Jordan's previous hold over them was never internationally recognized and that their fate must be determined in negotiations. Netanyahu praised the report for confirming the "legalization and legitimization of the settlement enterprise." Still, fearing international censure, among other things, Israel's government has not formally adopted the commission's conclusions.[51]

Later in 2012, Netanyahu's government announced that it would resume planning for 1,500 new units in the controversial West Bank "E-1" zone east of Jerusalem, an area where Israel had held off construction since at least 2009 under international pressure. This bold move came immediately

49. Ibid.
50. McCarthy, "Netanyahu visits Moscow."
51. Cumming-Bruce and Kershner, "U.N. Panel Says."

after the Palestinian Authority won a bid for non-member observer status at the UN. The Authority had lost its try for statehood in 2011 when the U.S. vetoed the move in the UN Security Council, but it won non-member status in November 2012 with the support of a large majority of the world's nations. Netanyahu's inflammatory response to this development provided more evidence that Israel is not interested in a two-state solution leading to a viable, contiguous Palestinian state. Building settlements in the "E-1" area effectively cuts the West Bank in half, separating Palestinians in the northern West Bank from those in Bethlehem and other areas to the south.[52]

The international community, with the exception of the United States, continued to oppose Netanyahu's settlement policies. On January 31, 2013, the UN Human Rights Council released a report on "the creeping annexation of the Palestinian territories" and declared that Israel had "committed multiple violations of international law, possibly including war crimes. . . ." Israel's response was to condemn the findings as "a political platform used to bash and demonize Israel."[53] In February 2013 German Chancellor Angela Merkel's office announced that it was withholding reparations to Holocaust survivors until there is a freeze on settlement-building in the occupied territories of the West Bank.[54] Later that year, in July 2013, the European Union issued a directive stating that all future agreements between the EU and Israel must explicitly exclude Jewish colonies in the West Bank, East Jerusalem, and the Golan Heights.[55] The directive was dubbed by Economy and Trade Minister Naftali Bennett as "economic terrorism." Others, calling the ruling a "diplomatic firestorm," charged that it would interfere with U.S. Secretary of State John Kerry's efforts to restart the peace negotiations.[56]

Netanyahu and the "Jewish State"

In the last decade, Benjamin Netanyahu has taken to calling for a "Jewish state" as an outcome of negotiations, a concept that has now become standard rhetoric. In October 2010, Glenn Kessler wrote an article in *The Washington Post* on the origin of this demand for a "Jewish State":

> Nine years ago, then-Secretary of State Colin L. Powell delivered a speech on the Middle East in which he briefly called on

52. "The E1 Plan and its implications for human rights in the West Bank," B'Tselem, at http://www.btselem.org/settlements/20121202_e1_human_rights_ramifications.

53. Cumming-Bruce and Kershner, "U.N. Panel Says."

54. Beck, "Germany Delays Holocaust Survivor Restitution."

55. Sherwood, "EU Takes Tougher Stance."

56. Also see Rosenberg, "The EU's Not-Quite Settlement Boycott."

Palestinians to recognize Israel as a "Jewish state." Powell doesn't recall how the phrase ended up in his speech, but David Ivry, then the Israeli ambassador to the United States, says he persuaded an aide to Powell to slip it in. From that small step—the first time a U.S. official took sides on the issue—a significant and potentially insurmountable hurdle has emerged, one that could scuttle President Obama's newly launched effort to promote a peace deal between Israel and the Palestinians.

President George W. Bush picked up the "Jewish state" concept in his speeches and used it in a controversial exchange of letters with Israeli Prime Minister Ariel Sharon in 2004. Obama has also adopted the phrase, most recently in a speech last month before the UN General Assembly.

Describing Israel as a "Jewish state" may seem like standard boilerplate in the United States, often used in newspaper articles and television programs. But words can carry deep meanings, especially in Middle East diplomacy.

For the Israeli government of Prime Minister Binyamin Netanyahu, Palestinian recognition of Israel as a "Jewish state" would mean acceptance that the Jews have existed in the Middle East for thousands of years—and that Palestinian refugees have no claim to return to property they fled or were forced to flee when Israel was founded six decades ago.

> Palestinians see their "right of return" as a sacred tenet. They regard a "Jewish state" as a trap, a new demand that did not come up during years of negotiations in the 1990s or in peace treaties reached with Egypt and Jordan. The Palestinian Liberation Organization recognized the State of Israel as part of the Oslo Accords in 1993. . . . Moreover, Palestinian and Arab officials contend that labeling Israel a "Jewish state" calls into question the rights of Palestinians with Israeli citizenship, who comprise 20 percent of Israel's population.[57]

In short, a "Jewish state" legitimizes racism and discrimination in favor of Jews in all areas of public life and denies many national rights to non-Jewish citizens of Israel.

Since the Powell speech, this insistence on a "Jewish state," which fits with the Zionist vision, has become almost routine, but it is new language for negotiations and for the international community. In less than a decade, the phrase has become part of the American lexicon and appears to be settled American policy, judging by U.S. presidential campaigns and UN speeches. This demand presents a major obstacle for peace because, just as

---

57. Kessler, "Defining Jewish State."

Jews want a "right of return" to the land, so too do the millions of Palestinian refugees who have languished in refugee camps for three generations. Moreover, as a demanded outcome, it requires Palestinian negotiators to delegitimize those whom they represent in order to become acceptable at the table. Non-Zionists point out that a Jewish state with non-Jewish citizens is an *ethnocracy*, not a democracy.[58]

Discriminatory Laws Within Israel Proper

Most international attention is focused on the brutality of the Israeli military occupation of Palestinian territories rather than on discrimination against Palestinian Israelis. We sometimes forget that 20 percent of the citizens of Israel are Palestinian. (For political reasons, Israel calls them Arabs, not Palestinians. They are both and include Muslims, Christians, a small Samaritan community, and Druze.) From the beginning in 1948, Zionism has enacted racial and ethnic discrimination into law, segregating Palestinians and rendering them second-class citizens. Even before the 2009 to 2013 term of Netanyahu as prime minister, there were over thirty discriminatory laws severely restricting Arab (Palestinian) rights in Israel proper. For example, the Absentees' Property Law was instituted in 1950, shortly after 750,000 Palestinians fled for their lives from the Israeli army. The effect of this and other land laws enacted over the next fifteen years was to transfer legal title to land formerly owned by Palestinians to the Jewish National Fund, which made it available to Jews for lease or purchase. Let us recall that in the opinion of the "founding fathers" of political Zionism, the Arabs "had to go."

Another law reserves 93 percent of the land in Israel for Jews only and bans non-Jews from leasing any of it. This land is owned by the Jewish National Fund and the State of Israel. Jews who make use of it do so as lessees. Again, the 2003 Citizenship and Entry into Israel Law prohibits family unification for those marrying spouses from the West Bank, Jordan, and elsewhere in the Middle East, which ensures that if a Palestinian who is an Israeli citizen marries a Palestinian who is not an Israeli citizen, they must either live apart, or leave Israel. The list goes on.

From 2009 to 2013 the Knesset passed more than a dozen additional discriminatory laws. The Association for Civil Rights in Israel notes that because of this "tide of anti-democratic" legislation "the basic principles of the Israeli democratic system are being undermined. There is an ongoing infringement on issues such as freedom of expression, human dignity, and equality; on the possibility of upholding the pluralism of views and

---

58. Halper, *An Israeli in Palestine*, 63–137.

thoughts; on freedom of assembly and protest; and on the very legitimacy of certain views and positions."[59] These laws illustrate the steady hardening of politics in Israel, re-oriented toward the right.[60] For example,

- A 2009 law confiscates Palestinian refugees' land to be sold to private Jewish investors and placed beyond future claims for restoration or restitution.

- A 2010 law prevents Palestinian citizens of Israel from submitting law-suits to reclaim confiscated land.

- Another 2010 law gives official status to about sixty individual Jewish settlements in the Negev, most of them established without permits and contrary to Israel's own planning laws, and provides them with all basic services. At the same time Bedouin villages in the Negev are denied official status and their ninety to one hundred thousand in-habitants, all citizens of Israel, go without most basic services. Many traditional Bedouin villages in the South Hebron Hills are now being destroyed and the land confiscated by government order.

- A 2011 law gives local towns built on state land in the Galilee and the Negev the right to exclude Palestinian Israelis and even Israeli Jews with different ideological convictions.

- The "*Nakba* Law" (2011) authorizes the ministry of finance to withhold funds from schools that commemorate the *Nakba* (the name Palestin-ians have given to the 1947–48 "Catastrophe" of their dispossession).

- The Anti-Boycott Law (2011) permits legal action against advocates of economic, cultural, and academic boycotts of Israel and the Israeli settlements in the West Bank, preventing Israeli citizens, including Palestinians, from participating in non-violent methods of resistance to legalized discrimination.

The intensifying crackdown on Palestinian and Jewish citizens who criticize Israel can also be measured by the type of bills introduced in the Knesset that did not become law. These far outnumber the laws that have been passed. They include:

59. "Anti-Democratic Initiatives," *The Association for Civil Rights in Is-rael,* at http://www.acri.org.il/en/category/democracy-and-civil-liberties/anti-democratic-legislation/.

60. For a list of these laws, see "New Discriminatory Laws and Bills in Israel," *Adalah, the Legal Center for Arab Minority Rights in Israel,* June 2011, updated October 2012, at http://adalah.org/Public/files/English/Legal_Advocacy/Discriminatory_Laws/Discriminatory-Laws-in-Israel-October-2012-Update.pdf.

- A bill to impose a loyalty oath on all Israeli citizens, including Palestinians, at age sixteen, requiring them to swear loyalty to Israel as a "Jewish, Zionist, and democratic state, to its symbols and values."

- A 2010 bill, occasioned by the Goldstone Report on Israel's possible crimes against humanity in its assault on Gaza in 2008 and 2009, "to outlaw associations that provide information to foreigners or are involved in litigation abroad against senior officials of the Israeli government and/or army officers for war crimes."

- A 2011 bill designed to reduce severely foreign funding for Israeli Jewish and Palestinian human rights organizations and other NGOs that are critical of Israel. This bill specifically exempts limits on foreign funds from four outside Zionist groups that collect vast sums outside of Israel each year, namely, the World Zionist Organization, the Jewish Agency for Israel, the United Jewish Appeal, and the Jewish National Fund.

- A retroactive bill "to exempt the state from its responsibility for injuries and damages inflicted on Palestinians in the Occupied Palestinian Territories . . . from 2000 onwards."[61]

Many of these bills are likely to be reintroduced during future sessions of the Knesset.

The January 2013 Election—Prospects for Change?

In January 2013, Netanyahu faced another election. Press reports indicated that a right-wing party called *Habayit Hayehudi* ("The Jewish Home"), led by Naftali Bennett, was gaining in popularity and would probably win several seats in the Knesset. The party had been formed by the merger of three smaller parties, the National Religious Party, *Moledet* ("Homeland"), and *Tkuma* ("Resurrection"), whose platforms supported the ethnic cleansing of Palestinians outright. Although everyone expected Netanyahu to win, predictions were that he would need to build a coalition from the top vote-getters which would push the Likud party even further to the right.[62]

Bennett's extreme-right Jewish Home party won eleven seats in the 120-member Knesset, while Netanyahu's *Likud* party lost eleven seats (dropping from forty-two to thirty-one); but the major surprise was the ascendancy of a centrist party, *Yesh Atid*, or "There is a Future," which won nineteen seats. Its candidate, Yair Lapid, won support for his agenda to

61. Ibid.

62. Remnick, "Letter from Jerusalem."

reduce the financial and social inequality in Jewish society in Israel. Peace with Palestinians was not high on the agenda of Lapid or any major party.

Netanyahu's cabinet members seem determined to continue the rush to the right of recent governments. As Middle East expert Geoffrey Aronson noted, "Eitan Haber, a confidant of [former prime minister] Yitzhak Rabin, described the ruling coalition as 'the most right-wing government that Netanyahu could have assembled. The settlers . . . are inside the key positions and are closer to the decision-making process than ever before.'"[63] The influence of settler power was quickly demonstrated in March 2013, when the new finance minister, Yair Lapid, announced a major plan to build an additional sixteen thousand housing units in the illegal settlements[64] and on March 27, when the new minister of economics and trade, Naftali Bennett, called the two-state solution "beautiful statements" but "sadly detached from reality."[65] Given Netanyahu's background and deep convictions, it is hard to believe that basic change will emerge under his leadership. His lip service to a two-state solution appears to be a smokescreen for his actions. As long as there is no peace agreement, and no effective push-back from the U.S., he is free to continue the takeover of all of Palestine by authorizing thousands of new settlement units.

Moreover, Netanyahu's worldview continues to be shaped by both the "Iron Wall" doctrine of Revisionist Zionism and a nationalist appropriation of the Bible as history. While he does not claim to be religious, Netanyahu is quick to take advantage of the Zionist belief that emerged when the second generation of Zionists moved away from secular ideology and adopted a religious one, namely, that Jews were "promised" the land of Israel by God as it is described in the Torah/Bible. Here is where "political Zionism" and "religious Zionism" merge. Divine redemption is now seen as national redemption through human struggle. In May 2012, *Prophecy News Watch* reported that Netanyahu had "resurrected" the Bible Study Circle of Ben-Gurion:

> "The Bible is a parable for humanity," Netanyahu said at the outset in English, giving a powerful sound bite to the cameras invited to film just the opening of the study circle. "If the Jews are able to cross the river of time, and in their vast odyssey cross the

---

63. Aronson, "President Obama's trip," 1.

64. "Israel plans 16,000 more illegal settlement units in the West Bank and Jerusalem," *Middle East Monitor*, March 21, 2013, http://www.middleeastmonitor.com/news/middle-east/5546-israel-plans-16000-more-illegal-settlement-units-in-west-bank-and-jerusalem.

65. Podolsky, "Bennett Promises."

chasm of annihilation and come back to their ancestral home, that means there is hope for humanity."[66]

Mitri Raheb, pastor of the Christmas Church in Bethlehem, refers to this practice by secular Zionists as an intentional effort to *brand* the State of Israel as a "biblical entity."[67] The confusion meant that most Christians were not able to distinguish between biblical Israel and the newly created State of Israel.

> . . . Studying the book of Ruth, Netanyahu made clear what the message was:
>
> Ben-Gurion and Begin believed that the Bible should be the heritage of the entire nation—secular and religious, young and old, men and women. The Bible is the foundation of our existence. It unites the Jewish people, as it has throughout the generations. It also serves not only as a foundation but also as a map and compass, he said.[68]

Recent scholarship has examined this belief and how it is used in Israeli schools. Shlomo Sand's new book, *The Invention of the Land of Israel: From Holy Land to Homeland,* looks at this directly: "I don't think the religious affinity to the land gives you historical right. And after two thousand years, to pretend that the land is your land, if we continue with this logic, we can't accept the right of the whites, blacks and Latinos to live in New York. It's something dangerous, this idea."[69] Sand calls the presentation of a Jewish metaphysical relationship to the land "Zionist historiography." The transition has been made from "the Bible as theology" to "the Bible as history," and it is now taught as such in Israeli schools. Sand identifies three Jewish moral arguments used to establish the land of Israel as a national territory: the Bible is an accurate historical text; Jews were forcibly exiled from the Land in the year 70 CE (or a bit later); and most modern Jews were "racially" or "ethnically" descended from the ancient Hebrews.[70]

Nurit Peled-Elhanan, Hebrew University professor of language and education, describes this historiography as responsible for the hard-line views of young Israeli Jews. She says it is responsible for "a clear socialization

66. "Netanyahu Resurrects Ben-Gurion's Bible Study Circle," *Prophecy News Watch,* May 29, 2012, at http://www.prophecynewswatch.com/Archive2012/May29.htm.

67. Raheb, *The Invention of History,* 18–19.

68. "Netanyahu Resurrects," *Prophecy News Watch.*

69. Shlomo Sand, interview by Philip Weiss, "Shlomo Sand on Zionism, post-Zionism, and the two-state solution," *Mondoweiss,* December 13, 2012, http://mondoweiss.net/2012/12/shlomo-sand-on-zionism-post-zionism/.

70. Sand, *The Invention of the Land of Israel,* 203.

process" guided by a "racist education system." Peled-Elhanan is the author of *Palestine in Israeli Schools,* the most comprehensive study to date of the portrayal of Palestinians and the Israel-Palestine conflict in Israel's high school history and geography textbooks. In an interview Peled-Elhanan described the process of indoctrination:

> By the time Israeli kids go to the army, they have learned nothing about their Arab neighbors. Young Israelis are not even taught where the borders of their country are, so it is only natural that they think that the Palestinians are intruders on their land.
>
> "You begin with a Zionist narrative and it goes on and on and on through the ceremonies, through the media, and then through the army, with intense indoctrination," Daniel Bar-Tal, an internationally renowned professor of political psychology at Tel Aviv University, remarked to me. . . . So when you take into account all this information, it's not surprising that there is a right-wing consensus in Israel today.[71]

When we contrast the worldview of Netanyahu and the right-wing consensus in Israel today with the conditions for peace that would be acceptable to Palestinians and the wider Arab world, the gulf appears to be expanding rather than narrowing. In the wake of the 2013 elections, Rami Khouri, columnist for the *Beirut Daily Star* and a Palestinian Christian, observed that the new government would not begin to close this gap:

> I see no evidence that a majority of Israeli citizens has repudiated or even softened its position on the five critical issues that define Israeli-Palestinian and wider Arabism-Zionism interactions: Israel's positions on settlements and continued colonization, sharing Jerusalem, withdrawing from all lands occupied in 1967 (with swaps to be agreed), negotiating a mutually agreed and law-based resolution of the Palestine refugee issue (along with any claims by Jewish refugees, also to be based on the same laws and principles) and giving full rights to Palestinians with Israeli citizenship.[72]

This disheartening trend is taking a toll on Palestinian hopes for a just solution to the occupation. Daniel DePetris, who writes for the Institute for Policy Studies in Washington, DC, says the results of the latest two polls taken among Palestinians reveal "a stark and disturbing malaise in the Palestinian territories." He adds, "The numbers can best be summarized by Ali

71. Blumenthal, "Why the Israeli Elections."
72. Khouri, "Consolidating Its Center or Its Criminality?"

Najjar, an eighteen-year-old Palestinian who lives in a refugee camp. 'In my view,' he said, 'what was taken by force will only be returned by force.'"[73] His call for violent resistance reveals that many, old and young, are tired of waiting and want more immediate results. It also comes even as the non-violent BDS (Boycott, Divestment, and Sanctions) movement continues to gain traction in Palestine, Israel, and around the world.

There is a growing consensus everywhere, except in the U.S. and Israel, that an existing one-state situation/solution is irreversible and that the Israeli form of apartheid (segregation and separate development) is becoming more and more entrenched. Brant Rosen, a Reconstructionist congregational rabbi in Evanston, Illinois, co-chair of the Jewish Voice for Peace Rabbinical Council, and a contributing author in this book, was recently interviewed by Mark Karlin about his new book, *Wrestling in the Daylight: A Rabbi's Path to Palestinian Solidarity* (Just World Books, 2012). Asked if he thought "that Israel is in the process of becoming an apartheid state," he replied:

> It's not just a potential risk; I think we're witnessing the cost of this apartheid process every day. Even so, most Zionists are unable or unwilling to admit that this is what inevitably comes from fusing Judaism and political nationalism [Zionism]. But if you really consider it, how could it be otherwise? At the end of the day, how can you have a Jewish state that does not somehow treat non-Jews as "other"? That does not discriminate between Jews and non-Jews? That does not, on some level, create a system of institutional racism that privileges Jews over non-Jews?[74]

For our study of political Zionism, we are left with this question: What went wrong *at the ideological level*? That is, how did a project of Jewish liberation morph into a system of apartheid that has become a form of bondage for both Palestinians and Israelis? And here is another question: How can theology and ethics contribute to dismantling the ideological justifications for perpetuating this systemic bondage?

---

73. DePetris, "The Depth of Malaise in Palestine."

74. Rosen, interview by Karlin, "A Rabbi's Path," *Truthout*, October 10, 2012, at http://truth-out.org/opinion/item/12009-a-rabbis-path-to-palestinian-solidarity.

The Dream vs. the Reality: "By their fruits you shall know them."[75]

"If you will it, it is no dream," Herzl had declared.[76] But in 1896 when he first proposed a Jewish state, most people thought he was nothing more than a dreamer. The Zionists disagreed. Herzl's declaration became a popular slogan of the Zionist movement, and a half-century later the Jewish State of Israel came into being. Zionism has transformed a diverse collection of Jews from all over the world from a dispossessed people into a society with a modern economy, a relatively open and free culture and political system for its Jewish citizens, and a nuclear-armed military that ranks number four in the world. One of its most remarkable achievements is the creation of the modern Hebrew language, a feat that baffles other nations that have tried and failed to resurrect their ancient language. And who can deny the role of Zionism in creating a "new Jew," not only in Israel, but around the world? Even Zionism's critics recognize its astounding achievements. "Modern Israel is an incredible antithesis of the dry bones of Jewish existence two hundred years ago. In creating it, Zionism has performed a miracle," writes Haifa University Professor Benjamin Beit-Hallahmi, author of *Original Sins.*[77]

From the standpoint of national power and territorial expansion, there can be no doubt that Zionism has been successful. Judged by international law, human rights covenants, and UN resolutions—that is, judged by the democratic standards of a decent respect for the opinions of humankind—Zionism has been a dismal failure. Its consequences, whether intended or unintended, have raised fundamental questions about the long-term viability of Zionist ideology and Israel as a Zionist state. To put it bluntly, in today's world, is Zionism self-delegitimizing and therefore self-destructive? "Israel's major problem," writes Beit-Hallahmi, "is how to survive in a hostile world: many Israelis would see in that an extension of the Jewish condition" that Zionism set out to change.[78] The reason is obvious: Israel continues the expansion of its colonial settler project to seize control of Palestinian land and to dispossess the Palestinians. British social historian Tony Judt, who had once been an ardent Zionist, shocked the Jewish world in 2003 when his article, "Israel: The Alternative" appeared in *The New York Review of Books:*

75. Matt 7:20 (NKJV).

76. These stirring words appeared on the frontispiece of older editions of Herzl's novel, *Altneuland* (*Old New Land*). See Goldberg, "A Dream World."

77. Beit-Hallahmi, *Original Sins,* 210.

78. Ibid., 214.

The problem with Israel, in short, is not—as is sometimes suggested—that it is a European "enclave" in the Arab world; but
rather that it arrived too late. It has imported a characteristically late-nineteenth-century separatist project into a world that
has moved on, a world of individual rights, open frontiers, and
international law. The very idea of a "Jewish state"—a state in
which Jews and the Jewish religion have exclusive privileges
from which non-Jewish citizens are forever excluded—is rooted
in another time and place. Israel, in short, is an anachronism.[79]

Like other forms of European colonialism, the seed of its own corruption was embedded in Zionism from the beginning. Zionism shared the
dreams as well as the prejudices of nineteenth-century colonial imperialism. Those whose land they would colonize were regarded as "backward
races" without the same rights and privileges of the colonizers. In 1885, only
a decade before Herzl wrote *The Jewish State,* the major European powers
met in Berlin to divide up Africa and launch another chapter in the "civiliz-
ing mission" which Rudyard Kipling lampooned in his poem "The White
Man's Burden." After World War I, the victors drew the map of the Middle
East without consulting the people of the region.

How ironic for Zionism that the State of Israel was created in 1948
by the newly formed United Nations, whose charter rejected all forms of
colonialism and racial-ethnic discrimination, in part because of the Nazi
racism that led to the Holocaust. Zionism's failure—and perhaps inability—
to come to terms with "The Palestinian Question" that it helped create has
only reinforced Israel's ideological rigidity. At the same time that Zionism
has solved one aspect of the "Jewish Question" (a relatively secure homeland
for Jews), it has created for the world "The Israeli Question," which is how
to end Israeli apartheid and the Zionist ideology that sustains it.[80] And since
many Diaspora Jews today prefer not to live in or even travel to Israel, the
question has to be asked if the project has succeeded in providing a secure
homeland for Jews.

The Zionist movement that Herzl launched gained much of its support
from the history of humiliation and shame engendered by European persecution and Christian anti-Semitism and from the fear that no Jew anywhere
would ever be secure without a Jewish state. The Holocaust reinforced this
fear, turning it into a central Zionist doctrine. The new State of Israel acted
on this fear-based doctrine in 1950 by passing the Law of Return, granting

79. Judt, "Israel."

80. A survey conducted by Dialog, an academia-based peace and civil rights group
headed by Tel Aviv University professor Camil Fuchs, on September 16, 2012, found
that 58 percent of Israelis believe "there is apartheid in Israel." See Levy, "Survey."

the right of citizenship to all Jews who immigrate to Israel. Successive Israeli governments have mastered the art of manipulating this fear for political advantage in both domestic and foreign policy issues. In light of this persistent fear, one may ask: Has fear become a self-fulfilling prophecy, creating a self-perpetuating downward spiral of anxiety among political Zionists? How does one escape from the debilitating anxiety that fear produces, if the Zionist definition of the human condition—the never-ending hostility of non-Jews toward Jews—is a cornerstone of one's identity? Rabbi Brant Rosen comments:

> The Jewish state is now the only place in the world where Jewish people feel collectively endangered. Given Theodor Herzl's original vision, it's tragic to consider that the Jewish state has become a kind of Jewish ghetto of its own making—an over-militarized garrison state that is literally building higher and higher walls between itself and the outside world.[81]

In addition to fear, the Zionist movement, like other colonial movements, required collective denial of what was being done to Palestinians, a denial that may even be characterized as self-imposed blindness. The major American Jewish organizations[82] bear considerable responsibility for spreading this fear and blindness by their uncritical support for Israel over the years, especially since 1967.[83] In 1975 Fouzi El-Asmar invited I. F. Stone to write a preface to his book, *To Be an Arab in Israel*. As Wheatcroft tells it in *The Controversy of Zion*, Stone "accepted the author's charge: 'You have done to my people what others did to you.' . . . And he grasped that Zionism had involved a psychological act of denial along with a physical act of displacement; 'Jewish life went on *as if the Arabs weren't there*. In a profound sense, the *yishuv*, the Jewish community, had to pretend the Arabs

81. Rosen, interview by Karlin, "A Rabbi's Path."

82. For a list of the fifty-one member organizations, see the website of the Conference of Presidents of Major American Jewish Organizations, http://www.conferenceof-presidents.org/.

83. In his book *The Crisis of Zionism*, Peter Beinart discusses the role of American Jewish organizations that began their work on the left of the political spectrum but are now on the far right because of their hawkish support of the far-right Israeli government. Organizations like the American Jewish Congress and the American Jewish Committee were tasked with providing access to power for American Jews. By the 1970s, when Jews were well assimilated and were elected to the U.S. Congress in large numbers, the raison d'etre of such groups began to disappear. Rather than declare victory and fold, these organizations with multi-million dollar budgets changed their purpose to one of unconditional support for Israel and its government, even as it lurched further and further to the right. This stance is a cultural anathema for most of the American Jewish community, who are traditionally social justice Democrats.

weren't there or confront ethical problems too painful to be faced."[84] Stone's observation raises a fundamental question: Has the centuries-old legacy of humiliation and shame, often called victimhood, merged with the fear about survival to produce an institutional as well as a personal blindness that blocks the ability to examine Zionism's ethical contradictions and may actually contribute to its own self-destruction?

Anglican Archbishop Desmond Tutu chaired the South African Truth and Reconciliation Commission that helped his nation begin a process of healing after half a century of brutal apartheid. His book describing this process is entitled *No Future without Forgiveness*. In the case of Israel/Palestine, there is a prior step before forgiveness can begin: no future without moral truth.[85] Speaking moral truth will require both courage and compassion. The time has come for us all to name the Christian theological and ethical failures that gave rise to Zionism, as well as the Jewish theological and ethical failures that Zionism has produced. Each of the following chapters will address aspects of these theological and ethical challenges we now face.

Bibliography for Introduction and Chapters One and Two

Books and Periodicals

Alam, M. Shahid. *Israeli Exceptionalism: The Destabilizing Logic of Zionism*. New York: Palgrave Macmillan, 2009.

Aronson, Geoffrey. "President Obama's Trip: Masterful Rhetoric, but No Concrete Peace Proposals." *Settlement Report* 23/2 (March–April 2013) n.p.

Asmar, Fouzi El-. *To Be an Arab in Israel*. Beirut: Institute for Palestine Studies, 1978.

Ateek, Naim, et al., eds. *Challenging Empire: God, Faithfulness and Resistance*. Jerusalem: Sabeel Ecumenical Liberation Theology Center, 2012.

Avineri, Shlomo. *The Making of Modern Zionism*. New York: Basic Books, 1981.

84. Wheatcroft, *The Controversy of Zion*, 346.

85. Donald W. Shriver Jr., President Emeritus of Union Theological Seminary, is one of the few social ethicists who has examined the complex process of reconciliation between nations and groups within nations with a history of enmity. In his groundbreaking work, *An Ethic for Enemies: Forgiveness in Politics*, Shriver uses three case studies to illustrate four elements of narrative experience of groups committed to restored relationship. These are moral truth, forbearance, empathy, and commitment to repair fractured human relationships. "Forgiveness in a political context . . . calls for a collective turning from the past that neither ignores past evil nor excuses it, that neither overlooks justice nor reduces justice to revenge, that insists on the humanity of enemies even in their commission of dehumanizing deeds, and that values the justice that restores political community above the justice that destroys it" (9).

Avishai, Bernard. *The Tragedy of Zionism: Revolution and Democracy in the Land of Israel*. New York: Farrar Straus Giroux, 1985.

Baltzer, Anna. *Witness in Palestine: A Jewish American Woman in the Occupied Territories*. Boulder, CO: Paradigm, 2007.

Beck, Eldad. "Germany Delays Holocaust Survivor Restitution." *Ynetnews*, February 19, 2013. www.ynetnews.com/articles/0,7340,:L-4346776,00.html.

Beinart, Peter. *The Crisis of Zionism*. New York: Times Books, 2012.

Beit-Hallahmi, Benjamin. *Original Sins: Reflections on the History of Zionism and Israel*. New York: Olive Branch, 1993.

Ben-Gurion, David. *Ben-Gurion Looks at the Bible*. Translated by Jonathan Kolatch. Middle Village, NY: Jonathan David, 1972.

Ben-Gurion, David, and Thomas R. Bransten. *Memoirs: David Ben-Gurion*. New York: World, 1970.

Blumenthal, Max. "Why the Israeli Elections Were a Victory for the Right." *The Nation*, January 23, 2013.

Braverman, Mark. *Fatal Embrace: Christians, Jews, and the Search for Peace in the Holy Land*. Austin, TX: Synergy, 2010.

———. *Verhängnisvolle Scham: Israels Politik und das Schweigen der Christen*. Foreword by Mitri Raheb. Translated by Bernardin Schellenberger. Gütersloh: Gütersloher, 2011.

Cohen, Naomi W. *The Americanization of Zionism, 1897–1948*. Hanover, NH: University Press of New England, 2003.

Cumming-Bruce, Nick, and Isabel Kershner. "U.N. Panel Says Israeli Settlement Policy Violates Law." *New York Times*, January 31, 2013.

DePetris, Daniel. "The Depths of Malaise in Palestine." *Foreign Policy in Focus*, February 13, 2013. http://www.fpif.org/articles/the_depths_of_malaise_in_palestine.

Ellis, Marc. *Beyond Innocence and Redemption*. San Francisco: HarperCollins, 1991.

———. *Judaism Does Not Equal Israel*. New York: The New Press, 2009.

Filc, Dani. *The Political Right in Israel*. New York: Routledge, 2010.

Flapan, Simcha. *The Birth of Israel: Myths and Realities*. New York: Pantheon, 1987.

Gitlin, Todd, and Liel Leibovitz. *Chosen Peoples: America, Israel, and the Ordeals of Divine Election*. New York: Simon & Schuster, 2010.

Goldberg, David J. *The Divided Self: Israel and the Jewish Psyche Today*. London: I. B. Tauris, 2006.

———. "A Dream World." *The Guardian*, May 2, 2008.

Goldmann, Nahum. *The Jewish Paradox: A Personal Memoir*. New York: Grosset & Dunlap, 1978.

Goren, Arthur A. *Dissenter in Zion*. Cambridge, MA: Harvard University Press, 1982.

Gorenberg, Gershom. "Benzion Netanyahu's Legacies." *Daily Beast*, May 1, 2012.

Halper, Jeff. *An Israeli in Palestine: Resisting Dispossession, Redeeming Israel*. London: Pluto, 2008.

Hasson, Nir, Yossi Verter, and Barak Ravid. "Benzion Netanyahu, Father of Prime Minister Benjamin Netanyahu, Dies at 102." *Haaretz*, April 30, 2012.

Hertzberg, Arthur. *The Zionist Idea: A Historical Analysis and Reader*. 2nd ed. Philadephia: Jewish Publication Society, 1997.

Hess, Moses. *Rome and Jerusalem: A Study in Jewish Nationalism*. Lenox, MA: HardPress, 2013.

Israel-Palestine Mission Network of the Presbyterian Church (U.S.A.). *Steadfast Hope: The Palestinian Quest for Just Peace.* Louisville: Israel-Palestine Mission Network, 2011.

Judt, Tony. "Israel: The Alternative." *New York Review of Books*, October 23, 2003.

Karlin, Mark. "A Rabbi's Path to Palestinian Solidarity." *Truthout*, October 10, 2012. http://truth-out.org/opinion/item/12009-a-rabbis-path-to-palestinian-solidarity.

Kessler, Glenn. "Defining Jewish State: For Many, Term Has Different Meanings." *Washington Post*, October 2, 2010.

Khalidi, Rashid. *Brokers of Deceit.* Boston: Beacon, 2013.

Khouri, Rami G. "Consolidating Its Center or Its Criminality?" *Beirut Daily Star*, January 25, 2013.

Landau, Susan J. *Thou Shalt Not Stand Idly By: Reclaiming Jewish Voices of Conscience on Israel-Palestine.* Philadelphia: Philadelphia Jews for a Just Peace, 2008.

Levy, Gordon. "Survey: Most Israeli Jews Would Support Apartheid Regime in Israel." *Haaretz*, October 23, 2012.

Louis, William Roger, and Avi Shlaim, eds. *The 1967 Arab-Israeli War: Origins and Consequences.* Cambridge: Cambridge University Press, 2012.

Martin, Douglas. "Benzion Netanyahu Dies at 102." *New York Times*, April 30, 2012.

McCarthy, Rory. "Netanyahu Visits Moscow in Secret to Obstruct Iran Missile Sale." *Guardian*, September 10, 2009.

Morris, Benny. *Righteous Victims: A History of the Zionist-Arab Conflict, 1881–2001.* New York: Vintage, 2001.

Myers, David. "Benzion Netanyahu: In Life and Death." *Jewish Journal*, May 15, 2012.

Pappé, Ilan. *The Ethnic Cleansing of Palestine.* Oxford: One World, 2006.

———. *The Forgotten Palestinians: A History of the Palestinians in Israel.* New Haven: Yale University Press, 2011.

Paulson, Amanda. "Commencement 2011: What 10 Eminent Speakers Told Graduates." *Christian Science Monitor*, May 31, 2011.

Peled, Miko. *The General's Son.* Charlottesville, VA: Just World, 2012.

Piterberg, Gabriel. *The Returns of Zionism: Myths, Politics and Scholarship in Israel.* London: Verso, 2008.

Podolsky, Philip. "Bennett Promises to Prevent Capitulation to Palestinians." *The Times of Israel*, March 29, 2013.

Raheb, Mitri. *The Invention of History: A Century of Interplay Between Theology and Politics in Palestine.* Bethlehem, Palestine: Diyar, 2011.

Remnick, David. "Letter from Jerusalem—The Party Faithful: The Settlers Move to Annex the West Bank—and Israeli Politics." *New Yorker*, January 21, 2013.

Rose, Jacqueline. *The Question of Zion.* Princeton: Princeton University Press, 2005.

Rosen, Brant. *Wrestling in the Daylight: A Rabbi's Path to Palestinian Solidarity.* Foreword by Adam Horowitz. Charlottesville, VA: Just World, 2012.

Rosenberg, Yair. "The EU's Not-Quite Settlement Boycott." *Tablet Magazine*, July 16, 2013.

Ross, Jack. *Rabbi Outcast: Elmer Berger and American Jewish Anti-Zionism.* Washington, DC: Potomac, 2011.

Sand, Shlomo. *The Invention of the Land of Israel: From Holy Land to Homeland.* London: Verso, 2013.

———. *The Words and The Land: Israeli Intellectuals and the National Myth.* Los Angeles: Semiotext(e), 2011.

Sherwood, Harriet. "EU Takes Tougher Stance on Israeli Settlements." *Guardian*, July 16, 2013.

Shlaim, Avi. *The Iron Wall: Israel and the Arab World*. New York: Norton, 2001.

———."The Likud in Power: The Historiography of Revisionist Zionism." *Israel Studies* 1/2 (Fall 1996) 278–93.

Shriver, Donald W., Jr. *An Ethic for Enemies: Forgiveness in Politics*. New York: Oxford University Press, 1995.

Solomon, Abba A. *The Speech, and Its Context: Jacob Blaustein's Speech, "The Meaning of Palestine Partition to American Jews," Given to the Baltimore Chapter, American Jewish Committee, February 15, 1948*. Self published. Inquiries: TheSpeech.and. ItsContext@gmail.com. 2011.

Teveth, Shabtai. *Ben-Gurion and the Palestinian Arabs: From Peace to War*. New York: Oxford University Press, 1985.

Tutu, Desmond. *No Future Without Forgiveness*. New York: Doubleday, 1999.

Wheatcroft, Geoffrey. *The Controversy of Zion: Jewish Nationalism, the Jewish State, and the Unresolved Jewish Dilemma*. New York: Addison-Wesley, 1996.

Williams, David. "I See Peace for Palestine within a Year—but Swiss Cheese Isn't Going to Work." *Daily Mail*, January 11, 2008.

World Council of Churches. *Current Dialogue*. December, 2012. Special issue on Jewish-Christian Relations.

Yadid, Judd. "Word of the Day/Tov lamut be'ad artzeinu." *Haaretz*, July 3, 2013.

Websites

Adalah, the Legal Center for Arab Minority Rights in Israel. http://adalah.org.

The Association for Civil Rights in Israel. http://www.acri.org.il.

Betar U.S.A. Zionist Youth Movement. http://www.betar.org.

B'Tselem–The Israeli Information Center for Human Rights in the Occupied Territories. www.btselem.org.

Conference of Presidents of Major Jewish Organizations. www.conferenceofpresidents. org.

Congregation Beth Torah. http://beth-torah.org/.

The Council for European Palestinian Relations. http://thecepr.org.

The Daily Beast. http://www.thedailybeast.com.

Daily Mail. http://www.dailymail.co.uk.

Foreign Policy in Focus. A Project of the Institute for Policy Studies. http://www.fpif.org.

Foundation for Middle East Peace. www.fmep.org.

FOXNews.com. http://www.foxnews.com.

Globalwebpost.com. http://www.globalwebpost.com.

The Guardian. http://www.guardian.co.uk.

Haaretz. http://www.haaretz.com.

Hebrewsongs.com. http://hebrewsongs.com/song-shirbetar.htm.

Institute for Middle East Understanding. http://imeu.net.

Israeli Committee Against House Demolitions. http://www.icahd.org.

Jewish Encyclopedia. http://www.jewishencyclopedia.com.

JewishGen: An Affiliate of the Museum of Jewish Heritage. http://www.jewishgen.org.

Jewish Journal. http://www.jewishjournal.com.

Jewish Virtual Library. http://www.jewishvirtuallibrary.org/.

JTA: The Global Jewish News Source. http://www.jta.org.

Konrad Adenauer Stiftung. www.kas.de/wf/en/.

Middle East Monitor. http://www.middleeastmonitor.com.

Modern History Sourcebook. Fordham University. www.fordham.edu/Halsall/mod/modsbooks.asp.

Mondoweiss. http://mondoweiss.net.

My Jewish Learning. www.myjewishlearning.com.

The Nation. http://www.thenation.com.

The New York Review of Books. http://www.nybooks.com.

Only a Northern Song. Blog. http://northernsong.wordpress.com.

Palestine Remembered: The Home of Ethnically Cleansed and Occupied Palestinians. http://www.palestineremembered.com.

ProCon.org. Pros and Cons of Controversial Issues. www.procon.org.

Prophecy News Watch. http://www.prophecynewswatch.com.

Reliefweb. A Project of the United Nations Office for the Coordination of Humanitarian Affairs. http://reliefweb.int/report/occupied-palestinian-territory/water-life-water-all.

Roger Hollander: News and Opinion. Blog. http://rogerhollander.wordpress.com.

Sixdaywar.co.uk. http://www.sixdaywar.co.uk.

Tablet Magazine. http://www.tabletmag.com.

Truthout. http://truth-out.org.

The Washington Post. http://www.washingtonpost.com.

Wesleying: Real Student Life at Wesleyan University. Blog. http://wesleying.org/.

Ynetnews. http://www.ynetnews.com.

Zionism and Israel Information Center. http://www.zionism-israel.com.

Films

Between Two Worlds. Directed by Alan Snitow and Deborah Kaufman. Snitow-Kaufman Productions, 2011–12. http://btwthemovie.org/.

Defamation. Directed by Yoav Shamir. First Run Features, 2009.

Chapter Three

Rising to the Challenge
A Jewish Theology of Liberation

Brant Rosen

As a rabbi, a person of faith, and an activist committed to the values of universal human rights, my religious thinking has been profoundly influenced by the ideals of Palestinian Christian Liberation Theology. While most Jews are unaware of this ideology (and most members of the Jewish institutional establishment are deeply threatened by it), I have come to believe that the faithful work of Palestinian Liberation theologians presents an important spiritual/political challenge to my community. In this brief essay, I want to explore the nature of this challenge and suggest some ways that Jewish theology might rise to meet it.

Palestinian Liberation Theology is perhaps most famously articulated through the theological teachings of the Sabeel Center and its founder, Canon Naim Ateek. When I first read Ateek's book *Justice and Only Justice: A Palestinian Theology of Liberation,* it touched me deeply as both a moving spiritual autobiography and as a faithful theological treatise. It challenged me, as a Jew, to confront the implications of the story of a Palestinian who was expelled and exiled from his home through the creation of a Jewish nation-state. And on a deeper level, this testimony of a Palestinian Christian compelled me to reexamine my own relationship to my inherited biblical tradition.

I was particularly struck by his following observation:

> For most Palestinian Christians, as for many other Arab Christians, their view of the Bible, especially the Hebrew Scriptures . . . has been adversely affected by the creation of the State of Israel. Many previously hidden problems suddenly surfaced. The God of the Bible, hitherto the God who saves and liberates, has come to be viewed by Palestinians as partial and discriminating. Before the creation of the State, the Old Testament was considered to be an essential part of Christian Scripture, pointing and witnessing to Jesus. Since the creation of the State, some Jewish and Christian interpreters have read the Old Testament largely as a Zionist text to such an extent that it has almost become repugnant to Palestinian Christians.[1]

Clearly, Ateek's experience of the *Nakba* (Catastrophe) challenged his relationship to a sacred canon that was, and continues to be, used to justify his own people's oppression. As a religious Jew, I would suggest that his challenge is ours as well. Quite simply, the testimony of Ateek and his fellow Palestinian Christian theologians calls upon us to confront the ways Zionism uses our sacred spiritual tradition to justify the oppression of another people.

Challenge Articulated

In *Justice and Only Justice*, Ateek suggests three distinct ideological streams emerging out of the Hebrew Bible: "the nationalist, the Torah-oriented, and the prophetic."[2] He identifies the nationalist tradition in those biblical passages that describe "the use of force to achieve the Israelites' national goals."[3] This tradition, which comes to full fruition in the conquest and settlement narratives of Joshua, Judges, 1 and 2 Samuel, and 1 and 2 Kings, describes Israel's unique and privileged relationship to their God and is largely characterized by a land-centric, militaristic ethos.

The "Torah-oriented" approach, according to Ateek, is a product of the Pharisaic tradition that eventually evolved into Rabbinic Judaism following the destruction of the Second Temple. Unlike the "nationalist" approach, Pharisaic Judaism viewed militarism and political power with profound ambivalence and opposed a Jewish return to the land through human agency. Jewish communal life would henceforth be guided by the "Torah-oriented observance of the law," while the return to the land was

---

1. Ateek, *Justice and Only Justice*, 75.

2. Ibid., 93.

3. Ibid., 94.

projected into a far-off future messianic age.[4] While Ateek suggests that the theology of the "Torah-oriented" approach offers evidence of a "maturing God," he nonetheless notes that Rabbinic Judaism had a "tendency toward legalism and isolation, especially with regard to an often hostile European Christianity" and that "[its] concept of God at times betrayed exclusivity."[5]

The third and final stream draws its inspiration from the great prophetic traditions of the Hebrew Bible. For Ateek, this tradition is the most spiritually evolved, expressing a "deep, profound and mature understanding of God."[6] The later prophets in particular were notable for their universal and inclusive theological message—one that rejected the idea of a tribal, national deity in favor of a God that ruled over and would eventually redeem *all* humanity. Even so, continues Ateek, the universalist ideals of prophets were often expressed within a "massive quantity of material that is narrow, nationalist and exclusive." He points out that even Second Isaiah (often held up as among the most universalist of all prophetic works) evokes a palpable intolerance of nations that do not demonstrate obeisance to the God of Israel.

As a Christian, of course, Ateek locates the apogee of the prophetic tradition in the figure of Jesus, whose "inclusive understanding of God . . . breaks through so many books of the Old Testament."[7] Though he is unapologetic about his Christian faith in this regard, Ateek makes it clear he understands that such a theological step is untenable for Jews:

> Most Jews would not accept the validity of our perception of the New Testament as continuation of the prophetic tradition; that I understand. . . . However, as I have already indicated, since the source of the three traditions—the nationalist, the Torah-centered, and the prophetic—is the Old Testament, that is, the Hebrew Scriptures, I hope I may at least ask to be heard by them.
>
> What is quite clear from a Palestinian Christian point of view and in light of the above analysis, is that the emergence of the Zionist movement in the twentieth century is a retrogression of the Jewish community into the history of its very distant past, with its most elementary and primitive forms of the concept of God. Zionism has succeeded in reanimating the nationalist tradition within Judaism. Its inspiration has been drawn not from the profound thoughts of the Hebrew Scriptures, but from those

4. Ibid.
5. Ibid., 95.
6. Ibid., 96.
7. Ibid., 100.

portions that betray a narrow and exclusive concept of a tribal god.[8]

Ateek's characterization of Jewish political nationalism has inevitably led to charges of anti-Semitism from a contemporary Jewish establishment that now regards Zionism as coterminous with Judaism itself. However, while Ateek's fundamental critique of Zionism is undeniably painful for many Jews to countenance, it is important to remember that prior to the establishment of the State of Israel, many quarters of the Jewish community leveled similar criticisms at the Zionist movement.

The most notable example is the American Reform movement, whose leaders famously disavowed Zionism in their Pittsburgh Platform of 1885:

> We recognize, in the modern era of universal culture of heart and intellect, the approaching of the realization of Israel's great Messianic hope for the establishment of the kingdom of truth, justice, and peace among all men. We consider ourselves no longer a nation, but a religious community, and therefore expect neither a return to Palestine, nor a sacrificial worship under the sons of Aaron, nor the restoration of any of the laws concerning the Jewish state.[9]

In addition to the Reform movement, other prominent Jewish figures, including Ahad Ha'am, Martin Buber, Hannah Arendt, Rabbi Judah Magnes, and Simon Rawidowicz, voiced similar concerns over the potential dangers posed by political Zionism. On the eve of the establishment of the state, for instance, Arendt warned that "[Israel] would degenerate into one of those small warrior tribes about whose possibilities and importance history has amply informed us since the days of Sparta."[10] Magnes likewise wrote in 1942: "It is true that Jewish nationalism tends to confuse people, not because it is secular and not religious, but because this is unhappily chauvinistic and narrow and terroristic in the best style of Eastern European nationalism."[11]

While these kinds of prophetic Jewish voices have been effectively silenced since the trauma of the Shoah and the ascendance of Zionist ideology in the Diaspora Jewish community, we may well be witnessing the reversal of this trend as Arendt's prophetic warnings of a "Jewish Sparta" in the Middle East have become increasingly more difficult to deny, i.e., the

8. Ibid., 100–101.

9. Mendes-Flohr and Reinharz, *Jew in Modern World*, 372.

10. Arendt, *Jewish Writings*, 397.

11. Goren, *Dissenter in Zion*, 385.

establishment of a Jewish state through the ethnic cleansing of hundreds of thousands of indigenous Palestinians; a polity that openly fears a "demographic threat" to the Jewish state; infrastructural discrimination between Jewish and non-Jewish citizens; a crushing military occupation over non-Jewish residents in the midst of a rapidly expanding settlement regime; and the rise of an over militarized garrison state that is literally building higher and higher walls between itself and the outside world.

Ateek's views have also subjected him to withering attack from some contemporary Jews and Christians who identify his views with supersessionism, a theological viewpoint that has been roundly discredited in the post-Holocaust era. Also known as "replacement theology," this belief affirms a new Christian covenant that has superseded or replaced God's covenant with the Jewish people. In liberal religious circles, the ideology of supersessionism is now accepted as a root cause of Christian anti-Semitism. Indeed, supersessionist ideology has been used as justification by the church for its persecution of the Jewish people over the centuries, citing the Jews' "tribal" resistance to God's covenant with the "New Israel."

As a result, disavowal of supersessionism has become among the most inviolate tenets of contemporary Jewish-Christian dialogue and postwar liberal Christian theology. Responding to the dark legacy of church anti-Judaism that culminated in Christian culpability during the Shoah, prominent Christian theologians such as Paul Van Buren, Franklin Littell and others have constructed dramatic new theologies that now suggest that a Christian covenant does not break with the Jewish covenant at all but should be viewed as fully continuous with the Abrahamic promises of the Hebrew Bible.

In such a theological climate, it is inevitable that ideas such as Ateek's would become the target of vicious criticism from the Jewish establishment. In many important ways, we might say that Palestinian liberation theology collides head on with some of the most delicate, even incendiary, theological issues of our day, particularly in its juxtaposition of "particularist" Judaism/Zionism with the prophetic universalism of Jesus's ministry.

While this is obviously delicate theological territory, Jews and Christians alike nonetheless do Ateek a slanderous disservice when they accuse him of propagating anti-Semitism. Such slurs are particularly pernicious when we consider that Ateek clearly addresses his Jewish readers in good faith, admitting he understands that Jews cannot and do not share his beliefs, and asks only "to be heard by them." While Ateek's theological ideas are painfully challenging for many religious Jews, he clearly offers them to us in the spirit of dialogue that seeks honest and open conversation on points of tension between our faith communities.

Moreover, while we must certainly confront the extent to which supersessionist ideology historically played a role in Christian anti-Judaism, this conversation should not eclipse the universal aspects of Jesus's message and the prophetic challenge he leveled at the religious tribalism of his day. One of the most important new Jewish voices on this subject is writer/activist Mark Braverman, who has courageously urged liberal Christians not to rush to embrace traditional Jewish theologies of exceptionalism in the name of religious rapprochement:

> If Christians want to find a way to reconcile with Judaism and to bring the faiths closer together, then let us together look forward and find a way to join in a universal family. If, however, progressive Christians lead with an affirmation of the Jewish people's specialness, refitting aspects of Christian theology to allow for this, they end up negating the very thing that Christianity was doing, which was superseding the tribal in favor of the universal.[12]

This, then, is Naim Ateek's challenge to religious Jews who also cherish values of universal justice and human rights: we simply cannot look away from the tragic legacy of Jewish political tribalism that is embodied by the State of Israel. In the twenty-first century, an era marked by the rise of religious fundamentalisms as well as the growth of unprecedented connections between nations and faith traditions, this challenge is more critical than ever. Just as Christians are called upon to confront the exceptionalism of their religious tradition, the challenge remains before the Jewish people: What is the Judaism we seek to affirm? Will it based be on values of Jewish triumphalism or on values of universal justice and dignity for *all* of God's children?

If the answer is indeed the latter, what would such a Judaism possibly look like?

Constantinian vs. Prophetic Judaism

Since the end of Shoah and the rise of the State of Israel, the major American Jewish denominations have come to embrace the marriage of sacred Jewish tradition to political state power. Although the American Reform movement, as noted above, was originally opposed to Zionism, Reform, along with the other mainstream American Jewish denominations, now unabashedly attributes redemptive meaning to Jewish political nationalism.

---

12. Braverman, *Fatal Embrace*, 115.

(Tellingly, the most recent prayer books of the Orthodox, Conservative, Reform *and* Reconstructionist movements all contain the traditional version of the Prayer for the State of Israel,[13] which refers to the establishment of the Jewish state as "the beginning of the flowering of our redemption.")

It has also been observed that Israel occupies a quasi-religious place in the civic life of the American Jewish community. In his landmark study of American Jewish "civil religion," scholar Jonathan S. Woocher claims:

> The role which Israel plays in the civil religion [of American Jews] is indeed central, if complex. In practical terms, an enormous proportion of the energies of the institutions of the Jewish polity is devoted to work of one sort or another on behalf of the state and people of Israel. For many activists, Israel is the prime motivator and focus of their involvement. It remains the central theme and cause in communitywide fundraising campaigns. Jewish unity, mutual responsibility, and Jewish survival all come together in Israel; it is the symbolic center of the civil Jewish universe, the place where the lines of Jewish existence—of Jewish history and tradition, of the modern Jewish condition and the response to that condition—intersect.[14]

The religious centrality of the State of Israel has also been reflected in the work of post-Holocaust theologians such as Elie Wiesel, Robert Rubenstein, Emil Fackenheim, and Rabbi Irving Greenberg, who have suggested that following the Shoah, we now live in an era of God's absence—and that Jewish physical survival is now the new redemptive paradigm. According to Greenberg, the Jewish people currently live in an era "marked by a higher level of human responsibility and authority and with a greater emphasis on holy secularity."[15] The State of Israel, naturally, represents the epitome of this "holy secularity."

A newer generation of progressive Jewish theologians such Rabbis Arthur Waskow, Michael Lerner, and Arthur Green are less inclined to idealize state power in such redemptive terms and have openly criticized the ongoing human rights abuses of Israel's occupation. Despite their powerful witness, however, their critiques are invariably expressed within a liberal Zionist context, and they remain unwilling to confront the essential problems inherent in the merging of Judaism with idolatrous political nationalism.

13. See, for example, the prayer book for Reconstructionist Judaism, *Kol Haneshamah: Shabbat VeHagim.*

14. Woocher, *Sacred*, 77.

15. Greenberg, *For the Sake of Heaven and Earth*, 29.

In the end, the only notable Jewish thinker willing to promote an unabashed Jewish theology of liberation is dissident scholar Marc Ellis. In his pivotal work *Toward a Jewish Theology of Liberation*, Ellis states unreservedly that "identification with Israel is not, in and of itself, a religious act" and that "the refusal to see Israel as central to Jewish spirituality is not, in and of itself, an offense warranting excommunication."[16] He goes on to label Zionism "Constantinian Judaism," reminiscent of the transformation that occurred when the Roman Emperor Constantine elevated a marginal, and sometimes persecuted, Christianity to the religion of the empire in the fourth century.[17] Regarding Judaism in the current age, Ellis writes:

> The twenty-first century presents us with a series of challenges. Will the Jewish prophetic voice survive Jewish empowerment? Where will that voice be spoken and to whom? . . . Will that voice testify to the power of God or to God's inability to address unjust power? Will prophetic critique of injustice testify to God's renewed presence in the world or to his continuing absence so deeply felt by Holocaust theologians?[18]

Ellis goes on to suggest that an authentic Jewish theology of liberation must "feel a distinct tension between particularity and universality," resist Jewish establishment pressure for "a moratorium on critique of the Jewish community," help Jews develop an ideological discipline that can "flourish in exile from mainstream Jewish life," and, perhaps most critically, serve as "a call to *teshuvah* (repentance), commitment, and solidarity."[19]

Finally, Ellis concludes:

> Prophetic Jewish theology, or a Jewish theology of liberation, seeks to bring to light the hidden and sometimes censored movements of Jewish life. It seeks to express the dissent of those afraid or unable to speak. Ultimately, a Jewish theology of liberation seeks, in concert with others, to weave disparate hopes and aspirations into the very heart of Jewish life.[20]

Among other things, Ellis's framework dramatically reminds us that religion has historically been at its best when it acts prophetically, when it holds power to account, and when it is leveraged on behalf of the powerless, the oppressed, and the voiceless. Conversely, we inevitably witness religion

16. Ellis, *Toward a Jewish Theology of Liberation*, 214.

17. Ibid., 206.

18. Ibid., 205.

19. Ibid., 205–6.

20. Ibid., 206.

at its very worst when faith becomes wedded to empire—when religion is used by powerful nations to justify the subjugation of others.

Marc Ellis has come closer than anyone else in the Jewish world to fleshing out a response to the theological challenges of Canon Naim Ateek. It is time for other Jews to follow his lead and construct a true Jewish theology of liberation that will level a faith-based challenge to the Constantinian Judaism of our day.

In Search of a Hermeneutic

In presenting his theology of Palestinian liberation, Ateek rightly notes that Palestinian Christians must use a hermeneutic that will "help them to identify the authentic Word of *God* in the Bible . . . lest it in turn become a mere instrument to oppose Jewish and Christian Zionists and support subjective Palestinian claims and prejudices."[21] Not surprisingly, Ateek's Christian hermeneutic is grounded in "the Word of God incarnate in Jesus the Christ [who] interprets for us the *word* of God in the Bible."[22]

Traditional Judaism, by contrast, has historically viewed revelation through rabbinical interpretation of the oral and written law, a process traced back to God's giving of the Torah to the Jewish people at Mt. Sinai. On a strictly hermeneutical level, then, we are presented with a daunting challenge at the outset. Although traditional Judaism undeniably espouses myriad universal values, these values ultimately exist within a decidedly exceptionalist context. True, God reveals divine law to humanity, but it is ultimately revealed within an exclusive covenant with God's Chosen People. True, the God of the Torah is a God that hearkens to the oppressed and frees the enslaved, but it is ultimately the Israelite/Jewish oppressed to whom God responds. And while Jewish tradition looks forward to a messianic age in which all nations will be united in service to one God, this messianic vision ultimately assumes a universal subservience to the God of Israel.

We must thus accept that *an authentic Jewish theology of liberation will not be realized through traditional Jewish hermeneutics but rather through a pedagogy that liberates Judaism from a context of exceptionalism.* Our hermeneutic simply cannot proceed from a standpoint of Jewish superiority. It must help us to understand Jewish values as universal values and connect Jewish liberation with the liberation of *all* nations.

For our purposes here, I will suggest a modern interpretative approach to Scripture that regards biblical tradition less as the literal, unadulterated

21. Ateek, *Justice and Only Justice*, 79.
22. Ibid.

word of God to Israel at Sinai than as an ancient, humanly-derived record of one people's sacred struggles. With such an approach, our hermeneutic will necessarily regard the text as potentially fallible and resist the temptation to rationalize or explain away the triumphalist or racist elements of our tradition. In other words, we will be prepared to read biblical values in a meaningful contemporary context, and we will be just as willing to disavow and reject those aspects of the biblical text that contradict that context.

This hermeneutic is perhaps most famously exemplified in the work of Rabbi Mordecai Kaplan,[23] who referred to this form of interpretation as "revaluation":

> Revaluation consists of disengaging from the traditional content those elements in it which answer permanent postulates of human nature, and in integrating them into our own ideology. When we revaluate, we analyze or break up the traditional values into their implications which can help us meet our own moral and spiritual needs; the rest may be relegated to archeology.[24]

When we revalue a text, we first attempt to understand religious ideas in the context of the world in which they emerged. According to Kaplan, we then "take into account the changes which have since taken place, and how they affect the validity of the idea or value of the institution under consideration." Thus, "some modification of the original idea will suggest itself" so that it can function for us in the context of our contemporary age just as meaningfully as it did for those who lived in the ancient world.[25] Other times, however, changes in our current social/political/intellectual context will have rendered biblical values ethically indefensible.

Our hermeneutic will thus view Scripture as "multi-vocal," taking its cue from the insights of modern biblical criticism which point out that the Bible is not a unified, seamless narrative but rather the product of many different authors writing in different historical contexts and expressing different ideological agendas. Rendering this insight in theological terms, we might put it this way: the Bible contains a variety of voices, including the limited, time-bound voices of humankind *as well as* the sacred, eternal word of God.

As another modern rabbi, W. Gunther Plaut,[26] has observed:

23. American rabbi and founder of Reconstructionist Judaism (1881–1983).

24. Kaplan, *Meaning of God*, 6.

25. Ibid., 7.

26. Reform rabbi, author, and Torah commentator (1912–2012).

The Torah is ancient Israel's distinctive record of its search for God. It attempts to record the meeting of the human and the Divine, the great moments of encounter. Therefore, the text is often touched by the ineffable Presence. . . . God is not the author of the text, the people are, but God's voice may be heard through theirs as we listen with open minds.[27]

Using such a hermeneutic in a contemporary liberatory context, we must affirm without hesitation that the voice of God speaks to us whenever the Torah exhorts us to pursue justice, to stand by the oppressed, to call out the oppressor, and to affirm universal values of dignity for all who dwell on earth. Conversely, we must be prepared to assert in no uncertain terms that those aspects of biblical and religious tradition that espouse triumphalism, xenophobia, and the extermination of indigenous peoples are not the voice of God at all, but are, as Rabbi Michael Lerner has suggested, "the voice of pain and cruelty masquerading as God."[28]

The late Catholic scholar Dr. Michael Prior (whose work we will discuss more thoroughly later) has pointed out that otherwise liberal theologians too often use biblical hermeneutics to mask the essential moral problems posed by sacred texts that advocate (and have historically triggered) persecution:

Many theologians sensitive to issues of human rights, especially those whose traditions depend heavily upon the Bible, face a dilemma. While they revere the sacred text, they see how it has been used as an instrument of oppression. They seek refuge in the view that it is the misuse of the Bible rather than the text of the Bible itself which is the problem. The blame is shifted from the non-problematical biblical text to the perverse predispositions of the biblical interpreter. This "solution" evades the problem. Examples from the past and the present indicate the pervasiveness, the persistence and the moral seriousness of the question. . . . [It is clear] that several traditions within the Bible lend themselves to oppressive interpretations and applications precisely because of their inherently oppressive nature.[29]

So, too, an authentic Jewish theology of liberation must avoid at all costs the temptation to hide behind its hermeneutic. The ultimate goal of biblical interpretation is not simply to harmonize the text on its own rarified, academic terms but to lift up the lives of real people in the real world.

27. Plaut, *The Torah*, xix.
28. Lerner, *Jewish Renewal*, 92.
29. Prior, *Bible and Colonialism*, 45–46.

Through such a hermeneutic, we may yet find that the sacred struggles of these ancient authors will invariably become our own—and the God of liberation may yet transform our lives and our world anew.

Peoplehood Without Tribalism

Any Jewish theology must start with the most basic building block of Jewish identity, namely, peoplehood. Indeed, it is a foundational concept rooted in the earliest chapters of the Bible. In Genesis 12:2[30] God tells Abram: "I will make of you a great nation (*am gadol*)"; when confronting Pharaoh in Egypt, God proclaims in Exodus 8:17: "Let My people go (*sh'lach et ami*) that they may serve Me"; and in Exodus 19:5–6 God tells the Israelites at Sinai:

> Now if you will obey Me faithfully and keep My covenant, you
> shall be My treasured possession among all the peoples. Indeed,
> all the earth is Mine, but you shall be to Me a kingdom of priests
> and a holy nation (*am kadosh*).

Through the development of rabbinic Judaism, the concept of *Am Yisrael* (the people of Israel) developed well beyond the biblical model of a territorially based Israelite nation. It is critical to bear in mind that Judaism as we know it today evolved and blossomed *outside* the land following the destruction of the Second Temple. Indeed, the Diaspora provided deeply fertile ground for a new spiritual group identity: a global Jewish peoplehood that eventually transcended national borders, ethnicities, and cultures.

At the same time, however, Jewish peoplehood became deeply invested with a religious exceptionalism that increasingly viewed the Jewish nation as God's exclusively Chosen People. While it could certainly be claimed that the Chosen People ideology was the understandable psychological/spiritual defense of a people experiencing significant persecution at the hands of powerful empires throughout its history, we cannot and should not gloss aspects of Jewish tradition that express a decidedly xenophobic belief in Jewish superiority over other peoples and religious traditions.

Confronting this ethical challenge, Rabbi Mordecai Kaplan has courageously written:

> We cannot fail to recognize in the claims of Jewish superiority a
> kinship and resemblance to the similar claims of other national

---

30. This and all subsequent biblical quotations in this essay are reprinted from the *Tanakh: The Holy Scriptures* by permission of the University of Nebraska Press. Copyright 1985, 1999 by the Jewish Publication Society, Philadelphia.

and racial groups which have been advanced to justify oppression and exploitation. Such claims have been used in defense of the imperialistic exploitation of the yellow and black races by the whites on the ground that they were "the white man's burden." They are the ground for the German persecution of Jewry. . . . They were in the past the grounds on which our own people rationalized their conquest and expropriation of the Canaanites. The highest ethical thought of our day views all such claims to the superiority of the one race, nation or caste as detrimental to the interests of humanity, and hence as essentially vicious.[31]

To put it plainly: a voice that affirms claims of theological superiority in the name of *one people* cannot be the voice of God. A voice that asserts God's word to humanity was vouchsafed *exclusively* to the children of Abraham cannot be the voice of God. A voice that looks to the messianic day in which all nations will ultimately serve the *God of Israel* cannot be the voice of God. If we seek an expression of Jewish peoplehood that reflects "the highest ethical thought of our day," we will, quite simply, have to search elsewhere.

Let us begin with the biblical episode in which Jacob wrestles with a night stranger and subsequently receives the name Israel (Genesis 32:25–33). This classic mythic moment identifies the birth of Jewish peoplehood in the personage of Jacob as he transforms from the trickster/schemer to the wounded/healed "One Who Wrestles with God." From a liberationist perspective, we might say the sacred element of this story is to be found in the Jewish people's eternally recurring process of struggle and transformation, and *not* in an exclusive promise to Abraham's descendants. That is to say, the defining aspect of Jewish peoplehood resides in our readiness to wrestle with divine meaning and purpose—to encounter God through cycles of struggle and change that inevitably lead Jacob, our people, and indeed *all* peoples, toward liberation and reconciliation.

Defining the name "Israel" in a spiritual rather than tribal sense will be daunting, particularly in a day and age in which this word has become almost exclusively associated with a Jewish nation-state. The classical Jewish value of *Ahavat Yisrael* (love of your fellow Jew) is similarly challenging. Traditionally meant to reflect the importance of internal Jewish communal support and cohesion (particularly during times of external threat to the community), this value, it must be admitted, has also served to reinforce the more overtly tribal, triumphalist aspects of Jewish identity.

---

31. Kaplan, *Meaning of God*, 95.

Is it even possible to understand the value of *Ahavat Yisrael* in a universal context? This is a particularly thorny question given what we now know about social identity construction. What does it mean to "love" members of your "tribe," knowing that national identities are culturally conditioned? This question is even more complicated in an era where increased intermarriage has helped to create a Jewish community that is more diverse and dynamic today than ever before. What does Jewish communal loyalty mean when the very definition of "who is a Jew" has become a subject of such profound intra-communal debate?

Since the very truth of our peoplehood is so complex and ever-changing, we simply must find ways to bestow a more universal meaning upon *Ahavat Yisrael*. We must actively question whether our solidarity should automatically extend to embrace those in our "tribe" who affirm exclusivist, xenophobic, or racist values. Conversely, the time may well have arrived for us to construct a model of peoplehood that makes room for "fellow travelers" who may not share our mythic bloodlines but with whom we share deep common bonds of conviction.

Again, our biblical story of Jacob/Israel offers some possible answers. As the word *Yisrael* literally means "Wrestles With God," we may render *Ahavat Yisrael* not simply as "love of your fellow Jew," but as "solidarity with those who struggle." In other words, we honor the value of *Ahavat Yisrael* when we love *all* who fight for freedom and justice and tolerance in the world; when we stand in solidarity with those who struggle against tyranny and are beaten, imprisoned, tortured, or killed for doing so; and when we throw our ultimate allegiance together with those who wrestle deeply with meaning in their lives and who seek to tear down the walls of religious dogma and ideological coercion.

Clearly, this new understanding will be too radical for many Jews to contemplate. But if *Ahavat Yisrael* is to be a *truly sacred* value, it must mean more than simple ethnic allegiance. True solidarity must ultimately be defined in terms of values and not mere tribal loyalties. The boundaries of Jewish peoplehood will have to be firm enough to instill a healthy sense of belonging, yet permeable enough for the Jewish people to find common cause with spiritual sisters and brothers who also struggle in the sacred quest for liberation.

This new understanding of *Ahavat Yisrael* is particularly critical in an era in which Jewish loyalty is too often understood as unblinking allegiance to the State of Israel. In the contemporary Jewish world, the sacred value *Ahavat Yisrael* is too often assumed to mean "love of [the State of] Israel." In the end, we must not forget that well before Jewish communal identity was reduced to political nationalism by the Zionist movement, Jewish peoplehood had always been defined as a multi-cultural, multi-ethnic, multi-lingual spiritual community without borders. We must therefore seek to reclaim this vision—and stand down the limiting vision of Jewish nation-statism—as the primary religious model for Jewish identity.

Exodus, Not Eisodus

If the story of Jacob/Israel is a transformational Jewish narrative in personal microcosm, the Exodus story presents this transformation on a collective scale. The Exodus is, of course, the sacred liberation story *par excellence,* in which God hearkens to the cry of the persecuted, rebukes the oppressor pharaoh and frees the enslaved. While this narrative is clearly presented within a particularist context (God hearkens to the cry of *God's* oppressed people), it has historically resonated with universal power. As the social and political scientist Michael Walzer has observed, a myriad of liberation movements have been indelibly marked with Exodus consciousness throughout the course of Western civilization.[32]

On the most basic level, then, a Jewish theology of liberation must necessarily view the Exodus as a particular narrative of a certain people *as well as* a universal narrative that encompasses all humanity. The oppression of the Jewish people must be understood as inseparable from the oppression of all peoples; likewise, the liberation of the Jewish people must be inextricably linked to the liberation of all peoples. While the historical events may differ in the details, they are all bound by a common sacred truth: the voice of the God of Liberation calls out in every language and in every generation to demand the liberation of the oppressed.

However, if we read the Exodus story honestly and unflinchingly, we must be ready to admit the presence of another, darker voice present in this narrative. The Exodus not only describes the liberation of an oppressed people from bondage but also contains the story of a journey toward and entrance into a "Promised Land" inhabited by other peoples, indigenous inhabitants whom the Israelites are commanded to dislodge and exterminate without pity.[33]

As difficult as it may be to read morally repugnant passages such as these in one's "sacred" text, it is even more unsettling when we consider that these imperatives are inextricably bound to our cherished liberation narrative. In a sense, the "Exodus" is only the first half of a much longer story, a saga that begins with the Israelites' exit from Egypt (Exodus) and ends with

---

32. Walzer, *Exodus and Revolution*, 4.

33. See, for instance, Deut 20:16–18 and Josh 6:21–26.

their entrance into Canaan (Eisodus). In other words, we cannot ultimately separate the Exodus from God's promise of the land, and this promise cannot be fulfilled without the Israelites' obedience to a commandment that demands nothing less than ethnic cleansing and even genocide.

The late Roman Catholic scholar Dr. Michael Prior has left us with a profoundly important and often devastating critique of the biblical Eisodus tradition. In a 2000 essay entitled, "Confronting the Bible's Ethnic Cleansing in Palestine,"[34] Prior described his "growing unease about the link between biblical spirituality and oppression" during his studies as a visiting university student in the West Bank in the 1980s. As a result of his witness, he felt compelled to examine the land traditions of the Bible more deeply and to confront the essential moral problems that lie at their core:

> By modern standards of international law and human rights, what these biblical narratives mandate are "war crimes" and "crimes against humanity." While readers might seek refuge in the claim that the problem lies with the predispositions of the modern reader, rather than with the text itself, one could not escape so easily. One must acknowledge that much of the Torah, and the Book of Deuteronomy in particular, contains menacing ideologies and racist, xenophobic, and militaristic tendencies. The implications of the existence of dubious moral dispositions, presented as mandated by the divinity, within a book which is canonized as Sacred Scripture, invited the most serious investigation. [Is] there a way of reading the traditions which could rescue the Bible from being a blunt instrument of oppression, and acquit God of the charge of being the Great Ethnic-Cleanser?[35]

Prior became committed to evaluating the land traditions of the Bible against "general ethical principles and criteria of human decency, such as are enshrined in conventions of human rights and international law," believing resolutely that "any association of God with the destruction of people must be subjected to an ethical analysis," demanding that we ask ourselves whether we *really* seek to apologize for biblical texts that portray God as "a chauvinistic, nationalistic and militaristic xenophobe."[36]

Prior's scholarship was guided by the conviction that "biblical studies and theology should deal with the real conditions of people's lives, and not satisfy themselves with comfortable survival in an academic or

34. Prior, "Confronting the Bible's Ethnic Cleansing," 1.

35. Ibid., 4–5.

36. Ibid., 12.

ecclesial ghetto." In particular, he was concerned "about the use of the Bible as a legitimization for colonialism and its consequences."[37] His subsequent scholarship thus examined the way the biblical land tradition inspired "the colonization by Europeans of Latin America, South Africa, and the Middle East" as well as "the history and development of Zionism."[38]

Prior concluded:

> Biblical scholars have the most serious obligation to prevent outrages being perpetrated in the name of fidelity to the biblical covenant. The application of the Bible in defense of the Crusades, Spanish and Portuguese colonialism, South African apartheid, and political Zionism has been a calamity, leading to the suffering and humiliation of millions of people, and to the loss of respect for the Bible as having something significant to contribute to humanity.[39]

As Prior's challenge makes all too clear, the moral problems of the biblical land tradition are not simply academic. They have had, and continue to have, real-life consequences for real people. Thus, those who cherish biblical tradition cannot equivocate on this point: we simply *cannot* lift up the Exodus tradition without also simultaneously calling out the Eisodus tradition. As Prior rightly pointed out, even liberation theologians themselves cannot be exempted from this challenge.[40]

The rabbis of the Talmud famously responded to biblical holy war tradition by honoring these precepts as eternal and divinely authorized commandments while at the same time creating legal restrictions that made them virtually inoperative in practice.[41] In our day, however, there can be no hesitation on this issue: a theology of Jewish liberation must celebrate the voice of God that demands freedom in the Exodus story *and* be prepared to reject the voice of human cruelty and oppression that calls for holy war against Canaan's indigenous peoples.

To be sure, this is a religious and moral duty for all liberation theologies, but for obvious reasons it is particularly critical for the Jewish people living in the age of Zionism. We cannot be unmindful that the land traditions of the Bible were central to the formation of Jewish political nationalism and have been used in various ways by early Zionist ideologues, by the political founders of the state, and by the present-day religious settler

---

37. Ibid.

38. Prior, *Bible and Colonialism*, 14.

39. Ibid., 292.

40. Ibid., 278–79.

41. See Firestone, *Holy War in Judaism*, 73–76.

movement.[42] The insidious comparison of Palestinians to the nations of Canaan has become particularly ubiquitous in the words of Israeli politicians, settler leaders, and ultra-religious rabbis alike. Statements such as these must not be dismissed as mere religious rhetoric. These theological linkages have enormous power, particularly when we consider the historical reality of the Zionist enterprise that includes the expulsion of Palestinians from their homes in 1947–48 and policies of displacement and transfer that continue to this very day.

This is not to say that an honest reckoning with the land tradition means simply ignoring or somehow "surgically excising" the Israelite Eisodus from biblical tradition. It *does* mean, however, that as suggested above, we recognize the voice that commands the genocide of others for what it is and what it is not. Through this recognition, these otherwise odious passages may yet become spiritually instructive to us, albeit in a decidedly different way.

As Prior has observed, "It is high time that biblical scholars, church people, and Western intellectuals read the biblical narratives of the promise of the land 'with the eyes of the Canaanites.'"[43] Prior admits that his consciousness on this point was raised after reading the comments of one Native American activist: "The obvious characters for Native Americans to identify with are the Canaanites, the people who already lived in the promised land. . . . I read the Exodus story with Canaanite eyes."[44] (This statement by one of the "Bible's victims" recalls Ateek's observation that the use of the Old Testament as a "Zionist text" has rendered it almost "repugnant to Palestinian Christians.")

Testimonies such as these call to us to encounter these texts in a new way—not through apology or disregard, but with *sacred empathy*. If we are truly to hear the sacred voice of liberation speaking through biblical tradition, we must be prepared, quite simply, to read the story of the Exodus through the eyes of the Israelites and the story of the Eisodus through the eyes of the Canaanites.

"All the Land is Mine"

Rabbi Meir Lau, former Chief Ashkenazi Rabbi of the State of Israel, tells of meeting David Ben-Gurion in 1973. Lau told Ben-Gurion that he had heard an interesting story about a 1937 meeting between Ben-Gurion and

42. See Masalha, *Bible and Zionism*, 135–64.

43. Prior, "Confronting the Bible's Ethnic Cleansing," 12.

44. Prior, *Bible and Colonialism*, 43.

Lord Peel, who was then in Palestine heading a British Royal Commission of Inquiry into partition of the land. According to the story, Lord Peel asked Ben-Gurion where he was born. Ben-Gurion replied that he was from Plonsk, Poland.

Lord Peel said, "Very strange indeed. All of the Arab leaders who have appeared before me were born in Palestine. Most of the Jewish leaders who have appeared before me were born in Eastern Europe. Mr. Ben-Gurion, the Arab people have a *Kushan* (Ottoman land deed) entitling them to this land. Do you have a document saying that Palestine belongs to you?"

At that point, Ben Gurion became aware of the Bible in his hand upon which he had previously sworn an oath to serve as witness to the commission. He held it up triumphantly and exclaimed, "Here is your *Kushan*. It is the world's most highly respected book, and I believe that you British regard it with much respect too. We must have this land."

Upon meeting Ben-Gurion in 1973, Rabbi Lau asked him, "Is this story really true? Did you hold up a Bible and say 'Here is your document'?" Smiling, Ben Gurion replied, "*Emet Veyatziv*" ("It is true and certain").[45]

Whether or not this story is "true and certain," it speaks to a central tenet of political Zionism that views the Bible as the essential justification for Jewish statehood in historic Palestine. For secular Zionists such as Ben-Gurion, the Bible is regarded as an ancient Jewish history book. It remains a mandatory aspect of Israeli public school curriculum to this day. For religious Israelis and Zionists such as Rabbi Meir Lau, it represents nothing less than the God's eternal "bill of sale" of the land to the Jewish people.

Leaving aside the problem of using an ancient, mythic and profoundly ahistorical document such as the Bible as the justification for founding a modern nation-state, let us look more carefully at the theological claim that regards the Bible as the Jewish people's "bill of sale" to the land.

From the very first verse in the Torah, it is established that ultimate ownership of the earth belongs to God and that humanity is created to be its stewards and caretakers. In Genesis 1:28 God tells the first man and woman, "Be fertile, and increase, fill the earth and master it; and rule the fish of the sea, the birds of the sky, and all the living things that creep upon the earth." The universal context of this commandment makes clear that human "mastery" of the world does not denote ownership or exploitation. Humanity is given dominion over the earth and may use it for its benefit. But the earth certainly does not *belong to* humanity; moreover, as the subsequent flood narrative makes perfectly clear, the future of human beings on the earth is radically dependent on *how they behave upon it*.

45. Lau, "Oxford Chabad Society Lecture."

Soon enough in the biblical narrative, of course, God will offer a certain piece of the earth to Abraham and his descendants.[46] While the Abrahamic covenants in Genesis are promissory in nature, by the time the Israelites enter into a formal covenant with God at Sinai, the promise has become decidedly conditional. From Exodus on, the Israelites are told they will "long endure on the land that the Lord your God is giving you"[47] *only if* they obey the terms of God's covenant.

In other words, Israel's mere presence on the land does not constitute "ownership." When God instructs the Israelites to institute the jubilee year, for instance, God says pointedly, "the land must not be sold beyond reclaim, *for the land is Mine; you are but resident aliens with Me.*"[48] The conditional nature of the covenant is driven home even further in Leviticus 18:26–28 when God warns the Israelites "not to do any of the abhorrent things . . . that were done by the people who were in the land before you, and the land became defiled. Let not the land vomit you out for defiling it." Later, in Deuteronomy, God similarly admonishes the children of Israel:

> When you have begotten children and children's children and are long established in the land, should you act wickedly and make for yourselves a sculptured image in any likeness, causing the Lord your God displeasure and vexation, I call heaven and earth to witness against you that you shall soon perish from the land that you are crossing the Jordan to possess; you shall not long endure in it but shall be utterly wiped out. The Lord will scatter you among the nations to which the Lord will drive you.[49]

These passages make it clear that in the biblical conception, the land does not and cannot "belong" to anyone but God. The Israelites, like all nations who dwell on the land, are temporary residents who stand in relation to the land not as "property/heir" but rather as "gift /recipient."[50]

After the fall of the Second Temple in 70 CE, the Jewish theological relationship to the land became even more complex. Rabbinic Judaism responded to the loss of the land by developing into a diaspora-based religion, broadening Jewish theology to allow for communion with God anywhere Jews may live. In a celebrated midrash, Rabbi Akiba taught, "Wherever the

---

46. See Gen 12:6–7, 13:14–17, 15:18–21, 17:5–8, 26:3–4, 28:4, 28:13–15, 35:12.

47. Exod 20:12.

48. Lev 25:23–24.

49. Deut 4:25–27.

50. Burge, *Jesus and the Land*, 7.

people of Israel were exiled, the Divine Presence was exiled with them."[51]
Teachings such as this indicate a dramatic post-Temple theological reconstruction that rejected a geographically specific God enthroned in the Jerusalem Temple in favor of a God in exile. In so doing, the rabbinic Judaism
transformed a land-based cultic practice to a global civilization, enabling
Jewish life to flourish and grow throughout the Diaspora.

Post-Second Temple Judaism, in other words, *spiritualized* the land by
refracting present Jewish experience through the mythic memory of biblical Israel. Throughout Talmudic literature, for instance, we find extensive
discussions of agricultural and sacrificial laws that apply exclusively to the
land. These rabbinic discussions served multiple functions: they helped
to maintain the memory of an idyllic, mythic past; they enabled rabbinic
exegetes to adapt these laws to ever-changing diasporic contexts; and they
served to keep alive laws that they believed would be reinstituted following
the messianic restoration to the land.

Despite these fundamental theological shifts, however, we can still de-
tect a palpable strain of religious entitlement to the physical land throughout
the course of Jewish tradition. One well-known example of this attitude may
be found in the commentary of the medieval Jewish commentator Rashi,[52]
widely considered by traditional Jews to be the most authoritative interpreter of biblical tradition. In a comment on Genesis 1:1, Rashi asks rhetorically
why the Torah begins its narrative with God's creation of the earth. Would
it not have made more sense to begin the Torah with the verse from Exodus
12:2, which contains the very first commandments to the people of Israel?

Rashi answers by quoting a famous midrash from Genesis Rabbah 1:2:

> [If] the nations of the world should say to Israel, "You are rob-
> bers, for you conquered by force the lands of the seven nations
> [of Canaan]," they will reply, "The entire earth belongs to the
> Blessed Holy One; God created it (this we learn from the story
> of the Creation) and gave it to whomever God deemed proper.
> When God wished, God gave it to them, and when God wished,
> God took it away from them and gave it to us."[53]

Most understand Rashi's interpretation here as a thinly veiled defense
against the European Christian nations' dismissal of Judaism as a tribal religion of violence and war. Nevertheless, by offering this defense, Rashi essentially reduces a universal cosmic narrative to an exclusivist polemic that
exists only to justify the Jewish people's claim to a physical piece of land. It is

51. Epstein, "Babylonian Talmud, Megillah 29a," 175.
52. Rabbi Shlomo Yitzhaki, Troyes, Champagne (1040–1104).
53. Rashi on Gen 1:1 (translation mine).

also notable that while Rashi sees God's gifting of the land to the Israelites as self-evident, he *fails* to make the next obvious statement: while according to the Torah, God did indeed "take the land away" from the Canaanite nations and "give it to the Israelites," God would eventually "take the land away" from the Israelites as well.

In the end, a Jewish theology of liberation must reject such attempts to treat the Jewish people's relationship to the land as any more self-evident than that of any other nation. We must affirm that our relationship to the land is not an inherent entitlement nor does it result from our superiority to other peoples. Rather, we must take our cue from the biblical notion of a conditional covenant and affirm that our future on the land—indeed, the future of any peoples—is radically dependent upon how we see fit to live *upon* the land.

Using our hermeneutic of revaluation, we can say that it is *conditionality* and not *entitlement* that is the inherently sacral element of the biblical land tradition. While in ancient times this conditionality focused primarily on idolatrous worship of the gods of other nations, in our day we may understand conditionality as dependent upon values such as human rights, equity and religious freedom for all who live on the land. We must take seriously the Bible's warning that Israel is no different from other nations inasmuch as the land can "vomit them out" just as easily as the nations that came before and after us.

In short, conditionality applies to all. If there is a covenant between God and Israel, it must extend to include a multiplicity of peoples who have lived on the land throughout the centuries and who live there still. In the end, it is a covenant that challenges these various faiths and nations to behave in such a way that *all* may long endure on the land that God has given them.

Judaism and Empire

Those who seek an authentic Jewish theology of liberation must also honestly reckon with the relationship between Judaism and state power. To return to our earlier point, a central tenet of liberation theology holds that religion is at its very worst when it is used as justification by empires to enable them to wield their power oppressively over others—and at its best when it holds power to account and leverages God's power on behalf of the powerless, the oppressed, and the voiceless.

It is fair to say that biblical tradition has a strong ambivalence toward the institution of what we would today call centralized state power. While, as noted above, the land tradition contains a troubling advocacy of brutal conquest, the eventual settlement envisioned in the Torah is essentially a decentralized tribal confederacy. The institution of kingship is eyed warily at best; in Deuteronomy 17:14 the laws pertaining to the Israelite monarchy begin thus:

> *If*, after you have entered the Land that the Lord your God has assigned to you, and taken possession of it and settled in it, you decide, "I will set a king over me as do all the nations about me."

This verse makes it clear that God's original intention was not for the ancient nation of Israel to be a kingship "like other nations" (*ke'chol ha'goyim*) but rather, as God told the Israelites earlier in Exodus, to be a "kingdom of priests and a holy nation."[54] Later, when the Israelite kingship is actually established in the book of 1 Samuel, it is notably portrayed as a *rejection* of prophetic leadership. The elders of Israel assemble before the prophet Samuel and demand, "We must have a king over us, that we may be like all the other nations: Let our king rule over us and go at our head and fight our battles."[55]

While Samuel is grieved by this request, God reassures him by explaining that this is not a failure of his prophetic leadership, but rather a rejection of God, characterizing their desire for a king as part of their overall penchant for idolatry: "Like everything else they have done since I brought them out of Egypt to this day—forsaking Me and worshiping other gods—so they are doing to you."[56] Not long after the Israelite kingship is established, of course, it becomes rife with corruption, focused on paranoid militarism, split in two, and inevitably overrun from within and without.

This ambivalent attitude toward Jewish empire was developed even more thoroughly by Rabbinic Judaism following the disastrous experiences of the Hasmonean dynasty (110–63 BCE) that ascended to power following the Maccabean revolt against the Selucid Empire. This event—much celebrated in Zionist mythos—was to become a brief and decidedly ignoble moment in Jewish history. The priestly Hasmonean dynasty viciously persecuted the rabbinic Pharisees, engaged in internecine warfare, and attempted ill-advised wars of conquest against surrounding nations. In the end, the Roman Empire would overthrow the Hasmoneans in 63 BCE, and this period of Jewish independence in the land lasted less than one hundred years.

54. Exod 19:6.
55. 1 Sam 8:19.
56. 1 Sam 8:8.

Perhaps because the rabbis were wary of those who would put their ultimate faith in political/military power, they were notably silent regarding the military adventures of the Maccabees in connection with the festival of Hanukkah. Their only mention of the revolt is a glancing, apocryphal story of the miraculous cruse of oil that lasted for eight days after the rededication of the Temple.[57] Notably, the rabbis chose as the prophetic portion for Hanukkah an excerpt from the book of Zechariah containing the classic line, "'Not by might and not by power, but by my spirit,' says the Lord of Hosts."[58]

So too, the rabbis were deeply ambivalent about the ill-fated Jewish revolts against Rome that had brought massive tragedy and ruin upon the Jewish people. Following the destruction of the Second Temple and the subsequent failure of the Bar Kokhba rebellion (132–136 CE), the Jewish sages explicitly suppressed the temptation toward militarism and war. Any attempt to bring about a return to Jewish sovereignty in the land through rebellion or revolution was considered to be a forcing of God's hand—"an act of disobedience that would only bring further divine wrath and additional disasters for the Jewish people."[59]

The rise of Zionism in the modern era, however, was a conscious rejection of this rabbinic ideology in favor of a new Jewish *realpolitik*. In the writings of Zionists dating back to Theodor Herzl, we can clearly discern the strong impulse for a "Jewish return to history" and for the Jewish people, once again, to be "*ke'chol ha'goyim*"—"like other nations." While the central motivation for Zionism emerged from a very real, and not unfounded, concern over anti-Semitism as well as a desire for a national Jewish renaissance, it is poignant to recall God's words to the prophet Samuel when we now consider what Jewish political nationalism has wrought: the people should be careful what they wish for.

To be sure, the desire to be "like other nations" meant different things to different Zionists. For political Zionists like Theodor Herzl, it meant creating a liberal nation state similar to those in nineteenth century Western Europe. To Labor Zionists such as A. D. Gordon, it meant the creation of a viable Jewish working class. To cultural Zionists such as Ahad Ha'am, it meant a cultural/spiritual center for world Jewry. For Revisionist Zionists such as Ze'ev Jabotinsky, it meant the maintenance of a Jewish military force dedicated to Jewish self-defense.

But while it is important to understand the emergence of Zionist ideology in historical context, it is even more critical that we confront the

---

57. Epstein, "Babylonian Talmud, Shabbat 21b," 91–92.

58. Zech 4:6.

59. Firestone, *Holy War in Judaism*, 75.

reality of Zionism in its current reality: the State of Israel is now the living embodiment of Judaism as empire. It demonstrates, all too tragically, the consequences of this quasi-Faustian bargain we have made with political nationalism. The Jewish people, for centuries the victims of empire *and* the guardians of a sacred tradition that promoted a spiritual alternative to the veneration of human power, has betrayed its unique spiritual vision in favor of idolatrous nation-statism and militarism.

In this sense, then, a Jewish theology of liberation would represent a return to certain profound religious strains in biblical and rabbinic tradition. It would mean affirming, as 1 Samuel would have it, that the overweening desire for national power is itself a kind of idolatry and a turning away from God. It would mean responding to national tragedy as the rabbis did: with the affirmation that mighty empires may come and go, but the Jewish people have survived because we have affirmed a transcendent power much greater than any human power.

And, conversely, it would affirm that when we put our faith in the power of empire, we may well be sowing the seeds of our own destruction.

Toward a New Interfaith Covenant

I have offered above what I hope might be a new kind of response to the daunting challenges presented by Palestinian Liberation Theology to the Jewish faith community. I have done so with the realization that my responses will be enormously difficult, if not impossible for many in my community to countenance. Still, there are emerging indications that the growth of Jewish Liberation Theology may not be as unthinkable as previous generations may have assumed.

Ellis writes that "Jewish theology must help Jews develop a discipline that can flourish in exile from mainstream (Constantinian) Jewish life."[60] While this is certainly true, there is every indication that a new generation of Jews is taking root in the fertile ground Ellis has helped to cultivate. In recent years, we have witnessed the growth of alternative Jewish institutions such as Jewish Voice for Peace,[61] organizations that are challenging the American Jewish establishment's Constantinian hegemony on Israel. This new flourishing is leading, in turn, to new interfaith coalitions of conscience

---

60. Ellis, *Toward a Jewish Theology of Liberation*, 206.

61. Jewish Voice for Peace is a progressive, grassroots-based American Jewish organization founded in 2006. According to its mission, JVP is "inspired by Jewish tradition to work together for peace, social justice, equality, human rights, respect for international law, and a U.S. foreign policy based on these ideals."

that we might well view as the emergence of an exciting new interfaith covenant.

As stated above, a central pillar of post-war interfaith dialogue was the disavowal of theological supersessionism in favor of a view that regarded the Christian covenant as continuous with the covenant with Abraham in the Hebrew Bible. While this new formulation may have served to assuage Christian guilt over centuries of Church anti-Semitism, it has failed to address the problematic exceptionalism of the original covenant. Just as troubling, these interfaith negotiations inevitably have led to what Ellis and others call an "ecumenical deal"[62] in which liberal American Christians have been theologically blackmailed into silence over Israel's human rights abuses.

It seems, however, that this deal is starting to fray at the edges and that a new kind of grassroots interfaith covenant is beginning to emerge. In 2012, a group of Christian lay leaders, academics, and clergy convened to found Kairos USA, a response to the landmark 2009 *Kairos Palestine* document.[63] As did the signers of *Kairos Palestine*, the founders of Kairos USA drafted their document as an act of witness to the "sin of the occupation." As part of their witness, the Christian signatories made a confession that included an acknowledgement of Christianity's "shameful role in the historic persecution of the Jewish people" as well as church complicity in the Holocaust. However, their confession also went on to include a painful admission of past silence on Israel's treatment of Palestinians and a new readiness to work for a just peace that respects a commitment to "the dignity and human rights of the Palestinians" and affirms "a dedication to the humanity of their Jewish sisters and brothers."[64]

Inevitably enough, the Kairos USA statement was excoriated by professional Jewish establishment institutions such as the Jewish Council for Public Affairs, which hysterically condemned its "extreme rhetoric" and referred to it as a "false witness."[65] However, this time abject dismissal was not to be the final word of the Jewish community. In a public letter, the Kairos USA statement was openly embraced by members of the Jewish Voice for Peace Rabbinical Council:

> We are inspired by the confessional nature of the Kairos document for past sins against the Jewish people. Thank you for

---

62. Ellis, *Unholy Alliance*, 54.

63. Released in 2009, *Kairos Palestine* was signed by prominent Palestinian Christian leaders as a faith-based call for justice in Israel/Palestine.

64. Kairos USA, "Call to Action."

65. Jewish Council for Public Affairs, "Jewish Council for Public Affairs."

acknowledging your role in Jewish suffering. As Jews, the Christian confession awakens a responsibility to consider and confess our own sin, the sin of occupation. We cannot stand idly by when members of our extended Jewish family ask us to support dispossession, land confiscation, the destruction of homes and property, military invasion, torture, and the building of separation walls on the basis of shared identity. Our *vidui* (confession) must include ways in which we have privileged Jewish suffering over and against Palestinian suffering and the ways in which we use the claim of anti-Semitism to silence those who criticize Israel's violation of human rights. We share this perception with Kairos USA.[66]

While these rabbis represent but a small fraction of the American Jewish clergy so far, their willingness to respond publicly in such a way to the witness of their Christian sisters and brothers indicates the emergence of a new kind of interfaith covenant, not one that glosses over difficult issues or engages in emotional blackmail or theological bartering but one that finds common cause on issues of human rights in a land that holds deep religious significance for both faith traditions.

This new covenant does not view its primary work through the rarified and carefully controlled discourse of "interfaith dialogue" but rather through real-world activism that seeks nothing less than the transformation of an oppressive status quo. To this end, Jewish clergy and activists are increasingly voicing support for church divestment efforts that seek to shift the balance of power in Israel/Palestine. An important statement in this regard may be found in the 2012 Rabbis' Letter, a statement of twenty-six Jewish clergy and leaders who publicly supported attempts within the Methodist and Presbyterian churches to disengage their financial holdings from corporations that profit from Israel's occupation:

> There is in fact a growing desire within the North American Jewish community to end our silence over Israel's oppressive occupation of Palestine. Every day Jewish leaders—we among them—are stepping forward to express outrage over the confiscation of Palestinian land, destruction of farms and groves and homes, the choking of the Palestinian economy and daily harassment and violence against Palestinian people. Members of the Jewish community are increasingly voicing their support for nonviolent popular resistance against these outrages—including the kind of cautious, highly-specified divestment such

66. Jewish Voice for Peace Rabbinical Council, "Honor the Courage, Clarity, and Sensitivity of Kairos USA."

as the United Methodist   Church and the Presbyterian Church (USA) are preparing to undertake. . . .

As Christians, you have your own particular stake in the land to which both our traditions have long attachments of faith and history. We particularly acknowledge the oppression of Palestinian Christians under Israeli occupation and the justice of your efforts to relieve the oppression directed against your fellows.

To advocate for an end to an unjust policy is not anti-Semitic. To criticize Israel is not anti-Semitic. To invest your own resources in corporations which pursue your vision of a just and peaceful world, and to withdraw your resources from those which contradict this vision, is not anti-Semitic. There is a terrible history of actual anti-Semitism perpetrated by Christians at different times throughout the millennia and conscientious Christians today do bear a burden of conscience on that account. We can understand that, with your commitment to paths of peace and justice, it must be terribly painful and inhibiting to be accused of anti-Semitism.[67]

The increasing number of Jewish leaders who are willing to take a public stand to draft and sign statements provides a hopeful indication that our community may well be ready to meet the challenge presented to us by Canon Naim Ateek and his colleagues at Sabeel. We hope and pray that this new covenant will inspire us to find the courage to do God's work together so that we may help to hasten the day in which true liberation is proclaimed throughout the land to *all* the inhabitants thereof.

Bibliography

Ateek, Naim Stifan. *Justice and Only Justice: A Palestinian Theology of Liberation.* Maryknoll, NY: Orbis, 1989.

Arendt, Hannah. *The Jewish Writings.* Edited by Jerome Kohn and Ron H. Feldman. New York: Schocken, 2007.

Braverman, Mark. *Fatal Embrace: Christians, Jews and the Search for Peace in the Holy Land.* New York: Beaufort, 2010.

Burge, Gary M. *Jesus and the Land: The New Testament Challenge to "Holy Land" Theology.* Grand Rapids: Baker Academic, 2010.

Ellis, Marc. *Toward a Jewish Theology of Liberation: The Challenge of the 21st Century.* Waco, TX: Baylor University Press, 2004.

———. *Unholy Alliance: Religion and Atrocity in Our Time.* Minneapolis: Fortress, 1997.

67. Jewish Voice for Peace, "Rabbis' Letter."

Epstein, I., ed. "Babylonian Talmud, Megillah 29a." In *The Babylonian Talmud: Seder Moed in Four Volumes*. Vol. 4, *Tractate Megillah*. London: Soncino, 1938.

———. "Babylonian Talmud, Shabbat 21b." In *The Baylonian Talmud: Seder Moed in Four Volumes*. Vol. 1, *Tractate Shabbat*. London: Soncino, 1938.

Firestone, Reuven. *Holy War in Judaism: The Fall and Rise of a Controversial Idea*. New York: Oxford University Press, 2012.

Goren, Arthur A., ed. *Dissenter in Zion: From the Writings of Judah L. Magnes*. Cambridge, MA: Harvard University Press, 1982.

Greenberg, Irving. *For the Sake of Heaven and Earth: The New Encounter Between Judaism and Christianity*. Philadelphia: Jewish Publication Society, 2004.

Jewish Council for Public Affairs. "Jewish Council for Public Affairs Shocked by Extreme Rhetoric of Kairos USA Document." June 21, 2012. http://engage.jewishpublicaffairs.org/blog/comments.jsp?blog_entry_KEY=6389.

Jewish Voice for Peace. "Rabbis' Letter." 2013. http://www.rabbisletter.org/.

Jewish Voice for Peace Rabbinical Council. "Honor the Courage, Clarity, and Sensitivity of Kairos USA." http://kairosusa.org/?q=node/53.

Kairos USA. "Call to Action: U.S. Response to the *Kairos Palestine* Document." http://www.kairosusa.org/images/kairosusabooklet.pdf.

Kaplan, Mordecai M. *The Meaning of God in Modern Jewish Religion*. Detroit: Wayne University Press, 1994.

Kol Haneshamah: Shabbat VeHagim. Jenkintown, PA: Reconstructionist, 1994.

Lau, Meir. "The Oxford Chabad Society Joseph Graham Memorial Lecture." St. Anne's College, May 7, 2006. http://www.oxfordchabad.org/templates/articlecco_cdo/aid/384600/jewish/Rabbi-Israel-Lau-Lecture-for-Chabad-Society.htm.

Lerner, Michael. *Jewish Renewal: A Path to Healing and Transformation*. New York: HarperPerennial, 1994.

Masalha, Nur. *The Bible and Zionism: Invented Traditions, Archaeology and Post-Colonialism in Israel-Palestine*. London: Zed, 2007.

Mendes-Flohr, Paul, and Jehuda Reinharz, eds. *The Jew in the Modern World: A Documentary History*. New York: Oxford University Press, 1980.

Plaut, W. Gunther, ed. *The Torah: A Modern Commentary*. New York: Union of American Hebrew Congregations, 1980.

Prior, Michael. *The Bible and Colonialism: A Moral Critique*. Sheffield: Sheffield Academic Press, 1997.

———. "Confronting the Bible's Ethnic Cleansing in Palestine." *The Link*, newsletter of Americans for Middle East Understanding 3/5 (December 2000).

Tanakh: The Holy Scriptures: The New JPS Translation According to the Traditional Hebrew Text (NJPS). Philadelphia: The Jewish Publication Society, 1985.

Walzer, Michael. *Exodus and Revolution*. New York: Basic, 1986.

Woocher, Jonathan, S. *Sacred Survival: The Civil Religion of American Jews*. Bloomington: Indiana University Press, 1986.

Chapter Four

Eastern Orthodox Perspectives on Zionism and Christian Zionism

Voices from the Ancient Church, from Modern America, and from the Middle East Today

Carole Monica Burnett

The author would like to express gratitude to Marilyn Rouvelas, Anne Glynn-Mackoul, and Gabriel Habib for providing sources for this essay.

IN THE VALLEY BETWEEN Mount Gerizim and Mount Ebal (see Josh 8:30–35), in the northern part of the West Bank, is an ancient well known as "Jacob's Well" (in Arabic, *Bir Yacoub*), which is believed to be the site where Jesus conversed with the Samaritan woman (John 4). The property has been in Christian hands since the days of the Roman Empire. Surrounding and protecting the well are the walls of a Greek Orthodox church, which is open to tourists and pilgrims.

On the night of November 29, 1979, intruders vandalized the interior of the church and murdered the parish priest, Father Philoumenos, by hacking the shape of a cross into his face with vertical and horizontal blows of a hatchet. In addition, they chopped off the three fingers of his right hand that he had used for blessings. Although the identity of the marauders has not been established, a strong indicator is provided by the fact that fanatical Zionist settlers had menacingly confronted Father Philoumenos a few days earlier, claiming the well as Israeli property and demanding the removal of

Christian artwork from the premises. Father Philoumenos has since been canonized as an Orthodox saint and a martyr for the faith.[1]

It is evident that the tangible effects of Zionism are acutely felt by Orthodox Christians. Relatively large in size among the Holy Land churches,[2] the Orthodox Church has much to lose in terms of harm to people and property. Moreover, walls and checkpoints impede access to churches and holy sites; for example, a middle-aged Palestinian couple (known personally to the author of this chapter) living about five miles from Jerusalem can no longer visit the Orthodox church on the Mount of Olives where their teenage and young adult children were baptized as infants, because of the prohibitive Israeli restrictions on travel. A more conspicuous example is that of the Orthodox School of Bethany operated by the Russian Orthodox Convent of Saint Mary Magdalene on the Mount of Olives in Jerusalem. A former principal of the school, Mother Agapia Stephanopoulos (sister of the well-known Greek-American television news commentator George Stephanopoulos), has worked vigorously, through public lectures and visits to U.S. Representatives and Senators on Capitol Hill, to arouse concern about the hardship imposed on the school, which serves both Christian and Muslim students, and about the suffering inflicted on the Palestinian population by the Israeli wall, which she characterized as "worse than the Berlin wall." When the government of Israel erected its "Separation Barrier" (part-wall, part-fence, snaking through the West Bank and East Jerusalem, separating farmers from their fields and family members from each other), Mother Agapia's school was cut off from the homes of 25 percent of its students and of some of its teachers. Merely getting to school became a difficult challenge for these students and teachers. Moreover, the economy of the town of Bethany has suffered drastically because the wall, which not only separates Bethany from Jerusalem and its tourists, but also slices across the main street, separates businesses from many of their former Palestinian clientele. Such crises have been multiplied throughout the West Bank as the erection of the barrier has proceeded.[3]

It is no wonder that the Christian population of the Holy Land is slipping away, migrating to other countries, after nearly two thousand years

---

1. Online: http://orthodoxwiki.org/Philoumenos_(Hasapis)_of_Jacob's_Well and http://www.allsaintsofamerica.org/martyrs/nmphilou.html.

2. Online: "FACT SHEET: Palestinian Christians in the Holy Land," at http://imeu.net/news/article0023369.shtml; also, "FACTBOX—Christians in Israel, West Bank and Gaza," at http://uk.reuters.com/article/2009/05/10/uk-pope-mideast-christians-sb-idUKTRE5491FH20090510.

3. Tsine, "Israeli Settlement Barrier." For the bisection of the main street, see McCarthy, "Bethany."

of continuous Christian witness in the land of Christ's birth. Yet the Orthodox Church has not adopted an official position on the dilemma posed by aggressive Zionism. This may seem puzzling, but is understandable in light of the fact that the collegiality of the Orthodox bishops as well as the self-governance of the various ethnic jurisdictions do not provide for a monarchical leader or central bureaucracy authorized to speak on behalf of all of the world's Orthodox Christians. This absence of centralization, however, can be a source of strength because it allows room for a chorus of voices.

The voices of the Orthodox Church include clergy and lay folks of diverse ethnicities. In the case of Zionism, it is primarily Arabs and Arab-Americans who have spoken out, although the Greek Orthodox Archdiocese in the United States has also been engaged in the issue. This essay will introduce the reader to some of these thinkers, hierarchs, and activists. First, however, it is necessary to delve into the theological foundations on which Orthodox thought and action are based. Since the Orthodox Church listens attentively to the voices of the past, heeding its centuries of tradition,[4] no discussion of Orthodoxy would be complete without an excursion into historical theology.[5]

Theological Foundations

The teachings of the Orthodox Church are based on Scripture as interpreted in the ancient, time-tested writings of the church fathers and mothers and the statements of the seven Ecumenical Councils (which took place between 325 and 787 CE in what is now modern Turkey). Since the Ecumenical Councils did not address issues that can be linked to questions raised by the modern Christian Zionist movement,[6] let us look at the works of

4. The word "tradition" may ring jarringly in the ears of some Christians. It is employed here to refer to the church's cumulative experience throughout history in interpreting and endeavoring to live out the tenets of Holy Scripture. The Orthodox Church gives special attention to the early centuries as the most formative ones.

5. The scope of this chapter is confined to the Orthodox churches that stand in agreement with the Council of Chalcedon (451 CE), which identified two natures in Christ, human and divine. After this council, a grievous schism ruptured the church, and today there are churches that include the word "Orthodox" in their names but are not part of the Chalcedonian branch of the church. Some examples are the Coptic, Syriac, Armenian, and Ethiopian Orthodox churches. The author of the present essay is warmly inclined toward these churches, but does not discuss them in this chapter both because of space limitations and because of the language barrier, which impedes research.

6. See note 14 below.

the early Christian theologians, each of whom was grappling with specific theological problems generated in a particular historical context.

The presence of anti-Jewish rhetoric in some of the ancient Christian writings may give pause to some readers. Therefore, a few words of clarification are in order. First, it must be stressed that the anti-Semitism of the twentieth century, which was based on genealogy and theories of racial inferiority, has nothing to do with the theological debate of the early centuries of the Common Era. The fathers and mothers of the church welcomed all believers of all ethnicities. Secondly, it is clear from the writings of the bishops Ignatius of Antioch (martyred ca. 110 CE), Melito of Sardis (late second century), and John Chrysostom (late fourth century) that these Christian leaders were concerned about Christians who participated in Jewish rites and festivities or sought wisdom from Jewish sources; in sermons and letters they asserted that church members should maintain a single-minded loyalty to their own family of faith.[7] In the process of strenuously discouraging Christians from engaging in any sort of dual membership, the homiletic remarks of Melito and John Chrysostom extended to harsh invective against the Jewish community. Other ancient Christian writers, too, pointed to their local Jewish communities as examples of behavior to be avoided. Although the horrific events of subsequent eras must not be excused, it is necessary to understand, in regard to the ancient church leaders, that within the context of the rhetorical techniques commonly employed in the time of the Roman Empire, *ad hominem* language targeting one's theological or political adversaries was regarded as normal; in fact, Christians on opposite sides of a theological controversy (such as the fourth-century debate on the relationship of the Father and Son) typically attacked each other with insults that would be considered scandalous in today's marketplace of ideas.

Without ignoring these considerations, let us now look at some of the issues confronting the early theologians. It was natural that the emergence of a new faith community would elicit questions that had not yet been encountered. A pressing issue was the status of the Old Testament. As Joseph Trigg has remarked, "The status of the Old Testament for Christians was a delicate question because Patristic authors had to maintain a balance between the positions of Jews and Gnostics."[8]

On the one hand, the predominantly Jewish composition of the early church compelled its leadership to identify which of the precepts of the Old Testament (such as those regarding circumcision and dietary regulations, as

7. See Ignatius of Antioch, *Epistle to the Magnesians*, 8–10 and *Epistle to the Philadelphians*, 6–9, 96–97, 109–11; Melito of Sardis, *On Pascha*; John Chrysostom, *Homilies against Judaizing Christians*.

8. Trigg, *Biblical Interpretation*, 19.

well as ethical norms such as those of the Ten Commandments) should be honored; this discussion is found in the New Testament, especially in Acts 15 and in the Epistle to the Galatians. Moreover, after the destruction of the Jerusalem Temple in 70 CE, both Jews and Jewish Christians were forced to reassess the importance of the cultic practices dependent on the Temple; such a discussion is found in the Epistle to the Hebrews. An even more foundational issue was that of covenant and chosen-ness: if the Jews were God's chosen people, what had become of God's fidelity to his own promises, and where did the church, which was experiencing an influx of Gentile believers, fit into God's plan? Paul wrestled with these matters in Romans 8–11, and these troubling issues persisted well beyond Paul's time, as seen in the pseudonymous *Epistle of Barnabas* and in Justin Martyr's *Dialogue with Trypho the Jew,* both written in the mid-second century. A resolution was sought in a Christocentric approach to the Old Testament. By means of this approach, which was a standard feature of patristic exegesis (the biblical interpretation of the church fathers), the entire Bible with both of its Testaments was perceived as an integral whole, and therefore any portion of it could be interpreted by the application of any other portion; thus the teachings of the New Testament were used as a key to unlock the meaning of the Old Testament.

On the other hand, there were second- and third-century Christian groups that rejected the Old Testament—groups such as Gnostics and Marcionites—finding it impossible to believe that the warlike God depicted in it could be the same as the loving Father of Jesus Christ. Some Gnostics even went so far as to say that the Creator of our material world had committed an evil act by generating bodies with physical limitations that hinder spiritual existence. Surely the spiritual entity at work in Genesis 1–2 could not be a force for good. In response to these groups also, church fathers utilized a Christocentric method of interpretation that retained the Old Testament in the canon of sacred Scripture but also pointed to Christ as its underlying principle of unity and meaning.

The particular exegetical approach that maintained a crucial role for the Old Testament in the church, yet pointed to God's revelation in Christ as its linchpin, was that of typology and allegory, which are closely related to each other and rely on symbolism.[9] Allegory is the description of spiritual realities, such as Christian virtues and vices, in accounts of tangible, concrete events. For example, the stories of battles between ancient Israelites and various tribes in the land of Canaan could be seen as metaphorical

---

9. A symbolic approach to exegesis had been employed by the first-century Jewish scholar Philo, whose writings influenced early Christian theologians.

descriptions of battles between fidelity to God and the temptations to sin against God. Typology is the symbolism whereby the events and characters of Old Testament stories function as foreshadowing, or prefiguration, of the events and characters in the story of the incarnation, earthly ministry, crucifixion, and resurrection of Jesus Christ, or in the life of the church. Below are some examples of the ways in which allegory and typology served to provide a Christocentric view of the Old Testament, based on the uniquely Christian assumption that Christ is the source of meaning, the *raison d'être,* of the Old Testament. These examples have been chosen for this chapter because they have a bearing on the perspectives of early Christian thinkers on the "Promised Land," the land granted to ancient Israel and now claimed by the modern State of Israel.

The New Testament itself contains examples of the use of typology and allegory. In 1 Cor 10:1–4 Paul depicts the cloud and the Red Sea of the Exodus story as symbolizing baptism, and the rock from which water flowed as symbolizing Christ, thus perceiving Old Testament narrative elements as types of Christ and of Christian initiation. To the Galatians, Paul specifically names his method as "allegory," employing the Greek participle *allēgoroumena* to describe what he is about to impart, namely, that Hagar the slave and her children represent those who are under the Law, whereas the freewoman Sarah and her descendants symbolize those who live by the Gospel (Gal 4:21–31). In addition to Paul's writings, the anonymous Epistle to the Hebrews, with its Platonic concept of ideal forms and imperfect copies, presents the Israelite priesthood and sacrificial cult as transitory precursors of Jesus, the perfect high priest, who sacrificed himself once and for all (Heb 7–10).

Continuing this New Testament approach, the *Epistle of Barnabas,* written by an unknown author probably between 130 and 140, utilizes typology extensively, portraying the scapegoat of Yom Kippur as a type (prefiguration) of Christ, who took our sins upon himself; the boy Isaac, being led to the sacrificial altar by his father Abraham, as a type of the crucified Son of God; and Joshua as a type of Jesus (the two names being the same in Greek: *Iēsous*). Entry into the Promised Land is the transformation of the human being as a new creature in Christ.[10]

Likewise, the Christian philosopher Justin Martyr (martyred ca. 165 CE) in his *Dialogue with Trypho the Jew* expounds an intensely Christocentric exegesis that regards Christ's advent, ministry, death, and resurrection, as well as the life of the church, as the message and purpose of the Old

---

10. *Epistle of Barnabas,* 6.8–17, 7.3, 7.6–11, 12.8–10.

Testament.[11] Justin highlights the parallel between the *Iēsous* (Joshua) of the Old Testament and the *Iēsous* (Jesus) of the New Testament, but also contrasts the two, pointing out that the land distributed to ancient Israel by Joshua was merely a transitory gift whereas the heavenly dwelling-place promised by Christ is for eternity. Moreover, he notes, the eternal gift is for all the peoples of the earth, not merely for a single ethnic group. Justin's words are clear: the land grant to ancient Israel was tied to a particular era of history and is surpassed by salvation in Christ.[12] The inheritance promised to Abraham will be bestowed upon all people of any ethnic group who believe in Christ and renounce sin, "because by our similar faith we have become children of Abraham."[13]

Although Justin believed in an eschatological thousand-year reign of Christ with his followers in Jerusalem,[14] as certain of today's evangelicals do, he believed that the timeframe of one thousand years was based on numerical symbolism indicating a temporal period of some fixed duration, rather than being a number to be taken literally. More importantly, the millennial Jerusalem that he envisioned would not be a restoration of the ancient Israelite Jerusalem but is something entirely new, that is, a Jerusalem where the Christian faithful will live joyfully regardless of ethnicity; this renewed Jerusalem, though not permanent, is more compatible with the description of the city of God in the book of Revelation than with the Jerusalem of King Solomon or King Herod.[15] In the next generation after Justin, the Christian bishop Irenaeus (late second century) also discussed the thousand-year reign of Christ, but his eschatological expectation was similar to Justin's, and in addition he extends the joyous renewal to embrace the whole creation, not merely Jerusalem or Israel.[16] These expectations differ from that of Christian Zionists, whose goal is to restore the ancient Israelite city.

11. Simonetti, *Biblical Interpretation in the Early Church*, 20–21.

12. Justin Martyr, *Dialogue with Trypho*, 75, 113.1–5, 139.4–5.

13. Ibid. 119.4–5; quoted words are in 119.5.

14. Millennialism (also called chiliasm) was not adopted into the tradition of the Orthodox Church. Although it was embraced by Justin Martyr and Irenaeus (both of whom are second-century saints of the church), it was not swept along with the tide of tradition, and sank out of sight. Other features of Justin's and Irenaeus's thought have been valued highly by the church, but not their millennialism. Although some modern scholars have stated that one or another of the early church councils, specifically, either the Council of Constantinople (381) or the Council of Ephesus (431), condemned millennialism, no compelling evidence exists for this assertion; see Gumerlock, "Millennialism and the Early Church Councils," 83–95. On the absence of millennialism from Orthodox eschatology, see Harakas, *Orthodox Christian Beliefs about the Bible*, 207–10.

15. Justin Martyr, *Dialogue with Trypho*, 80–81.

16. Irenaeus, *Against Heresies*, 5.33.3–4, 5.36.1.

A century after Justin, Origen, not a saint but a respected biblical scholar of the third-century church who is much studied today, explained the rationale and application of the allegorical method. Every Scripture text can have as many as three meanings: literal, moral, spiritual. Although the majority of texts are actual historical accounts, he says, there are some that are simply implausible, such as texts that portray God in a way that is unworthy of divinity, or texts that contradict each other. For example, one text that cannot be taken literally is that which depicts God as walking in the Garden of Eden, and Adam as hiding from him: how can the omnipresent God walk, and how can the omniscient God not see someone? Such texts must have a symbolic significance that is morally edifying or that describes spiritual truths about God, or both. Of course, it is possible that an Old Testament story that is literally true may also have moral and spiritual meanings because the actual events themselves may bear deeper significance.[17]

Applying his method to the Old Testament texts narrating the entry of the ancient Israelites into the Promised Land, Origen sees in the River Jordan a symbol of the spiritual nourishment of souls that thirst. In regard to the book of Deuteronomy, Origen states that Joshua is a type of Jesus; here again we see the congruence of the Greek version of the two names at work.[18] The spiritual significance of the Promised Land is that it symbolizes Christian perfection, in contrast to the wilderness experience of the Hebrews, which symbolizes a life of sin.[19] The value of these texts for Christians, then, resides on the spiritual level, and the factuality or non-factuality of the story is irrelevant. Elsewhere Origen specifies unequivocally that the offspring of Abraham to whom God has promised the conquest of cities in Gen 22:17 is best understood if the reader perceives the offspring of Abraham as Jesus Christ, the cities as human souls who become the possessions of Christ, and the enemy forces as sins.[20]

There are many examples of allegorical and typological exegesis in the writings of the church fathers, including not only the Greek but also the Latin fathers, such as Ambrose and Augustine.[21] Origen's interpretive approach left an enduring legacy that influenced Christian theology (though not necessarily popular devotion; see below) throughout the era of the

17. Origen, *On First Principles*, 4.2–3. For the example of God walking in the Garden, see *On First Principles*, 4.3.1.

18. Ibid., 4.3.12.

19. Origen, *Homilies on Joshua*, 4.4.

20. Origen, *Homilies on Genesis*, 9.3.

21. For more examples, see Burnett, "Early Christians." The present discussion of patristic exegesis has been adapted from portions of that essay.

post-Constantinian Roman Empire and beyond.[22] Two examples of fourth-century (post-Origen) writings will illustrate the application of this kind of exegesis.

Cyril of Jerusalem, the bishop of his city in the middle of the fourth century, is known for the baptismal instructions that he delivered to the candidates for baptism and the newly baptized. Cyril explains that Moses was a prefiguration of Christ, both of whom liberated their people from oppression—Moses, from slavery in Egypt, and Christ, from bondage to sin. Like the waters of the Red Sea, which drowned Pharaoh, the waters of baptism vanquish the tyrannical power of the devil over the human being.[23] And while teaching his pre-baptismal class in the city of Jerusalem, he indicates the nearby ruins of the Jewish Temple, an everyday sight in that locale, drawing a parallel between the destruction of the Temple in the first century and the precipitous collapse of the city of Jericho in the Old Testament. The earlier event was caused by the first Jesus (Joshua), and the more recent one was prophesied by the True Jesus (though not caused by him, Cyril says—because the cause was the sins of the people).[24]

Another example is the highly allegorical *Life of Moses* by Gregory of Nyssa, a bishop and theologian of the late fourth century, and one of the three Cappadocian Fathers, whose thought was essential to the articulation of the doctrine of the Trinity. Gregory presents Moses as the prototype of the enlightened believer seeking union with God. The wise Moses understands that his and his people's experiences are typological foreshadowings of what is to come in a later age. Gregory interprets various features of the Exodus and the Israelites' wilderness experience typologically and allegorically, in ways similar to what we have already seen in other ancient writers. What is striking about this work, however, is that Moses's upward journey toward intimacy with God does not culminate in possession of the Promised Land; rather, the metaphor that Gregory employs is the ascent of Moses up the slope of Mount Sinai, into the darkness of the cloud at its summit. The journey toward God, according to Gregory, has no end-point in this life, but is an unending ascent toward the infinite and unknowable God; the goal is to keep moving. Moses never entered the Promised Land, and the Promised Land is not even an object of interest in Gregory's story. It is Moses's constant perseverance in the process of journeying that accorded him the honor of becoming a friend of God. Gregory states, "We consider

22. Wilken, *The Land Called Holy*, 65–78.

23. Cyril of Jerusalem, *Mystagogical Catechesis*, 1.3.

24. Cyril of Jerusalem, *Catechesis* 10.11. The demise of the Jerusalem Temple was sometimes used by church fathers as evidence that the Old Covenant had reached its end since the types had been fulfilled by the reality that they had prefigured.

becoming God's friend the only thing worthy of honor and desire. This, as I have said, is the perfection of life."[25] Clearly the occupation of a plot of land is not the goal of a godly life.

In the preceding examples it is obvious that the patristic tradition assigns a symbolic significance to the land of milk and honey, or, as in the case of Gregory of Nyssa, simply ignores the land. The focal point is conformity to God's will, not the procurement of earthly goods. Today's Orthodox thought is grounded firmly on this patristic root.

Nevertheless, a tradition of pilgrimage arose, capturing the religious imagination of devoted Christians seeking a tangible connection with biblical narratives through visiting the locations where they were said to have occurred.[26] In particular, the sites linked to the stories of Christ inspired the construction of shrines[27] and the development of liturgical celebrations at them. Examples can be found in the journal of the late fourth-century pilgrim Egeria.[28] It should be noted, however, that pilgrimage has not been considered to be a religious obligation in Orthodoxy, nor is it a component of Orthodox doctrine.[29] A similarly ambivalent attitude toward pilgrimage is found in the Latin writings of Jerome (who died in Bethlehem in 420); on the one hand, he expends much ink in descriptions of the land and urges others to travel to the holy sites, but in debate with Jewish exegesis he maintains, on the other hand, that the Old Testament "land of promise" is the heavenly kingdom of God, not Palestine.[30]

The tradition of popular devotion to the holy sites thus gained momentum without acquiring doctrinal status. By contrast, the Orthodox Church has embraced unequivocally the writings of the church fathers on social justice. Basil, Bishop of Caesarea (died in 379), who exhorted his congregation to share their resources unstintingly with the poor, specifically condemned the practice of land seizure and home demolition committed by the wealthy against their social inferiors.[31] John Chrysostom, at first a priest in Antioch and then the Bishop of Constantinople at the turn of the fifth century, boldly proclaimed the obligation of the wealthy to share generously

25. Gregory of Nyssa, *The Life of Moses*; for the quoted words see section 320, p. 137.

26. The attitudes toward pilgrimage discussed here are those of the ancient church, not those of medieval western Europeans.

27. Helen, the mother of the emperor Constantine (both of them Orthodox saints), is identified by ancient church historians as a driving force behind such construction; Wilken, *Land Called Holy*, 98.

28. See Egeria, *Egeria*.

29. Wilken, *Land Called Holy*, 101.

30. Ibid., 120–22, 128–31. Also Jerome, *Letters* 46, 47.2, 129.1–6.

31. Basil, *Homily 7* ("To the Rich"), 41–58, esp. 50.

with the less fortunate. Indifference to suffering he denounced as absolutely unacceptable in God's eyes; moreover, a benefactor should not discriminate among possible beneficiaries on the basis of their personal characteristics but should give to anyone who is needy.[32] Among the early Latin-speaking fathers, Ambrose, Bishop of Milan (died in 397), composed a vehement treatise on the greedy King Ahab's disgraceful seizure of Naboth's vineyard (1 Kgs 21).[33] It is strikingly clear, then, that the church fathers' affinity for symbolic interpretation of the Promised Land plus their abhorrence of greedy acquisitiveness, combined with their advocacy for the poor, add up to a patristic tradition that offers no support for the current Zionist perpetration of land seizure, expulsion of residents, and repopulation in the West Bank.

Today's Orthodox Christian pilgrims and residents of the Holy Land include not only devotees of the biblical sites but also socially concerned believers whose advocacy for the oppressed and marginalized constitutes an additional mode of physical, practical connection to the region. Orthodox leaders do not ignore the sufferings of the people—Jewish, Muslim, and Christian people—who currently are trying to earn livelihoods in that land. They also support the right of access to holy sites for members of all three of the Abrahamic faiths. Let us now meet some of today's Orthodox theologians and church leaders who have explored the implications of their faith for today's Christians in the Holy Land.

Contemporary Orthodox Voices

The leading Orthodox figures introduced below have been selected because they are involved in the issues of Palestinian suffering and Zionism either here in the United States or in the Middle East. Of course there are actively concerned Orthodox Christians in other countries as well, but this chapter is confined to those two locations. It is hoped that the North American readers of this book will travel to Palestine and Israel, where they may have the opportunity to meet some Holy Land Christians.

---

32. John Chrysostom, *St John Chrysostom: On Wealth and Poverty*, esp. "Second Sermon on Lazarus and the Rich Man," 39–55.

33. Ambrose, *On Naboth*, 117–44.

Metropolitan George Khodr

The Orthodox hierarch since 1970 of Mount Lebanon, a district in the country of Lebanon, Metropolitan George Khodr has combined both a contemplative orientation and significant involvement in the cause of human rights. His weekly newspaper articles have reflected on the large questions of the Christian faith, with a focus on love of God and neighbor. As a student at the Institut de Théologie Orthodoxe Saint-Serge in Paris in the early 1950s, Metropolitan George immersed himself in the apophatic theology of the Fathers, especially of Gregory of Nyssa (see above) and of modern Russian theologians.[34] Apophatic theology asserts the unknowability of God and the resultant inability of human language to characterize God's essence. Orthodox theology holds that, while the essence of God is inaccessible to us, we can know God's energies, and it is the profound, all-powerful energy of love that became Metropolitan George's focus early in his career. In a recent article he has noted that since Scripture calls God by the name "love" (1 John 4:8), we can therefore apply the word "love" to God's own self and even (in a radical assertion) to God's essence.[35] The union of God and the human being, called "deification" or "divinization" in the Orthodox tradition, is a two-way process, says Metropolitan George: God has descended into our world in the incarnation of Christ and continues to abide in us and with us, and at the same time we move toward God by opening ourselves to loving God and others.

What are the social implications of this thinking? Metropolitan George clearly does not perceive deification as a duet played out between God and a single individual; religious individualism has no part in his teachings. Instead, he envisions communion between the divine in oneself and the divine in the other. He says, "If we realize that the meeting between people is the meeting of the divine in me and the divine in the other, then the question of how to love my neighbor as my own self disappears. I and my neighbor are both the dwelling places of God."[36]

Metropolitan George's genius in combining love of neighbor with a strong contemplative life in God is seen in a translated article that first appeared in Arabic in 2000, during the Second Intifada (the second Palestinian uprising, which lasted from 2000 to 2004). His synthesis is apparent in

---

34. The information in this paragraph about Metropolitan George's theology is taken from Avakian, "The Mystery of Divine Love in the Apophatic Theology of Bishop George Khodr."

35. Khodr, "God is Love," "Between Love and Friendship," and "Why Do I Write?"; all of these are cited in Avakian, "The Mystery of Divine Love," 43–44.

36. Khodr, "Love of the Self," cited in Avakian, "The Mystery of Divine Love," 57.

his ardent concern for social justice in Palestine. He draws a clear distinction between the desire of some people for land, on the one hand, and, on the other, the quest for God. He perceives the Holy Land not as an end in itself but as an icon, a window to God's reality. He points out that the Jewish exiles in Babylon longed not for Jerusalem but for "the Divine Presence in its Temple," and that in the Christian era Jerusalem became a symbol of the eschatological city of God yet to descend from heaven. He states that Christ's "Gospel and His presence in the Holy Gifts [the Eucharist] is much more precious than the earth of Jerusalem," and also remarks that since the 1960s Arab Christian theologians have been "overlooking the land and focusing on the man." Embracing this focus on the people of the Holy Land, Metropolitan George lists three very practical demands: a Palestinian state to include East Jerusalem; a halt to settlement expansion; the right of return for Palestinian refugees. He praises the unarmed Palestinian youth who have resisted the Israeli forces, sometimes at the expense of their lives.[37] His chief desire for the city of Jerusalem is that Jews, Muslims, and Christians share it as a home to all. In his book *Jerusalem* he states, "I cannot accept this international injustice against the Palestinian people. My dream is for these three religions to co-exist in real love, and this is possible if countries find a solution for Jerusalem."[38]

Patriarch Ignatius IV

The late Patriarch Ignatius IV of the Antiochian Orthodox Church (the same branch of Orthodoxy that his friend Metropolitan George Khodr serves) had a voice that resounded around the world. His church traces its inception to New Testament times (Acts 11:26: "in Antioch the disciples were for the first time called Christians," RSV). Centuries later the patriarchate of the ancient Syrian city of Antioch was compelled to move to Damascus when the Mamluks from Egypt conquered Antioch in 1268. With its Patriarch still residing in Syria, the church has attracted converts overseas, especially in the United States. The statements of the Patriarch, therefore, have been heard both throughout and far beyond the Middle East.

Patriarch Ignatius IV, who was born as Habib Hazim in Syria in 1921 and died in 2012, studied at the American University of Beirut and the Institut de Théologie Orthodoxe Saint-Serge in Paris, and founded the University of Balamand in Lebanon. In his speeches and interviews he has highlighted the diversity of religious practice and spirituality in Jerusalem and

---

37. Khodr, "Jerusalem and the Glory."
38. Quoted by Joanna Azar in "George Khodr: The Poet Bishop."

has emphasized the relationship of the entire human race, not merely Christians, with God. He characterized every human being as "the bearer of a divine breath, and as the dwelling-place of love without limit or restriction."[39] In a similar vein he remarked in a commencement address, "The book that must be read is in the other person whom we encounter in love."[40]

The Patriarch's respect for human diversity caused him to reject utterly all Israeli attempts to introduce ethnic and religious uniformity by means of "the Judaization of Jerusalem." Although he cherished the Christian sites in the Holy City, he stated unequivocally, "People, not stones, are our concern in Jerusalem, which must remain a city of peace and an example of co-existence among religions and peoples."[41] With this as his mission, Patriarch Ignatius IV urged his listeners to speak out: "Voices must be raised. . . . We must arise with all our might."[42]

Metropolitan Philip Saliba

Metropolitan Philip Saliba, the Primate of The Antiochian Orthodox Christian Archdiocese of North America since 1966, is known as a dynamic and outspoken leader. Born as Abdullah ("servant of God") Saliba in rural Lebanon, he studied in Balamand, Lebanon (for high school); Homs, Syria; Damascus; Nottinghamshire, UK; London; Boston; and St. Vladimir's Seminary in Crestwood, New York. In addition to theological studies, he has pursued the field of English literature. Such breadth of experience and study may be one of the factors contributing to his bold vision and forthright speech. In addition to statements on the Middle East, Metropolitan Philip has also spoken out against Marxism and has urgently promoted the cause of Orthodox unity in North America, which will require, among other things, the use of English in all liturgies.[43]

Metropolitan Philip has called attention to the unjust sufferings of the Palestinians and has commented in regard to Zionism, "God is no longer in the real estate business." Perturbed by the biblical exegesis generated by Christian Zionists, Metropolitan Philip stated, "My plea is that modern

---

39. From an interview with the newspaper *al-Safir*, quoted in Ignatius IV, *Orthodoxy and the Issues of Our Time*, 111.

40. Quoted by Economos Antony Gabriel, "A Farewell to Patriarch Ignatius IV," 30.

41. From an interview with the magazine *an-Nahar al-'arabi wa-l-duwali*, quoted in Ignatius IV, *Orthodoxy and the Issues of Our Time*, 111–12.

42. From an interview with the newspaper *al-Anwar*, quoted in Ignatius IV, *Orthodoxy and the Issues of Our Time*, 112.

43. Curtiss, "Metropolitan Philip Saliba." Since the writing of this essay, Metropolitan Philip has entered his repose (March 19, 2014).

Protestant theologians and students of Scripture take a critical and objective look at how the Church has interpreted the Bible throughout history." In this latter statement he is expressing not only dismay about Christian Zionism but also his solidarity with the continuity of Orthodox theological tradition.[44]

Believing that Israelis and Palestinians can and should share the Holy Land without either group exploiting the other, in 1968 (the year after the Six-Day War and the beginning of the Israeli Occupation of Palestine) Metropolitan Philip offered a three-part plan for resolving the situation. His three proposals were as follows: (1) a democratic state where Muslims, Jews, and Christians can live in equality and in security to be provided by the powerful nations; (2) the cessation of hostilities on the part of the Arabs; (3) an end to the Occupation and a provision for Palestinian refugees to return to their homeland. Unfortunately, Metropolitan Philip's views were not received sympathetically by U.S. politicians, including President Lyndon Johnson in a personal interview with the Metropolitan, and were regarded with apathy by Arab diplomats in Washington.[45]

Most recently Metropolitan Philip has signed, along with thirty-five other Christian leaders of various churches, a letter to President Obama. Dated January 7, 2013, the letter reminds the President of the disappointment caused by the failure of the 1993 Oslo Accords and the lack of trust that has ensued. While acknowledging the stiff challenges faced by prospective peace brokers, it nevertheless urges the President to exert every possible effort toward achieving a sustainable two-state solution that will meet the needs of both Israelis and Palestinians for security and justice.[46]

Archbishop Theodosios (Atallah Hanna)

The career of Archbishop Theodosios, an archbishop of the Greek Orthodox Patriarchate of Jerusalem, has been distinguished for his dedicated activism on behalf of all Palestinians. Born in the Upper Galilee as an Israeli citizen and named Atallah Hanna, he studied for the priesthood in Thessalonica, Greece, and was ordained in 1991 at the Church of the Holy Sepulcher in Jerusalem. As the official spokesperson for the Jerusalem Patriarchate under the late Patriarch Diodoros, he addressed the United Nations Commission

---

44. Ibid. The Metropolitan's statement about biblical interpretation is quoted also in Gillquist, *Metropolitan Philip*, 141. The remark about God and the real estate business is quoted also in Gillquist, "The Nation of Israel in Prophecy," 7.

45. Gillquist, *Metropolitan Philip*, 140–44.

46. The letter is reproduced in its entirety in *The Word* 57:3, 24–25.

on Human Rights at a conference convened by the World Council of Churches in 2000, where he described candidly the human rights violations inflicted on the Palestinian people. He also delivered a highly acclaimed speech at an assembly of Arab presidents and royalty at an Islamic summit meeting in Doha, Qatar.

Father Atallah Hanna's nonviolent but ardent activism did not escape the notice of the Israeli authorities. In August 2002 the Israeli police arrested him and interrogated him at the Al-Maskobiya Prison in Jerusalem. From 2002 to 2006 he was prohibited from traveling.

Fr. Atallah Hanna was appointed in 2005 as the Archbishop of Sebaste, a town not far from Nablus in the West Bank. Now named Archbishop Theodosios, he has the unusual distinction of being the only Arab to attain such a high office in a predominantly Greek hierarchy. He continues untiringly to plead the case for justice and human rights for Palestinians.[47]

In an interview Archbishop Theodosios has stated the following:

> I am very sorry to hear about some religious groups in the United States that support the Israeli Occupation of the Palestinian territories. Such support cannot be justified from a Christian point of view. . . . These groups need to re-read their Bibles, because the Bible calls us to stand with the marginalized and the oppressed and not with the oppressors. For those who use the Bible to support Israel need to differentiate between God's promise and the Balfour promise, because the Occupation is the result of a promise given to the Israelis by Lord Balfour and not by God.[48]

The Greek Orthodox Archdiocese of America and SCOBA

As Ecumenical Officer of the Greek Orthodox Archdiocese of America, Bishop Dimitrios of Xanthos participated in an ecumenical fact-finding trip to Palestine and Israel in December 2000, three months after the start of the Second Intifada ("second uprising"). In a press interview Bishop Dimitrios deplored not only the violence and destruction but also the economic privation being suffered by Palestinians, including high unemployment caused by the shutdown of tourist-dependent businesses. Shortly after receiving the report of the ecumenical delegation, the Standing Conference of Canonical

47. The information on Archbishop Theodosios that has been presented up to this point was taken from Shamir, "The Biography of Theodosius (Atallah) Hanna, Archbishop of Sebaste."

48. Harb, "Exclusive Intifada Interview."

Orthodox Bishops in the Americas (SCOBA) issued a statement expressing "grief" for the suffering of all Palestinians and Israelis, and their "urgent concern" about the plight of Christians in the Holy Land. SCOBA specifically named "the violence," "the ongoing confiscation of homes and land and the establishment of new Israeli settlements," "prohibitions against travel," and "massive unemployment." Both the ecumenical delegation's report and the SCOBA statement urged U.S. government officials to consider political steps toward peace, as well as much-needed humanitarian aid.[49] As the Second Intifada continued, SCOBA issued another statement in 2002, pleading for peace-making efforts and the harmonious co-existence of Judaism, Christianity, and Islam in a shared land.[50] Still persevering in his endeavor toward peace, Bishop Dimitrios in 2005 participated in an interfaith initiative presenting a proposal to President George W. Bush urging him to take specific steps toward a resolution of the Israeli-Palestinian conflict.[51]

Since that time, SCOBA has been replaced by the Assembly of Orthodox Bishops, but Greek Orthodox involvement in the Middle East situation has continued. Father Mark Arey, the successor of Bishop Dimitrios as Greek Orthodox Ecumenical Officer, is engaged in the work of Churches for Middle East Peace (CMEP) and the National Inter-religious Leadership Initiative for Peace in the Middle East (NILI). In December 2009 Fr. Mark visited the Holy Land as a member of a NILI delegation, which subsequently issued a statement, signed by each participant, calling for "achieving an effective, sustainable ceasefire, including international measures to prevent resupplying of rockets; for allowing the flow of urgently needed humanitarian and economic assistance to the people of Gaza; for continuing good efforts to improve the capacity of the Palestinian Authority to increase security and economic development; and for further reducing the number of checkpoints and freezing all settlement expansion in the West Bank and East Jerusalem."[52] Recently Fr. Mark signed the letter to President Obama from thirty-six Christian leaders, calling for strenuous efforts on the part of the Obama Administration toward a just peace (see under "Metropolitan Philip Saliba," above).

49. "Bishop Dimitrios Part of Delegation."

50. "SCOBA Statement on Crisis in the Holy Land."

51. McDonough, "Bishop Demetrios Joins Interfaith Coalition."

52. Rouvelas, "Ministering to Our Fellow Orthodox Christians." The quoted words are drawn from the 2009 NILI statement at http://nili-mideastpeace.org/downloads/2009_12_NILI_Trip_Statement.pdf.

Gabriel Habib

Gabriel Habib, a native of Lebanon, served as the Secretary General of the Middle East Council of Churches from 1977 to 1994. In addition, he has participated in various projects of the World Council of Churches on an *ad hoc* basis, has worked with the National Council of Churches of the USA, and from 1994 to 1998 served as one of the Presidents of the World Conference of Religions for Peace. The author of a booklet entitled *Aspects of Political Ethics in the Middle East Context* as well as innumerable articles, sermons, and lectures,[53] Mr. Habib's prolific writings can be characterized as social and political analysis presented in light of Christian ethical principles. Although he self-deprecatingly resists the title "theologian,"[54] his words reveal that he is steeped in both Testaments of the Bible.

In a meditation on Matt 22:34–40 (Jesus's statement of the two great commandments: love of God and love of neighbor), Mr. Habib recalls his youthful discovery that love is more powerful than revenge, in his account of his father's abduction and murder by a Muslim militia in Lebanon.[55] Sorely tempted to seek revenge, the young Gabriel Habib chose instead to dedicate himself to serving the same Muslim community that had spawned the murderers. In his writings he reflects that genuine Christians believe that their source of power is not any mode of violence, but rather is the Holy Spirit, who infuses love into hearts. His subsequent career has emphasized interfaith dialogue as a quest for shared values.[56]

In a sermon on Matt 2:1–12 (the visit of the Magi), Mr. Habib interprets the Nativity accounts as an expression of the reconciliation and inclusiveness of the Gospel of Christ. He notes that the Gospel of Luke, aimed

---

53. Habib, *Aspects of Political Ethics in the Middle East Context* is no longer in print. His other writings are collected in unpublished dossiers, four of which have been kindly provided to this author by Mr. Habib: "Theology in Global Context Association: Presentations from 1980 to 1992" (compiled in 2004); "World Council of Churches: Presentations from 1979 to 2004" (compiled in 2007); "MECC Dialogue with 'Western Evangelicals' through Evangelicals for Middle East Understanding (EMEU)" (2005); and "The Presbyterian Church in the USA: Sermons and Presentations on the Middle East Christians" (2005). An additional source is Mr. Habib's presentation "Christians in the Holy Land: Historical Background and Present Challenges," at http://www.pifras.org/Reports_Articles/RE_Christians_in_Holyland/re_christians_in_holyland.html.

54. Habib, "Theology in Global Context Association," 13.

55. Meditation delivered at the closing service of a meeting of the Commission of the Churches on International Affairs (of the World Council of Churches) in 2004, found in the dossier "World Council of Churches," 70. The account is also found in the dossier "Theology in Global Context Association," 21.

56. Habib, "MECC Dialogue," 50, 53, and idem, "The Presbyterian Church," 7–8; and the presentation "Christians in the Holy Land," section V.

at Gentile Christian believers, describes the devotion of Jewish shepherds, while Matthew, addressing Jewish Christians, identifies the earliest worshippers of Jesus as the Gentile Magi.[57] The universality of the Christian faith, embracing people of all ethnicities and cultures, is a prominent theme in Mr. Habib's writings, as is the equality of all human beings, who are created in the image and likeness of God.[58]

A contradiction to the principles of universality and equality appears in the Israeli concepts (a) of the exclusive election of the Jews as God's chosen people and (b) of the divine right of the Jews to occupy the Holy Land. Mr. Habib notes that election is now regarded as the bestowal of special privilege rather than as a call to mission and that the exercise of the belief in divine right does not allow for the human rights of the Christian and Muslim Palestinians as set forth in the UN Universal Declaration of Human Rights.[59] Moreover, the pre-eminence of the notion of divine right has led to a mindset conducive to the physical elimination of the "other" in the name of God or his people, which is reminiscent of King Herod's mass brutality in seeking the life of the infant Jesus.[60] A remedy for these conceptual distortions can be found in a concern for the spiritual welfare of Israeli Jews by holding them accountable to the ethical principles of the Hebrew prophets; clearly the idolatry of elevating special status and political power above God's universal sovereignty violates biblical precepts.[61] Mr. Habib rejects the belief of some Christian Zionists that the policies of the Israeli government must be exempt from critical assessment on the ground that the existence of the State of Israel is the fulfillment of God's will.[62]

Mr. Habib consistently promotes the Enlightenment principle of separation of religion and state, in opposition to what he calls "ethno-religious nationalism," the conceptual framework that undergirds the Zionist insistence on a Jewish state and that drives some Islamic movements today.[63] A peaceful, pluralistic society can and must be achieved. Civic life in the

57. Sermon delivered at a Presbyterian church in Detroit in 1996, printed in dossier Habib, "The Presbyterian Church," 33–34.

58. See, e.g., Habib, "The Presbyterian Church," 43.

59. Habib, "World Council of Churches," 7, 14, 66; "MECC Dialogue," 12; "The Presbyterian Church," 39, 55; "Theology in Global Context Association," 34.

60. Habib, "Theology in Global Context Association," 21.

61. Habib, "The Presbyterian Church," 27–28.

62. Ibid., 26, 41; "Theology in Global Context Association," 34; "World Council of Churches," 15; "Christians in the Holy Land," section I.

63. Habib, "MECC Dialogue," 25; "World Council of Churches," 14, 66; "Theology in Global Context Association," 1–2; "The Presbyterian Church," 4–5, 13–14, 24, 39, 55; "Christians in the Holy Land," section IV.

Middle East should be grounded upon values shared by Jews, Muslims, and Christians that can serve as the basis of harmonious co-existence and co-operation—values that can be defined and highlighted through interfaith dialogue.[64] Dialogue among the monotheistic religions would be significantly enhanced if Christians could attain unity among themselves, thereby boosting their credibility as discussion partners. Thus ecumenical dialogue among the churches, in addition to interfaith dialogue, is a moral imperative for Christians.[65]

The Very Rev. Dr. Paul Nadim Tarazi

Professor Emeritus Paul Nadim Tarazi of St. Vladimir's Seminary in Crestwood, New York, has taught and written prodigiously in the fields of both Old Testament and New Testament studies. The total corpus of his writings is too vast to summarize here; what is relevant for the purpose of the present chapter is his work on the Old Testament concepts of land and history. His book *Land and Covenant* investigates the uses of the Hebrew words 'eretz (translated by Dr. Tarazi as "earth") and 'adamah (which he translates as "ground"). His investigation demonstrates that God has consistently been in a faithful relationship with all the peoples of the earth, not exclusively with Israel.[66] In other books Dr. Tarazi has reassessed the commonly accepted theories assigning dates to portions of the Old Testament and has arrived at the conclusion that the Babylonian Exile was the formative influence that shaped the so-called "historical" narratives. Ezekiel, Jeremiah, and Isaiah are keys to understanding the Pentateuch and the books of Joshua, Judges, 1–2 Samuel, and 1–2 Kings. The intent behind the composition and compilation of the Old Testament narratives was to create a *mashal,* a cautionary statement or tale prophetically presenting examples of attitudes and behaviors to be adopted or avoided.[67] Thus it is the theme of obedience to God's will rather than nationalistic historiography that unifies the Old Testament, and the universalizing tendency so conspicuous in the prophets is present in the Old Testament as a whole.

Before the publication of *Land and Covenant,* Dr. Tarazi presented some of his findings at an international theological conference in 2008 in

64. See note 56 above.

65. Habib, "MECC Dialogue," 30; "The Presbyterian Church," 7–8, 36, 43; "Christians in the Holy Land," section IV.

66. Tarazi, *Land and Covenant.*

67. Tarazi, *The Old Testament: An Introduction,* 1:9–11, 15–25, 29–40; idem, *Joshua: A Commentary,* 21–25.

Bern, Switzerland, on the topic of "Promised Land," sponsored by the World Council of Churches, the Federation of Swiss Protestant Churches, and the Reformed Churches Bern-Jura-Solothurn. His presentation highlights the self-centeredness of humankind in its perception of God's will. He stated, "Only those who have ears *not to hear* [emphasis original] can come up with the monstrous idea that a piece of land would be deeded forever to a group of people by no less than God himself."[68]

Dr. Tarazi utilizes a linguistic approach, tracking and analyzing the uses of specific words in various scriptural texts. In continuity with the church fathers, who regarded the entire Bible as an interconnected whole, Dr. Tarazi compares Old Testament narratives with each other and with the prophetic pronouncements, and sets New Testament passages side-by-side with Old Testament texts. His conclusions are indisputably pertinent to the question of Zionism.

Father Peter Gillquist

The authoritative biographer of Metropolitan Philip Saliba and a strong supporter of the Metropolitan's views on the Middle East (see above), the late Fr. Peter Gillquist included some didactic sections in his biography of the Metropolitan, in which he expounded the views on the Middle East that he and Metropolitan Philip held in common. His writing makes it plain that the Orthodox Church categorically denounces all terrorism on either side of the Israeli-Palestinian conflict, that it does not challenge the existence of the State of Israel, and that it bears no animosity toward Judaism as a religious faith. Rather, it is the unjust treatment suffered by Palestinians and the expansionist agenda of today's Zionism that are under scrutiny. On the basis of history and of biblical texts, Fr. Peter Gillquist has stated and supported four major points: (1) "Palestinians Are the Native People"; (2) "The Old Covenant Has Ceased"; (3) "The Promises of God are for the Church"; (4) "There Must Be Justice for All."[69]

Fr. Peter Gillquist has also composed a pamphlet on Zionism for distribution in local churches. Entitled "The Nation of Israel in Prophecy," this

68. Tarazi, "The Promised Land."

69. Gillquist, *Metropolitan Philip*, 131–40. The second and third points may be regarded as supersessionist (that is, as proclaiming the replacement of ancient Israel by the Christian Church as God's chosen people). In Fr. Peter's defense, however, it must be noted that he never characterizes Jewish people as having been rejected; rather, it is the Old Covenant, the Old Testament mode of relationship with God, that has been replaced by the way of Christ, just as Paul envisioned the Gospel as replacing the works of the Law.

treatise explains, with proofs from Scripture (including, among others, Heb 8:13 and 10:1, 1 Pet 2:9–10, Gal 6:15–16, and the parable of the vineyard in Matt 21), that the Old Covenant has been fulfilled and the New Covenant is now the way forward for humanity's growth in the knowledge of God. Doctrines of millennialism and "the rapture" are novelties introduced by J. N. Darby in the nineteenth century (which is recent history for the Orthodox Church, with its emphasis on continuity through the entire sweep of the centuries since the incarnation of Christ). As far as the modern State of Israel is concerned, Fr. Peter has remarked, "Orthodox Christians know that if Israel wants to form a secular state and regroup as a people, they can certainly do so. But they cannot claim to be there by divine intent."[70]

Dr. Maria Khoury

Maria Khoury, Ed.D., is a Greek-American educator and author and the wife of David Khoury, the mayor of the West Bank village of Taybeh, renowned for the brewery owned by the brothers David and Nadim Khoury. A steadfast and creative advocate for Palestinian rights, Maria Khoury raises funds for new housing in Taybeh and for educational scholarships for Palestinians. Her speaking tours and her weekend conferences in the United States are aimed at educating American Christians about the facts on the ground in the West Bank, where she has resided with her husband since 1995. In addition to her children's books, she has penned *Witness in the Holy Land,* a compilation of eye-opening, heart-rending reports on life in Palestine during the Second Intifada.

By adhering to their decision to remain in David Khoury's native village rather than to reclaim the comfortable life they once enjoyed in the United States, the Khourys are persevering in their resistance to the encroachment of expanding Israeli settlements near Taybeh and the crippling restrictions on travel and transport (and hence on business) imposed by Israel. Guided by her Orthodox Christian faith, Dr. Khoury manages a church-affiliated website and sends informative and inspirational e-mails to her many friends and sympathizers on her listserve.[71]

In the midst of the uncertainties of the Second Intifada and the hardships imposed by martial law and curfews, Maria Khoury wrote the following words during the Christmas season of 2002:

---

70. Gillquist, "The Nation of Israel in Prophecy," 7.

71. See her website: http://www.saintgeorgetaybeh.org.

The spiritual joy in our hearts cannot be expressed [o]n a cultural or social level because violence and death continue to swallow us up. Daily destruction and oppression overwhelm our lives. For about a month now, the two main entrances to our village have been sealed off. . . . As Christians we will promote peaceful resolutions and seek nonviolent ways to [end] this terrible oppression. During this holy season we thank you for praying for the people of the Holy Land who suffer this terrible oppression. Christ is Born! Glorify Him![72]

Conclusion

This essay has presented a parade of Eastern Christian thinkers and activists, both past and present. None of these can be construed as supporting Christian Zionism. In fact, the exegetical approaches adopted by the church fathers in the early centuries as well as those employed by current Orthodox writers allow no space for the modern innovations of dispensationalism, restoration of the Jerusalem Temple, and rapture; moreover, the millennialism (chiliasm) taught by Justin Martyr and Irenaeus in the second century is not the same as that of Christian Zionism. An additional fact is that today's Orthodox Christian population in the Holy Land is suffering from the ravages of Zionist policies; from this it is obvious that Zionism, whether Jewish or Christian, is at odds both with the fourth-century church fathers' homiletic emphasis on economic justice and with the voices of modern Eastern Orthodox Christianity. By the grace of God, there are dedicated church leaders, both in the United States and in the Middle East, who are committed to replacing exploitation with social justice, marginalization with respect for human dignity, and war with peace.

Bibliography

Ancient Writings

Ambrose. *On Naboth*. In *Ambrose*, translated by Boniface Ramsey, 117–44. London: Routledge, 1997.

Basil. *Homily 7* ("To the Rich"). In *On Social Justice: St Basil the Great*, translated by C. Paul Schroeder, 41–58. Foreword by Gregory P. Yova. Crestwood, NY: St. Vladimir's Seminary Press, 2009.

72. Khoury, *Witness in the Holy Land*, 207–8.

Cyril of Jerusalem. *Catechesis 10.* In *St. Cyril of Jerusalem: Works, Volume I,* translated by Leo P. McCauley and Anthony A. Stephenson, 195–210. Fathers of the Church 61. Washington, DC: The Catholic University of America Press, 1969.

———. *Mystagogical Catechesis 1.* In *St. Cyril of Jerusalem's Lectures on the Christian Sacraments,* edited and translated by F. L. Cross, 53–58. Crestwood, NY: St. Vladimir's Seminary Press, 1986.

Egeria. *Egeria: Diary of a Pilgrimage.* Translated and annotated by George E. Gingras. Ancient Christian Writers 38. New York: Newman, 1970.

Epistle of Barnabas. In *Ancient Christian Writers,* edited and translated by James A. Kleist, 6:29–65. Mahwah, NJ: Newman, 1948.

Gregory of Nyssa. *The Life of Moses.* Translated with introduction and notes by Everett Ferguson and Abraham J. Malherbe. Preface by John Meyendorff. New York: Paulist, 1978.

Ignatius of Antioch. *Epistle to the Magnesians.* In *Early Christian Fathers,* edited by Cyril C. Richardson, 94–97. Translated by Cyril C. Richardson. Library of Christian Classics. New York: Macmillan, 1970.

———. *Epistle to the Philadelphians.* In *Early Christian Fathers,* edited by Cyril C. Richardson, 107–11. Translated by Cyril C. Richardson. Library of Christian Classics. New York: Macmillan, 1970.

Irenaeus. *Against Heresies* (Selections). In *Early Christian Fathers,* edited by Cyril C. Richardson, 358–97. Translated by Edward Rochie Hardy. New York: Macmillan, 1970.

Jerome. *Letters 46, 47, 129.* In *Nicene and Post-Nicene Fathers,* Second Series, vol. 6, edited by Philip Schaff and Henry Wace, 60–65, 65–66, 260. 14 vols. Grand Rapids: Eerdmans, 1989.

John Chrysostom. *Homilies against Judaizing Christians.* Translated by Paul W. Harkins. Fathers of the Church 68. Washington, DC: The Catholic University of America Press, 1979.

———. *St. John Chrysostom: On Wealth and Poverty.* Translated by Catharine P. Roth. Crestwood, NY: St. Vladimir's Seminary Press, 1981.

Justin Martyr. *St. Justin Martyr: Dialogue with Trypho.* Edited by Michael Slusser. Revised with new introduction by Thomas P. Halton. Translated by Thomas B. Falls. Selections from the Fathers of the Church 3. Washington, DC: The Catholic University of America Press, 2003.

Melito of Sardis. *On Pascha.* Translated with introduction and notes by Alistair Stewart-Sykes. Popular Patristic. Crestwood, NY: St. Vladimir's Seminary Press, 2001.

Origen. *Homilies on Genesis.* Translated by Ronald E. Heine. Fathers of the Church 71. Washington, DC: The Catholic University of America Press, 1982.

———. *Homilies on Joshua.* Edited by Cynthia White. Translated by Barbara J. Bruce. Fathers of the Church 105. Washington, DC: The Catholic University of America Press, 2002.

———. *On First Principles.* Translated by G. W. Butterworth. Gloucester, MA: Peter Smith, 1973.

Modern Sources

Antony Gabriel, Economos. "A Farewell to Patriarch Ignatius IV." *The Word* 57:1 (January 2013) 26–30.

Avakian, Sylvie. "The Mystery of Divine Love in the Apophatic Theology of Bishop George Khodr." *Theological Review* 33 (2012) 39–68.

Azar, Joanna. "George Khodr: The Poet Bishop." Al Akhbar English website. http://english.al-akhbar.com/node/11626.

"Bishop Dimitrios Part of Delegation on Mideast Peace Mission." *Orthodox Observer* (December 2000–January 2001) 6.

Burnett, Carole Monica. "Early Christians: Belonging Everywhere and Nowhere." In *Zionism through Christian Lenses: Ecumenical Perspectives on the Promised Land,* edited by Carole Monica Burnett, 69–106. Eugene, OR: Pickwick, 2013.

Curtiss, Richard H. "Metropolitan Philip Saliba and Christian Orthodox Unity in America." Originally published in *The Washington Report on Middle East Affairs* (July/August 1999). Posted at http://www.stmaryorthodoxchurch.org/orthodoxy/PHILIPunity.php.

Gillquist, Peter E. *Metropolitan Philip: His Life and His Dreams.* Nashville: Thomas Nelson, 1991.

———. "The Nation of Israel in Prophecy." Ben Lomond, CA: Conciliar, n.d.

Gumerlock, Francis X. "Millennialism and the Early Church Councils: Was Chiliasm Condemned at Constantinople?" *Fides et Historia* 36:2 (Summer–Fall 2004) 83–95.

Habib, Gabriel. *Aspects of Political Ethics in the Middle East Context.* Beirut, 1981.

———. "Christians in the Holy Land: Historical Background and Present Challenges." Presentation given on October 11, 2002, at the Eastern Church Traditions and Celebrations Seminar in Parma, Ohio. At http://www.pifras.org/Reports_Articles/RE_Christians_in_Holyland/re_christians_in_holyland.html.

———. "MECC Dialogue with 'Western Evangelicals' through Evangelicals for Middle East Understanding (EMEU)." Unpublished dossier compiled in 2005.

———. "The Presbyterian Church in the USA: Sermons and Presentations on the Middle East Christians." Unpublished dossier compiled in 2005.

———. "Theology in Global Context Association: Presentations from 1980 to 1992." Unpublished dossier compiled in 2004.

———."World Council of Churches: Presentations from 1979 to 2004." Unpublished dossier compiled in 2007.

Harakas, Stanley Samuel. *Orthodox Christian Beliefs about the Bible: Real Answers to Real Questions from Real People.* Minneapolis: Light and Life, 2003.

Harb, Elias. "Exclusive Intifada Interview with Archbishop Theodosios (Atallah) Hanna." Intifada Palestine website, July 23, 2010. http://www.intifada-palestine.com/2010/07/exclusive-intifada-interview-with-archbishop-theodosios-atallah-hanna/.

"Holy Hieromartyr Philoumenos." http://www.allsaintsofamerica.org/martyrs/nmphilou.html.

Ignatius IV, Patriarch of Antioch and all the East. *Orthodoxy and the Issues of Our Time.* Edited by Elie A. Salem. Translated by Shaun O'Sullivan. Balamand, Lebanon: University of Balamand, 2006.

Khodr, Georges. "Allah mahabbah" ("God is Love"). *An-nahar,* Jan. 21, 2012.

————. "Bayn al-mahabbah wal-sadaqah" ("Between Love and Friendship"). *An-nahar*, January 26, 2008.

————. "Jerusalem and the Glory." *An-Nahar*, October 14, 2000. Posted on the website of the Orthodox Research Institute: http://www.orthodoxresearchinstitute.org/ articles/misc/george_khodr_jerusalem_glory.htm.

————. "Limadza aktob?" ("Why Do I Write?"). *An-nahar*, July 31, 2010.

————. "Mahabbet al-nafs" ("Love of the Self"). In *Hadith al-ahad: al-insan fi masirihi wa akhlaqihi (Sunday's Word: Man in his Destiny and Morals)*, 3:65–66. Beirut: Manshurat al-nur, 1986.

Khoury, Maria C. *Witness in the Holy Land*. Ramallah, Palestine: CDK, 2003.

"Letter to President Obama." *The Word* 57:3 (March 2013) 24–25.

McCarthy, Pat, ed. "Bethany." http://www.seetheholyland.net/bethany/.

McDonough, Siobhan. "Bishop Demetrios Joins Interfaith Coalition in Appeal to President Bush." *The National Herald*, January 22, 2005.

National Interreligious Leadership Initiative. "Interfaith Delegation of American Jewish, Christian and Muslim Religious Leaders Travel, Pray Together and Meet with Jordanians, Israelis and Palestinians; Delegation Asserts Urgency Of U.S. Leadership in 2010 to Achieve Negotiated Peace." December 30, 2009. http://nili-mideastpeace.org/downloads/2009_12_NILI_Trip_Statement.pdf.

Rouvelas, Marilyn. "Ministering to Our Fellow Orthodox Christians in the Holy Land." *Orthodox Observer* (October–November 2010) 6, 22.

"SCOBA Statement on Crisis in the Holy Land." *The Hellenic Voice* (April 24, 2002) 7.

Shamir, Israel. "The Biography of Theodosius (Atallah) Hanna, Archbishop of Sebaste." http://www.israelshamir.net/Atallah/Atallah.htm.

Simonetti, Manlio. *Biblical Interpretation in the Early Church: An Historical Introduction to Patristic Exegesis*. Edited by Anders Bergquist and Markus Bockmuehl. Translated by John A. Hughes. Edinburgh: T. & T. Clark, 2001.

Tarazi, Paul Nadim. *The Old Testament: An Introduction*. Vol. 1, *Historical Traditions*. Rev. ed. Crestwood, NY: St. Vladimir's Seminary Press, 2003.

————. "The Promised Land: Old Testament Perspective." International Theological Conference on "Promised Land." Bern, Switzerland, September 10–14, 2008. http://www.oikoumene.org/en/resources/documents/wcc-programmes/public-witness-addressing-power-affirming-peace/middle-east-peace/promised-land-international-theological-conference-bernswitzerland-10–14-september-2008/the-promised-land-old-testament-perspective-promised-land-conference.html.

————. *Land and Covenant*. St. Paul, MN: OCABS, 2009.

————. *Joshua: A Commentary*. The Chrysostom Bible: A Commentary Series for Preaching and Teaching. St. Paul, MN: OCABS, 2013.

Trigg, Joseph W. *Biblical Interpretation*. Message of the Fathers of the Church 9. Wilmington, DE: Michael Glazier, 1988.

Tsine, Zoe. "Israeli Settlement Barrier 'Worse than Berlin Wall.'" *The National Herald*, April 23, 2005, 3.

Wilken, Robert. *The Land Called Holy: Palestine in Christian History and Thought*. New Haven: Yale University Press, 1992.

Chapter Five

The Vatican, Zionism, and the Israeli-Palestinian Conflict

Rosemary and Herman Ruether

Pre-Modern Attitudes to a Jewish Homeland

Jewish Zionism and the Israeli-Palestinian conflict are modern issues of the twentieth and twenty-first centuries. In ancient times a different political context shaped Christian attitudes toward Jews and the land of the Bible. During the early centuries of Christianity the Holy Land remained in the firm grip of the Roman Empire throughout its pre-Christian, its Constantinian, and its post-Constantinian eras. The pagan emperor Hadrian squelched the Jewish uprising known as the Bar Kokhba rebellion (132–35 CE) and prevented future Judean insurrections by banishing all Jews from Jerusalem and Judea and rebuilding Jerusalem as a Roman city named Aelia Capitolina, dotted with pagan temples, on the ruins of the former city. This political development and, even more significantly, the destruction of the Jewish Temple in the previous century (in 70 CE) provided ammunition for Christian polemicists in debates with Judaism.[1]

As early as the first half of the second century, Justin Martyr pointed to the Jews' exile from their holy city as divine punishment upon them.[2] Other

1. For detailed accounts of Roman destruction in response to Jewish uprisings (66–70 and 132–35 CE), see Armstrong, *Jerusalem*, 150–66.

2. Justin Martyr, *Dialogue with Trypho,* quoted by Ruether, *Faith and Fratricide,*

118

church fathers emphasized the Jews' inability to practice their Temple rites as proof of the divine termination of the Old Testament Covenant, and the sufferings of the Jews as punishment for the death of Christ. John Chrysostom in the late fourth century utilized a gospel text, Luke 21:24, to declare that by Christ's own decree Jerusalem would be ruled by Gentiles until the end of time.[3]

The Beginnings of Zionism

The traditional concept of permanent Jewish exile, having persisted from Roman antiquity through the Middle Ages, began to be reinterpreted in seventeenth-century English Protestant millennialism.[4] This school of thought, prevalent among English Puritans, emphasized the belief that the redemption of the world was dawning in their own movement, which would result in the reign of the true believers over the whole world. This redemption would include the conversion of the Jews, who would be gathered into the Promised Land. For some this conversion would happen before their restoration to the land, but for others it would happen only after they returned to their land. But, in either case, the restoration of the Jews to their land became a stock feature of millennialist Protestant views of a redemption of the world believed to be happening in their times.[5]

These beginnings of Christian Zionism took on further elaboration in nineteenth-century Europe. British Evangelicals taught that the restoration of the Jews to their land must be the first stage in the conversion of the whole world to Christ and the establishment of peace and justice over the earth. For Evangelical millennialists within the Anglican Church, such as Anthony Ashley-Cooper, Seventh Earl of Shaftesbury, this restoration of the Jews would take place through the British Empire, which would be the agent of a new reign of peace and justice on the earth. Lord Shaftesbury's Christian Zionism would be a spur to the decision of the Anglican Church to create an Anglican bishopric of Jerusalem in 1841. A Jew converted to Anglicanism, the Reverend Dr. Michael Solomon Alexander was selected to

---

148.

3. Ruether, *Faith and Fratricide*, 144–49, citing John Chrysostom, *Discourses Against Judaizing Christians* 5.1. The text of Luke 21:24: ". . . Jerusalem will be trodden down by the Gentiles, until the times of the Gentiles are fulfilled" (RSV).

4. The term "millennialism" refers to a belief in a thousand-year reign of Christ on earth at the end of time. The adjective "premillennialist" describes a subset of millennialist believers who expect Christ to return before, rather than after, the thousand-year period.

5. Ruether and Ruether, *Wrath of Jonah*, 72–74.

represent this vision as the first Anglican Bishop of Jerusalem. It was hoped that he would be the means of converting Jews to true Christianity (Anglican, that is) after their return to their land.[6]

In late nineteenth- and early twentieth-century America the restoration of the Jews to their homeland became a standard part of Evangelical Protestantism, proclaimed in Bible prophecy conferences and the teaching of premillennialist theological schools such as the Moody Bible Institute. In this apocalyptic vision, the Jews would first be restored to their land in an unconverted state. They would rebuild the Temple and restore the sacrificial cult. Then there would be a period of tribulation led by the Antichrist. Christ would then return, and the Jews would be converted to Christ. The Antichrist would be defeated, and the true Christians (including the converted Jews) would reign over the world in a thousand-year era of righteousness and peace.[7]

These views of Jewish restoration were not limited to Evangelical Protestants but had a wide influence on American culture, both Protestant and Catholic. A study published in 1987 showed that 57 percent of Protestants and 35 percent of Catholics believed that the founding of the State of Israel in 1948 was the fulfillment of a biblical prophecy that the Jews would be restored to their land.[8] However, these ideas of Jewish restoration to their land had no influence on official Catholicism, represented by the Vatican, which clung to the traditional teachings of Jewish exile in punishment for their denial of Christ. No restoration of Jews to the land was envisioned as part of a future, much less a dawning, messianic era.

An irony in the history of Zionism is that Christians began to develop a type of "Zionism" long before Jews. Traditional Judaism of the Babylonian Talmud had developed a doctrine that Jews must refrain from "forcing the end" and not seek to regain possession of the land but must accept their existence under the Gentiles for the time being. The land would eventually be restored to them, but this must be done by the Messiah, not by human effort.[9] Meanwhile, Jews should devote themselves to prayer and strict living according to Jewish law in order to hasten the coming of the Messiah. Some pious Orthodox Jews did return to live in Palestine in earlier centuries of the Christian era, but this was to pray and live a strict life more effectively in order to bring the Messiah, not to regain the land by themselves.

6. Ibid., 77–78.

7. Ibid., 81–82.

8. Stockton, "Christian Zionism—Prophecy and Public Opinion," cited by Ruether and Ruether, *Wrath of Jonah*, 82.

9. Rabkin, *Threat from Within*, 71–74.

Zionism and Nationalism

Reform Judaism, developed in the mid-nineteenth century, originally rejected Zionism.[10] It embraced the Enlightenment promise of a secular democratic state, where religion was to be privatized and people of many religions could co-exist as equals. Emerging European nationalism presented Jews with contradictory options. An Enlightenment nationalism called for ethnically, linguistically, and religiously differentiated groups to privatize these differences and to come together in secular states where all could share equal rights as citizens of a "nation." Jews could become equal citizens of Western democracies by surrendering any political standing as Jews, in terms of religion or culture. Privately they might practice Judaism, speak Hebrew in their religious gatherings, and study a historic religious culture, but publicly they would speak modern European languages such as French or English and would participate in modern Western cultures and political communities.

But another face of European nationalism insisted that belonging to a particular nationality was itself an ethnic identity historically rooted in and developed by biologically distinct people in particular lands and cultures. Because Jews were a distinct ethnic people with their own culture and "race," they could not assimilate into any European nationality. It was this exclusivist version of European nationalism that convinced some Jews that assimilation into European nations was impossible, given the racial nature of these nationalisms. Rather, Jews must recognize that they were indeed a separate race. They must claim their national identity as Jews and find a land of their own where they could build a Jewish nation. This perspective became the basis of Zionism.

This meant that Jewish nationalism (Zionism) was shaped in response to an ethnically or racially exclusivist, European nationalism and reproduced a similar racial-ethnic exclusivism of its own. Its plan for a Jewish state was for Jews only. Although some Zionists were willing to claim any land that might be available to them to buy and settle in, for most Zionists this must be Palestine, their historic homeland. Arab Palestinians resident in the land were seen as people to be removed from this land by encouraging them to migrate, or, as the early Zionist Theodor Herzl put it in his *Diaries*, "We shall try to spirit the penniless population across the border."[11]

Another early Zionist voice was Moses Hess, writing his manifesto, *Rome and Jerusalem,* in 1862. Hess argued that people have rights and

10. Ibid., 20.
11. Quoted by Rose, *The Question of Zion*, 62.

identities only as a part of national communities. Jews need to redevelop themselves as a national community by reclaiming their ancient national land in Palestine.[12] The major movements of Zionism, however, began in Eastern Europe after the anti-Semitic pogroms in Russia in 1881. Leo Pinsker wrote the foundational statement, *Auto-Emancipation*, in 1882, arguing that Jews are and have been essentially a nation, not a religious community. They needed to emancipate themselves by developing a national language and a national homeland.[13]

Pinsker's writing was followed in 1896 by Theodor Herzl's *The Jewish State*. Horrified by the outbreak of anti-Semitism in the Dreyfus case in France, Herzl became convinced that assimilation of Jews was impossible in Europe. He, too, sought the solution to anti-Semitism by the founding of a Jewish state in Palestine, which he hoped to facilitate by appealing to the great powers in Europe. He believed they would collaborate with this project in order to reduce what they saw as unwelcome numbers of Jews in their nations in Europe. In 1897 he gathered more than two hundred delegates in Basel, Switzerland, for the founding of the World Zionist Organization.[14]

The Catholic Response to Early Zionism

At the announcement of the meeting of the Zionist Congress in Basel, the Jesuit publication *Civilta Catholica* reacted negatively in language that reproduced the traditional Christian teaching of Jewish exile and subjugation to the Gentiles:

> 1827 years have passed since the prediction of Jesus of Nazareth was fulfilled, namely that Jerusalem would be destroyed . . . that the Jews would be led away to be slaves among the nations, and that they would remain in the dispersion until the end of the world. . . . According to the sacred Scriptures, the Jewish people must always live dispersed and wandering among the nations, so that they may render witness to Christ not only by the Scriptures . . . but by their very existence. As for a rebuilt Jerusalem, which could become the center of a reconstituted state of Israel, we must add that that this is contrary to the prediction of Christ himself.[15]

12. See Hertzberg, *The Zionist Idea*, 116–40.

13. Ibid., 178–98.

14. Ibid., 200–231.

15. *Civilta Catholica*, May 1, 1897, cited in Minerbi, *The Vatican and Zionism*, 96.

This response to the Zionist Congress by a leading Catholic journal reveals that the ancient and medieval view of Jewish punishment through permanent exile was still normative in Catholic thought in 1897.

Zionism remained a minority view among nineteenth- and early twentieth-century Jews, most of whom embraced other options, religious or secular. The American Jewish community, dominated by Reform Judaism, even reacted with outrage when Christian Zionists in 1891 appealed to President Harrison to support a renewed Jewish state in Palestine. Reform Rabbis of the Pittsburgh conference responded by saying, "We consider ourselves no longer a nation but a religious community, and therefore expect neither a return to Palestine nor a sacrificial worship under the sons of Aaron nor the restoration of any of the laws concerning the Jewish state." These American Jews saw in Christian Zionism a scheme for deportation that threatened their status as United States citizens. For these Reform Jews, Judaism was a universal religion of Jews who were citizens of many nations. They even deleted the prayer for messianic restoration to Jerusalem from their prayer book.[16] Only with the outbreak of Nazi anti-Semitism in the 1930s and the systematic effort to exterminate Jews in Europe did the majority of Jews become converted to the support of Zionism in the 1940s.[17]

The Vatican became aware of Zionism at the time of the founding of the World Zionist Organization in 1897. The pope may have read the negative reaction published in *Civilta Catholica* four months before the Congress actually took place. Immediately after the Congress the pope issued a circular letter protesting the idea that the Holy Places of Palestine might be occupied by Jews. The apostolic delegate in Constantinople, Monsignor Augusto Bonetti, was called to Rome to consult with the pope on "measures to be taken against the Zionist movement." The pope also consulted with the French Foreign Ministry to oppose any changes that would give the Jews occupation of the Holy Land. In addition he sent an envoy to the sultan in Constantinople appealing to him not to give Palestine to the Jews.[18]

Herzl became aware of these negative Vatican responses to Zionism through Italian and French newspapers after the Congress and immediately contacted the Vatican nuncio in Vienna for an audience. He hoped to

16. Rausch, *Zionism*, 88.

17. The postwar support for Zionism is being rethought by many Jews today in light of the conflict with the Palestinians, which is recognized as being rooted in Zionism as an ethnic-exclusive Jewish nationalism that has sought to eliminate the Palestinian people from the land claimed by Jews. For these Jews this exclusivist racial nationalism is seen as deeply contrary to Jewish values of justice. See Weiss, "It's Time for the Media."

18. See Minerbi, *The Vatican and Zionism*, 96–97.

explain Zionism to the pope as no threat to the Christian Holy Places. He finally received an audience with the nuncio in Vienna a year and a half later, in February 1899. The nuncio denied that there was any hostility toward the Jews on the part of the Holy See, who, he said, had always protected them throughout history. He also said that he personally was not unfavorable to the Zionist project.[19] But Herzl, recognizing that it was the pope who was his chief opponent, sought an audience with him.

In January 1904 Herzl was received by the Secretary of State of the Holy See, Cardinal Merry del Val. Herzl insisted that the Holy Places would be extra-territorialized and there would be no domination over them by the Jews in the Zionist project. But the cardinal insisted that the denial of Christ by the Jews made their rule over the Holy Land unthinkable:

> I do not quite see how we can take any initiative in this matter. As long as the Jews deny the divinity of Christ, we certainly cannot make a declaration in their favor. Not that we have any ill will toward them. On the contrary, the Church has always protected them. To us they are the indispensable witnesses to the phenomenon of God's term on earth. But they deny the divine nature of Christ. How then can we, without abandoning our own highest principles, agree to their being given possession of the Holy Land again?[20]

The cardinal arranged for Herzl to be received by Pope Pius X three days later, on January 25, 1904. The pope was equally stern in insisting that Jewish possession of the land could not be accepted because of Jewish denial of Christ.

> We cannot encourage this movement. We cannot prevent the Jews from going to Jerusalem—but we could never sanction it. The ground of Jerusalem . . . has been sanctified by the life of Jesus Christ. As the head of the Church I cannot tell you otherwise. The Jews have not recognized our Lord, therefore we cannot recognize the Jewish people.[21]

Herzl repeated his claim that the Holy Places would be extra-territorialized and would not be ruled over by Jews, but he recognized that the pope was not impressed by this assurance. In the pope's eyes Jerusalem's holiness resided in its identity as an integral whole, not as a collection of separate shrines and

---

19. Ibid., 97.

20. Entry of January 23, 1904, Herzl's *Diaries*, quoted by Minerbi, *The Vatican and Zionism*, 98.

21. Entry of January 26, 1904, Herzl's *Diaries*, quoted in ibid., 100.

churches. In this initial meeting of the Holy See with Herzl on Zionism, the Church's arguments against it focused entirely on theological reasons. These were seen as absolutely excluding any Jewish rule in Palestine.

Cardinal del Val's interview in *Die Welt* a few months after Herzl's audience with the pope seemed to open up a different option. He said:

> How can we deliver up the country of our Redeemer to a people of a different faith? . . . Yet the Church would do nothing to impede the Zionist's effort to obtain, "a home in Palestine secured by public law. . . ." For that is an entirely different matter. . . . If the Jews believe they can ease their lot in the land of their fathers, that is a humanitarian question in our view. The foundation of the Holy See is apostolic; it will never oppose an undertaking that alleviates human misery.[22]

What was meant here by a "home in Palestine secured by public law"? Del Val seems to be talking about Jews living in Palestine under a non-Jewish rule, as distinct from Jewish rule in Palestine. This, he claims, would be purely humanitarian, an option the Holy See would not oppose.

World War I and the Period Between the World Wars

The role of Zionism in Palestine took a decisive new step in World War I.[23] In this war the diminishing Ottoman Empire that was ruling Palestine allied itself with the Germans. Meanwhile the British sought an alliance with Arabs, represented by Husain ibn 'Ali, the grand sharif of Mecca, to split them from the Ottomans. The British High Commissioner for Egypt and the Sudan, Henry McMahon, promised the sharif an independent Arab state in exchange for his alliance with the British against the Turkish-German powers. These Arabs envisioned this state as incorporating the whole Arab-speaking region, including Palestine, although the British would later insist that it did not. On the basis of this correspondence, which the sharif understood as a firm agreement, the Arab armies revolted against the Ottoman Turks. With the assistance of British officers, such as T. E. Lawrence, they began a drive that captured the Arabian peninsula and pushed north and west from there.

During this period the British Foreign Office, represented by Sir Mark Sykes and Lord Arthur Balfour, entered into conflicting agreements with

22. *Die Welt*, April 1, 1904, quoted in ibid., 101.

23. For a detailed account of events narrated in this paragraph and the next, see Schneer, *The Balfour Declaration*, 165–236.

France and with the Zionists. In May of 1916 Sykes made a secret agreement with the French, represented by Charles Picot, to divide up the Arab region into five sections. Two would be under French administration and two under the British. The fifth area, Palestine, was to be under the three allied powers of Britain, France, and Russia, The Arabian peninsula was left to be a self-governing Arab state.

Meanwhile Lord Balfour made another agreement with the Zionists, promising Jews a "national home" in Palestine. The Arabs were outraged at what they saw as their betrayal by the British. The Balfour Declaration was issued on November 2, 1917, as General Allenby and his army completed the conquest of Palestine in a triumphal entry into Jerusalem. It asserted:

> His Majesty's government view with favour the establishment in Palestine of a national home for the Jewish people and will use their best endeavours to facilitate the achievement of this object, it being clearly understood that nothing shall be done which may prejudice the civil and religious rights of existing non-Jewish communities in Palestine, or the rights and political status of Jews in any other country.[24]

The Balfour Declaration would receive official international legal status in 1923, with the acceptance of the British Mandate for Palestine by the League of Nations. It has several notable features. The British promise only to facilitate a "national home" for the Jews, not a "Jewish state." Nothing is said about Jewish rule in this "home." In fact, the British intended to rule it themselves, giving Jews areas to live in, but not to rule. Arabs are not mentioned as a major part of the communities resident in Palestine, even though they comprised more than 90 percent of the population at that time. "Existing non-Jewish communities in Palestine" could have been intended to refer to them, but also to the Christian Holy Places presided over by Western Europeans and Greek Orthodox.

Though generally hostile to the Balfour Declaration, the Vatican was cautious about a response to it until its meaning became clear. Generally the Vatican did not oppose a "home" for the Jews in Palestine, if that was understood as areas to inhabit that would not interfere with either the Christian Holy Places or with the Palestinian Christian and Muslim population. It was deeply set against a Jewish sovereignty over the whole land. Cardinal Gaspari, Secretary to the Vatican, expressed his concerns about the British declaration to the Belgian diplomatic representative:

24. Ibid., 341.

Britain has apparently assumed an obligation towards the Jews to whom they will hand over a part of the administration of Palestine. Influenced by the big Jewish bankers of England and the United States, the British politicians do not sufficiently take into account the deep difference which exists between them and the Jewish people. It seems the British politicians fail to appreciate the dangers of this solution for Christian interests in the Holy Land.[25]

This situation was further confused in 1918 by a misquotation of a statement from James Cardinal Gibbons, leading Catholic churchman in the United States, that the pope supported the rights of the Jews in Palestine. This outraged the Arab Christians. Gibbons, who was strongly pro-Jewish, had responded to the Zionist Organization of the United States by saying, "It is with pleasure that I learn of the approval accorded by His Holiness, Benedict XV, to the plan providing a homeland in Palestine to the members of the Jewish race."[26] The distinction that the pope would have made between rule over some or all of Palestine and residence there under the British was not clarified in Gibbons' letter.

The pope later came to appreciate British rule in Palestine, perceiving that it treated the various communities of Palestine equally. The Vatican greatly increased its institutions in Palestine in the 1920s, building numerous churches, schools, orphanages, and hospitals. Many of these institutions, such as the schools and hospitals, served the Muslim population equally with the Christian. The papacy came to be concerned, not just about the Catholic Holy Places, but about the indigenous Palestinian population as well.[27]

This concern was aggravated in the 1930s as Nazi oppression of Jews in Germany grew and fleeing Jews created a greatly expanded Jewish immigration to Palestine. The growing Jewish population in Palestine bought up more and more land, creating agricultural communities and corporations that denied employment to the Arabs. Arabs, growing ever more destitute and marginalized, organized protests and then moved to armed rebellion against the British. The British responded by repressing the rising revolt under martial law, imposing massive arrests of leaders and collective punishment in villages. Many thousands of Palestinians died, were injured, or suffered imprisonment in this conflict (1937–38). The British found themselves having to commit massive funds and troops to put down the revolt as

25. Minerbi, *The Vatican and Zionism*, 122.

26. Ibid., 123.

27. Kreutz, *Vatican Policy*, 45–46.

a new world war was impending in Europe. This brought the British to the realization that they had to back away from this conflict and conciliate the Arabs, lest they ally themselves with enemies of Britain.

Meanwhile the British organized a royal commission, which reported in 1937 that the Palestinian Mandate was unworkable. The Peel Commission recommended the partition of Palestine into a small Jewish state occupying 20 percent of the land and a large Arab state joined with Jordan. But the Jewish state would have three hundred thousand Arabs in it; the commission recommended that they be transferred to the Arab state. The British would retain rule over the Jerusalem-Bethlehem area with a corridor to the sea, together with the ports, railroads, and airfields. The Palestinian leaders rejected this partition, which would have given the best agricultural land to the Jews. The Vatican added its voice to this situation with a letter to the British government, objecting to the partition of the land and calling especially for the protection not only of the Christian Holy Places, but also of the Christian minorities.[28]

In 1939 the British decided they could not afford this upheaval because of the prospect of impending war. They backed away from their commitment to the Zionists for a Jewish homeland and imposed a strict limit to Jewish immigration and land purchase in Palestine, declaring that this measure would be followed by the creation of a Palestinian state where Jews and Arabs would share government, not separate Arab and Jewish states. Zionists denounced the British for this move, and radical Zionist groups, such as the *Irgun* and the Stern Gang, began to turn their guns on the British. From 1939 to 1948 the British would rule Palestine without the cooperation of Jews or Arabs.[29]

After World War II: Humanitarian Concerns and Social Justice

During World War II Pope Pius XII spoke out many times against anti-Semitism but was later criticized for not being emphatic enough. Catholic institutions played a major role in the rescue of Jews in Europe. Although the papacy was supportive of the immigration of Jews to Palestine, it remained opposed to the Zionist goal of a Jewish state.[30] The war saw the emergence of the strongly pro-Zionist United States as a world power. With

28. Kreutz, *Vatican Policy*, 63–65.

29. For an account of political events in Palestine between 1936 and 1945, see ibid., 59–86.

30. Ibid., 75–84.

American support, the United Nations voted in 1947 for the partition of Palestine into a Jewish and an Arab state. The Arabs rejected the partition, as did the Vatican, while the Jews accepted it as the legal basis of a Jewish state, although they did not endorse the limits of the territory assigned to them in the plan.

As the British withdrew from the area in 1948, a war broke out between the newly declared Jewish state and Arab armies from Jordan and Egypt. The better organized and more determined Israelis soon pushed these Arab armies aside and expanded into more than half of the lands assigned to the Arabs, driving the residents of many Arab villages into exile. Jordan annexed the remaining part of the West Bank, and Egypt occupied the remainder of Gaza, causing the land designated for Arab state to disappear. A million Palestinians became refugees,[31] driven into the West Bank, Lebanon, Jordan, and Gaza. Israel also confiscated much of the Arab land in Israel, making many of these Palestinians refugees as well. Contrary to Israeli claims that the Palestinians "voluntarily" left, this was an intentional effort by the Israeli leaders to clear as much of the land as possible of Palestinians.[32]

The Vatican quickly became heavily involved in humanitarian aid to the Palestinian refugees, most of whom were Muslim. In June 1949 the pope established the Pontifical Mission for Palestine, creating more than 270 social welfare centers that distributed food, clothing, and medicine to the refugees and opening hundreds of schools for the children. Catholicism thus became firmly committed to the Palestinian people as a whole, calling for their repatriation and a just sharing of the land of Palestine between Israel and the Palestinians. The Vatican also refused to give official recognition to the State of Israel, on the grounds that its territorial borders were "undecided." This stance would last until 1993, and in the following year the Vatican also gave official recognition to the PLO as representative of the Palestinian people.

In January 1964 Pope Paul VI made a major pilgrimage to the Holy Land. It was the first time in history that a pope had personally confronted the realities of the Palestinian situation and the politics of the Middle East. He was able to see for himself the deep suffering and misery that displacement and marginalization were imposing on the Palestinian people, and this experience made a deep impression on him. He could see what their needs were and determine what the Church's humanitarian services should

31. The United Nations Relief and Works Agency for Palestine Refugees was aiding one million registered refugees in 1949; Ruether and Ruether, *Wrath of Jonah*, 103.

32. For historical research on the Zionist agenda at that time, see Pappé, *Ethnic Cleansing*.

include. Many of the pope's later remarks and initiatives were shaped by his experience at that time.[33]

After his pilgrimage the pope arranged with the Christian Brothers to set up Bethlehem University, which exists today as a major educational institution for Palestinians in the West Bank, the majority of whom were and are Muslims.[34] In October and November of 2006 Herman Ruether spent considerable time in Bethlehem, especially at Bethlehem University, and was impressed by the prevalence of Muslims at the school and their warm identification with it. In 2010 Rosemary Ruether spent some days visiting with families in a refugee camp in the Bethlehem area, all of whom are Muslim. The young people in this camp spoke English fluently and were able to interpret for us. They were proudly attending Bethlehem University.

In 1962 Pope John XXIII convoked the Second Vatican Council (1962–65), which was subsequently continued after his death by Paul VI. This council would have a major impact in church renewal and in the creation of a new relationship of the Catholic Church with social justice issues worldwide. In consideration of the Holocaust, European delegates were very anxious that the Council issue a major statement on Judaism, repudiating anti-Semitism. Delegates from the Middle East, however, were worried that such a statement would be seen as endorsing Zionism. The Vatican assured them that this statement would be purely religious, not political. On October 15, 1965, on the eve of the final vote on the declaration, Paul VI even personally assured Father Ibrahim Ayyad, a Roman Catholic priest deeply committed to the Palestinians, that the Council "would not allow its decision to be exploited by the Israelis," and the decision would not adversely affect "the legitimate rights of the Palestinian people."[35]

As a result, the statement on Judaism was rethought and recast more broadly in the *Declaration on the Relation of the Church to Non-Christian Religions* (*Nostra Aetate*, October 28, 1965), which included Hinduism, Buddhism, Islam, and Judaism.[36] This declaration did not attack or criticize any of these religions, but rather lifted up what was regarded as positive aspects of each of them, in an ascending order, with Islam and Judaism seen as closest to Christianity.

Concerning Islam, the declaration said of Muslims, "They adore the one God . . . merciful and all-powerful, the Creator of heaven and earth

33. Kreutz, *Vatican Policy*, 114.

34. Irani, *The Papacy and the Middle East*, 32.

35. Kreutz, *Vatican Policy*, 119.

36. The declaration can be found on the Vatican website: http://www.vatican.va/ archive/hist_councils/ii_vatican_council/documents/vat-ii_decl_19651028_nostra-aetate_en.html. The words quoted from it below are drawn from sections 3 and 4.

. . . they take pains to submit wholeheartedly to even His inscrutable de-crees. . . . Though they do not acknowledge Jesus as God, they revere Him as a prophet. They also honor Mary, His virgin mother. . . . [T]hey await the day of judgment. . . . Finally, they value the moral life and worship God es-pecially through prayer, almsgiving, and fasting." The Council acknowledged that there had been many "quarrels and hostilities" between Christians and Muslims in the past, but urged that all "forget the past" and work for "mutual understanding" and "social justice."

The strongest and the longest statement is reserved for Judaism. The Church affirms that the "beginnings of her faith and her election are found already among the Patriarchs, Moses, and the prophets." Although "the Jews in large number [did not] accept the Gospel. . . . Nevertheless, God holds the Jews most dear for the sake of their Fathers. He does not repent of the gifts He makes." Alluding to the idea that the Jews would repent at the end of history, the declaration says that "the Church awaits that day, known to God alone, on which all peoples will address the Lord in a single voice." Never-theless, the Jews are to be revered for their patrimony and not discriminated against in any way.

The statement rejects any right to use the conflict that occurred at the time of Christ as a basis for discrimination against Jews today. It says that although "the Jewish authorities and those who followed their lead pressed for the death of Christ; still, what happened in His Passion cannot be charged against all the Jews, without distinction, then alive, nor against the Jews of today. Although the Church is the new people of God, the Jews should not be presented as rejected or accursed by God, as if this followed from the Holy Scriptures. . . . [M]indful of the patrimony she shares with the Jews and moved not by political reasons but by the Gospel's spiritual love, [the Church] decries hatred, persecution, displays of anti-Semitism, directed against Jews at any time and by anyone."

As we have seen in this essay, the claim that Jewish rejection of Christ was the reason why the Church rejected Zionism was prominent in the first responses of the Church to this movement in 1904, at the time of Herzl's audience with Pope Pius X. Although this claim was not cited thereafter, the viewpoint remained in the background because it had not been repudi-ated. But after 1965 this argument could no longer be used. The Vatican II statement removed from Catholicism any use of Jewish rejection of Christ as a basis for anti-Zionism. Criticism of Israel then became clearly political and ethical, not theological. Social justice for the Palestinians and the need to find a solution to the conflict by equal sharing of the land between the two people became the focus of the Vatican reservations toward the State of Israel.

Another important development of the Vatican II period, although independent of the Council's declarations, were papal declarations on behalf of global social justice. On April 11, 1963, Pope John XXIII issued the encyclical *Pacem in Terris* (*On Establishing Universal Peace in Truth, Justice, Charity, and Liberty*).[37] The foundation of well-ordered societies, according to the encyclical, is the principle that every person is endowed by nature with intelligence and free will and has rights and obligations flowing from this nature that are universal and inviolable and cannot be in any way surrendered.

Human rights, according to this encyclical, include the rights to life, to bodily integrity, to the means suitable for the development of life, food, clothing, shelter, rest, medical care, and social services. There is also the right to security, in cases of sickness, inability to work, widowhood, old age, unemployment, and any other case that deprives a person of the means of subsistence. Persons should be free to choose their state of life and have the right to set up a family, with equal rights and duties for men and women. They have a right not only to work, but to go about work without coercion. This right includes working conditions where physical health or morals are not endangered. All humans have the rights of private property, of assembly and association, of movement and residence in their country, of emigration to another country, and of participation in public affairs, as well as juridical protection of these rights.

The pope then goes on to comment upon the emergence of various groups of oppressed people, including the working classes, women, and colonized nations, all of whom should share equally in such human rights. For example, on women he says, "Women are gaining an increasing awareness of their natural dignity. Far from being content with a purely passive role or allowing themselves to be regarded as a kind of instrument, they are demanding both in domestic and in public life the rights and duties which belong to them as human persons." Especially relevant to the Palestinian plight are the pope's remarks on refugees:

> The deep feelings of paternal love for all mankind which God
> has implanted in Our heart makes it impossible for Us to view
> without bitter anguish of spirit the plight of those who for politi-
> cal reasons have been exiled from their own homelands. There
> are great numbers of such refugees at the present time, and many
> are the sufferings—the incredible sufferings—to which they are

37. The encyclical *Pacem in Terris* is on the Vatican website: http://www.vatican.va/holy_father/john_xxiii/encyclicals/documents/hf_j-xxiii_enc_11041963_pacem_en.html. The words quoted from it below are drawn from paragraphs 41, 103, 105, and 172.

constantly exposed. . . . [I]t is not irrelevant to draw the attention of the world to the fact that these refugees are persons and all their rights as persons must be recognized. Refugees cannot lose these rights simply because they are deprived of citizenship of their own States.

The encyclical is addressed not only to the priests and leaders of the Catholic Church but to all "men of good will."

This stirring document was followed by an insightful encyclical from Paul VI dated March 26, 1967, namely, *Populorum Progressio* (*On the Development of Peoples*).[38] This document is addressed particularly to the needs of developing nations emerging from colonialism. The pope cites his experiences of traveling to Latin America, Africa, India, and Palestine as grounding his concerns on this issue. These nations need more than political independence. The disparity between rich and poor nations must be overcome. Here the pope even endorses the right to expropriate landed estates from the wealthy when they are "unused or poorly used, bring hardship to peoples, or are detrimental to the interests of the country," and when this serves the "common good." "Unbridled liberalism" (*laissez-faire* capitalism), in which private property is seen as having no limits or social obligations, is condemned, in the phrase that Paul VI quotes here from his predecessor Pius XI, as an expression of the "international imperialism of money."

Generally the pope calls for transformations of these situations through reform rather than violent revolution, although acknowledging that sometimes revolution is necessary when there is "long-standing tyranny." He calls for world powers "to set aside part of their military expenditures for a world fund to relieve the needs of impoverished peoples." In this remarkable encyclical, which goes on for many pages, the Holy See takes the side of developing nations vis-à-vis the rich and powerful nations of the world. By mentioning Palestine along with India, Africa, and Latin America, he includes the Palestinian people among those whose needs should be addressed by the whole world.

After the Second Vatican Council the Holy See began to grant audiences to leaders of the State of Israel. In January 1973 Pope Paul VI met with Golda Meir; this was the first time a pope had met with an Israeli Prime Minister. A communiqué issued immediately after this meeting said that the pope,

---

38. The encyclical *Populorum Progressio* is on the Vatican website: http://www.vatican.va/holy_father/paul_vi/encyclicals/documents/hf_p-vi_enc_26031967_populorum_en.html. The words quoted from it below are drawn from sections 24, 26, 31, and 51.

> . . . having recalled the history and suffering of the Jewish people,
> explained the viewpoint of the Holy See on questions that touch
> most closely its humanitarian mission, such as the problem of
> the refugees and the situation of the various communities living
> in the Holy Land . . .[39]

The director of the Vatican Press office, Federico Alexandrini, clarified further that there was no change in the relation of the Vatican to Israel or to the Palestinians as a result of the meeting.

> The attitude of the Holy See with regard to Israel remains . . . un-
> changed. The Pope had accepted the request of Mrs. Golda Meir
> because he considers it his duty not to miss any opportunity to
> act in favor of peace, for the defense of human rights and those
> of the communities, . . . and in order to aid especially those who
> are the weakest and those who are defenseless, in the first place
> the Palestinian refugees.[40]

This mention of the Palestinians by the Holy See deeply angered Meir and caused an uproar in Israel.

From 1974 the PLO, with Yasir Arafat as its head, gained increasing international respectability as the representative of the Palestinian people. The Soviet Union influenced the PLO to abandon a claim to all of Palestine and to accept a Palestinian state in the West Bank and Gaza, a position partly endorsed in the Palestine National Congress meeting in June and July of 1974. In November of 1974 Arafat addressed the United Nations General Assembly. Arafat concluded his detailed remarks on the causes of the Palestinian oppression with these words: "Today I have come bearing an olive branch and a freedom fighter's gun. Do not let the olive branch fall from my hand."[41] Following his address, the United Nations voted in favor of granting the PLO observer status at the UN by Resolution 3237 (XXIX), and the PLO's permanent observer mission was established at that time.[42] Its status did not entail any designation of statehood.

In December 1987 the Vatican appointed Michel Sabbah, a Palestinian, as the Latin Patriarch of Jerusalem. Although the Latin Patriarchate had been established in 1099, at the time of the Crusades, it was marginalized by the fall of the Crusader states and eventually located in Rome. It was reestablished under the Ottoman sultan in 1847, but the office of Latin

---

39. Irani, *The Papacy and the Middle East*, 38.

40. Ibid., 39.

41. Arafat, "Yasir Arafat Addresses," 10.

42. "Background Paper Related to Palestine Status."

Patriarch was held by Westerners. Thus the appointment of a Palestinian as Latin Patriarch changed the official face of Roman Catholics in Israel and Palestine.

Born and educated in Palestine, Michel Sabbah held the position of General Director of the Roman Catholic schools in the region and subsequently that of President of Bethlehem University. As Latin Patriarch, an office he held for twenty years (1988–2008), he represented the Vatican and served as the spiritual leader of all Catholic Christians in Israel and Palestine. He has spoken out strongly for Palestinian human rights, the end of occupation, the return of the refugees, and a two-state solution.[43] His successor, Fouad Twal (2008 to the present), is also a Palestinian and has continued this call for Palestinian rights, the end of the Wall and the checkpoints, and a Palestinian state. Thus the Latin Patriarchate has become an insistent voice for Palestinian rights.

The United States, with Israel, has boycotted any direct relations with the PLO, labeling it a "terrorist organization." This view, however, became increasingly isolated from the world at large. The Vatican, along with most nations, recognized the PLO as the national representative of the Palestinians. On December 30, 1993, the Vatican moved to grant a "fundamental agreement" with the State of Israel, officially recognizing it and clarifying the rights of the Church in that country. Specifically named are the Church's rights to educational, health care, and media organizations as well as respect for the status quo of the Holy Places, Catholic institutions, and the promotion of pilgrimages in Israel.[44]

To make clear that the Holy See had in no way backed away from its commitment to the rights of the Palestinians, less than a year later, on October 26, 1994, the Vatican met with Palestinian representatives and entered into official relations with the PLO. The agreement calls for "a just and comprehensive peace in the Middle East . . . and a peaceful solution to the Palestinian-Israeli conflict, which could realize the inalienable national legitimate rights . . . of the Palestinian people." The PLO affirmed the equality before the law of the three monotheistic faiths in Jerusalem and its "permanent commitment to uphold and observe the human rights to freedom of religion and conscience, as stated in the Universal Declaration of Human Rights." The Holy See, in turn, affirmed its own commitment to

43. See Sabbah, *Faithful Witness*, with its biographical introduction by Christiansen and Sarsar.

44. *Fundamental Agreement between the Holy See and the State of Israel* (1993), at http://mfa.gov.il/MFA/MFA-Archive/1993/Pages/Fundamental%20Agreement%20-%20Israel-Holy%20See.aspx.

these equal rights of the different religious communities.[45] Pope John Paul II had previously met with Yasir Arafat in 1982 and again in 1988.[46]

John Paul II, who became pope in 1978, and his successor, Benedict XVI, installed in 2005, had different backgrounds and experiences of the Middle East than Paul VI. John Paul II, as a Pole, grew up with close relations with Jews and was shaped by the struggle against Nazi oppression of the Jews and the Poles in World War II. Benedict XVI, as a German, is sensitive to charges of anti-Semitism and of German responsibility for the Holocaust. Yet both popes maintained the Holy See's commitment to the Palestinians and their rights to equal sharing of the land with the Israelis. It was John Paul II who met with Arafat twice and entered into the agreement with the PLO, alongside that with Israel.

In December 2012 Pope Benedict XVI spoke out in praise of the United Nations' vote that made Palestine a non-member observer state of that body. This UN decision recognizes Palestine as a nation-state, and not simply as an "entity" (as in 1974). This is the same status enjoyed by the Holy See. One hundred thirty-eight members voted on November 29, 2012, for this change of status, while only nine, most notably the United States, Canada, and Israel, voted against it. Several close allies of the U.S., such as Britain and France, chose to abstain rather than support the "no" vote. The Vatican declared that the enhanced status of the Palestinians at the UN "does not constitute, per se, a sufficient solution to the existing problems of the region." This would require "effective commitment to building peace and stability, in justice and in the respect for legitimate aspirations, both for the Israelis and the Palestinians."[47]

The official views of the Catholic Church on the Israeli-Palestinian conflict are more in line with the views taken by developing nations than with those of the United States. This was evident in a 2010 statement promoting just peace in Palestine, issued by church leaders in the Philippines. The first signature was that of Bishop Deogracias Iniguez, Co-Chair of the Ecumenical Bishops Forum and Chair of the Episcopal Commission on Public Affairs of the Catholic Bishops Conference of the Philippines. This statement, signed by thirty-six church leaders of the Philippines, decried Israel's violence against international peace activists aboard the Freedom Flotilla bringing humanitarian aid to Gaza. The statement went on to say:

45. "The PLO-Vatican Agreement," at http://www.jerusalemquarterly.org/View-Article.aspx?id=233.

46. Kreutz, *Vatican Policy*, 158, 162.

47. Glatz, "Vatican Praises."

It is time to end Israel's illegal occupation of Palestinian lands. It's time for Israel to stop bulldozing Palestinian homes and to urgently implement a freeze on all settlement construction as a first step towards the dismantlement of all settlements. It's time to end the dispossession of the Palestinian people and the violation of their human rights and dignity. It's time for the Palestinians to exercise their right to self-determination. It's time for Palestinians who have been refugees for sixty years to have the right to return to their homes. It's time to do away with apartheid and double standards. The Separation Barrier is a grave breach of international and humanitarian law and must be removed from occupied territory. It's time to stop discrimination, segregation, and restrictions on movement. It's time to stop the recent Israeli military order that will categorize tens of thousands of Palestinians living in the West Bank as "infiltrators"—ostensibly because they lack proper permits—and give military officers sweeping control over their deportation. . . . It's time for healing to begin in the land called holy. Jerusalem must be an open, inclusive, and shared city in terms of sovereignty and citizenship. The rights of its communities must be guaranteed—Muslim, Jewish, and Christian, Palestinian and Israeli—including access to Holy Places and freedom of worship. Now is time for each of us to speak out and act, fulfilling our Christian vocation as peacemakers. It is time for freedom from *oppression and occupation*."[48]

This impassioned and comprehensive statement on behalf of Palestinian rights and shared rights to the Holy Land reflects the views of Christian leaders in a developing nation, led in this endeavor by a Catholic bishop. It is much in accord with the views that have come from the Holy See. Since then, a new pope, Francis, was elected in 2013. It is not yet known what his views on Palestine are, but his commitment to the poor and to the people of developing nations suggests that he will be sympathetic to papal precedents promoting social justice.

Bibliography

Arafat, Yasir. "Yasir Arafat Addresses the United Nations." In *Palestinian Visions: A Documentary Account of the Peace Initiative*, edited by Palestine Human Rights Campaign, 10. Chicago: Palestine Human Rights Campaign, 1990.

Armstrong, Karen. *Jerusalem: One City, Three Faiths*. New York: Ballantine, 1996.

48. "Philippine Church Leaders' Statement."

"Background Paper Related to Palestine Status." Permanent Observer Mission of the State of Palestine to the United Nations website. http://www.un.int/wcm/content/site/palestine/pid/11550.

Declaration on the Relation of the Church to Non-Christian Religions (Nostra Aetate). October 28, 1965. http://www.vatican.va/archive/hist_councils/ii_vatican_council/documents/vat-ii_decl_19651028_nostra-aetate_en.html.

Fundamental Agreement between the Holy See and the State of Israel. Jerusalem, 1993. http://mfa.gov.il/MFA/MFA-Archive/1993/Pages/Fundamental%20Agreement%20-%20Israel-Holy%20See.aspx.

Glatz, Carol. "Vatican Praises New UN Status for Palestine, Urges Full Sovereignty." *Catholic News Service,* November 30, 2012. http://www.catholicnews.com/data/stories/cns/1205029.htm.

Hertzberg, Arthur. *The Zionist Idea: A Historical Analysis and Reader.* New York: Meridian, 1960.

Irani, George E. *The Papacy and the Middle East: The Role of the Holy See in the Arab-Israeli Conflict, 1962–1984.* Notre Dame, IN: The University of Notre Dame, 1986.

John XXIII. *Pacem in Terris (On Establishing Universal Peace in Truth, Justice, Charity, and Liberty).* April 11, 1963. http://www.vatican.va/holy_father/john_xxiii/encyclicals/documents/hf_j-xxiii_enc_11041963_pacem_en.html.

Kreutz, Andrej. *Vatican Policy on the Palestinian-Israeli Conflict: The Struggle for the Holy Land.* New York: Greenwood, 1990.

Minerbi, Sergio I. *The Vatican and Zionism: Conflict in the Holy Land, 1895–1925.* New York: Oxford University Press, 1990.

Pappé, Ilan. *The Ethnic Cleansing of Palestine.* London: Oneworld, 2006.

Paul VI. *Populorum Progressio (On the Development of Peoples).* March 26, 1967. http://www.vatican.va/holy_father/paul_vi/encyclicals/documents/hf_p-vi_enc_26031967_populorum_en.html.

"Philippine Church Leaders' Statement for Just Peace in Palestine." June 2010. http://globalministries.org/news/eap/philippine-statement-palestine.html.

"The PLO-Vatican Agreement." *Jerusalem Quarterly* 8 (Spring 2000) n.p. http://www.jerusalemquarterly.org/ViewArticle.aspx?id=233.

Rabkin, Yakov M. *A Threat from Within: A Century of Jewish Opposition to Zionism.* Translated by Fred A. Reed. London: Zed, 2006.

Rausch, David A. *Zionism within Early American Fundamentalism, 1879–1918.* New York: Edwin Mellen, 1979.

Rose, Jacqueline. *The Question of Zion.* Princeton: Princeton University Press, 2007.

Ruether, Rosemary Radford. *Faith and Fratricide: The Theological Roots of Anti-Semitism.* Eugene, OR: Wipf & Stock, 1996.

Ruether, Rosemary Radford, and Herman J. Ruether. *The Wrath of Jonah: The Crisis of Religious Nationalism in the Israeli-Palestinian Conflict.* 2nd ed. Minneapolis: Fortress, 2002.

Sabbah, Michel. *Faithful Witness: On Reconciliation and Peace in the Holy Land.* Edited with introduction by Drew Christiansen and Saliba Sarsar. Foreword by Cardinal Theodore E. McCarrick. Hyde Park, NY: New City, 2009.

Schneer, Jonathan. *The Balfour Declaration: The Origins of the Arab-Israeli Conflict.* New York: Random House, 2010.

Weiss, Philip. "It's Time for the Media to Talk about Zionism." December 4, 2012. http://mondoweiss.net/2012/12/its-time-for-the-media-to-talk-about-zionism.html.

Chapter Six

The Mainline Protestant Churches
and the Holy Land

Donald E. Wagner

Introduction

An intense debate on Israel and Palestine has been underway within main-line U.S. Protestant denominations for nearly one hundred years. The debate has taken place during a period of profound change within the churches themselves, continuing conflict in Israel-Palestine, and seismic shifts in the religious landscape of the United States. This chapter will examine that debate and lift up several of the highlights, major figures, and theological and political issues that have framed the debate as it enters a new and controversial phase.

Following World War I, mainline Protestant leaders had extraordinary influence in American society, including access to the centers of power in Washington, D.C. Their churches were filled, their clergy and theologians received the utmost respect, and most congressional leaders and every president came from this tradition. However, by the late 1950s, these same Protestant churches began to decline in membership and influence to be replaced by the more conservative evangelical and fundamentalist branches of Protestantism.[1] The debate over Palestine and Israel has taken place dur-

---

1. The term "evangelical" represents a broad umbrella movement within Protestant Christianity with a membership of close to ninety million Americans. Fundamentalists

ing this period of change in U.S. religious life, and the following account describes the ebb and flow of this discussion within the American Protestant tradition(s). It includes the polarization of theological and political perspectives, various political strategies of politicians and Protestant leaders, the rising power of the Zionist movement in the United States, and, until recently, the near-eclipse of the Palestinian narrative.

1. The United States and Its Founding Mythologies

A brief review of North American settlers reminds us that, although thousands of African slaves arrived on these shores against their will, many Europeans came of their own will seeking religious freedom. Most believed they were "called" by God to fulfill a divine mission as a community of Christian believers sailing to the "new world." They understood their mission in biblical terms, linking their journey to that of the ancient Israelites.

On March 29, 1630, a boat carrying British Puritans left Southampton, England, with several important leaders, including John Winthrop, who would become the first governor of the Massachusetts Bay Colony. The departure sermon was delivered by John Cotton, who referred to their journey as a "divine calling" and summarized the core beliefs undergirding their perilous voyage. He turned to 2 Samuel 7:10: "And I will appoint a place for my people Israel and will plant them, so that they may live in their own place, and be disturbed no more." (NRSV) Cotton drew a direct parallel between the Puritans' mission and that of ancient Israel in its journey from Sinai to the "Promised Land." For the Puritans, their mission and journey were no less important nor were they any less divinely inspired than Moses and the Israelites. These "new Israelites" believed God would guide them and had in fact gone before them, preparing their way and granting a divinely ordained entitlement to a land that was already inhabited.

Several other colonizers would arrive in what they also called the "new world," with a similar sense of entitlement to that land—Roman Catholics, Methodists, Anglicans, Lutherans, Quakers, Presbyterians, and others. For all of the European settlers there was a relatively consistent embrace of themes of entitlement (often stated as a "divine right") to the land and its

---

are the most conservative wing of evangelicalism and include the Southern Baptist Convention and many independent Bible churches, some of which adopt premillennial dispensationalism (end-time theology). Others are hyper-Calvinists, or strict followers of the reformer John Calvin. All fundamentalists believe the Bible is without error and must be interpreted literally; however, dispensationalists are selective in the chapters and verses they emphasize, reading them with a predictive approach to the prophetic texts.

resources and superiority over the native people, or what political scientists call "settler colonialism."[2]

However, the entitlement did not extend to all citizens but only to a select group. Theologian Rosemary Radford Ruether reminds us that the United States was established on a fundamental contradiction: "Although claiming to be based on the 'universal rights of man,' as affirmed in the Declaration of Independence, the founders held an implicit and often explicit assumption that these rights were for their peculiar legacy of Anglo-Saxon Protestant males."[3] Catholics and Jews, women, Hispanics, blacks, Arabs, and other people "of color" would have to endure a long and costly struggle for equal rights and acceptance into the community, and some are still far from possessing full rights. Many Native Americans, Latino immigrants, and Muslims continue to experience significant discrimination, as they find it more difficult to realize the American "dream" than white Euro-Americans. Thus the United States was established on a fundamental contradiction: the claim of universal equality and the founding myths of entitlement, inequality, and conquest. The roots of these threefold privileges are anchored in a highly selective and distorted reading of the Hebrew scriptures and the New Testament. It has taken generations to begin to correct the moral and theological imperfections of these founding myths within the United States, let alone in western Christian theology. In fact, the history and ideology of settler colonialism have been so central to the political history of the United States that it has at times predisposed both political and religious leaders in the United States (and elsewhere) to embrace other settler colonial ideologies such as the Zionist movement and apartheid in South Africa.

Ruether's observation concerning various dangers inherent in these contradictory claims (that is, proclaiming the equality of citizens while allowing considerable privileges for white Anglo-Americans, males in particular) continues to challenge the United States to this day. Religious and political support for exclusivity and economic or territorial gain usually trumps what is legal and moral. As this history unfolds, we will observe that the same contradictory policy decisions were played out in the halls of Congress and the executive branch in U.S. policies in relation to the Israeli and Palestinian conflict, with the privileging of one side (Israel) over the Palestinians. Beginning with Woodrow Wilson and continuing to the present day, successive U.S. Presidents and Congress have chosen political

---

2. Settler colonialism is defined by Cavanagh and Veracini as "a global and transnational phenomenon and as much a thing of the past as well as a thing of the present. Settlers 'come to stay': they are founders of political orders who carry with them a distinct sovereign capacity" ("Definition"). See also Rodinson, *Israel*.

3. Ruether, *America, Amerikka*, 41.

expediency and the support of exclusive claims, whether for political or religious reasons. Usually their decisions came at the expense of what was moral, just, and legal. It should not be surprising that like our political leaders, many Christian clergy, academics, and business leaders also embraced theological and political doctrines of exceptionalism that supported Zionism's exclusive claims.

2. The Modern Era: Two World Wars and their Troubling Legacies

Some historians argue that United States and Protestant foreign policy interests in Israel-Palestine date back to the 1820s, when the Protestant churches commissioned the first American missionaries to Syria, Egypt, and Palestine. While there is a kernel of truth in this, the influence of the missionaries was limited, and they had little or no impact on U.S. foreign policy. The first significant political decision confronting the U.S. government in what was then called Palestine occurred during World War I, when England adopted the Zionist movement's formula by issuing the Balfour Declaration on November 2, 1917. The document states that the British government supported "a national home for the Jewish people in Palestine."[4] While this sounds like a wonderful idea, it must be noted that Jews were around 6 percent of the population in Palestine and Palestinian Muslims and Christians were over 90 percent. In effect, the Balfour Declaration enabled the Zionist movement to gain its initial international legitimacy while simultaneously displacing the rights and very existence of the majority Palestinian population. Thus begins the dominance of the Zionist narrative in Western political and religious thought and the negation of the Palestinian narrative, not to mention Palestinian political and human rights.

President Woodrow Wilson was persuaded to adopt the Balfour language and support its insertion in the treaties ending World War I, thus subverting his own "Wilsonian Principles." One of the most important of Wilson's principles asserted that the former Ottoman colonies would be granted the right to self-determination based on the desires of the majority population within a given territory.

---

4. Smith, *Palestine and the Arab-Israeli Conflict*, 71–72. The text reads: "His Majesty's Government view with favour the establishment in Palestine of a national home for the Jewish people, and will use its best endeavours to facilitate the achievement of this object, it being clearly understood that nothing shall be done which may prejudice the civil and religious rights of existing non-Jewish communities in Palestine, or the rights and political status enjoyed by Jews in any other country."

Several of Wilson's foreign policy advisors argued against the Balfour Declaration, claiming it would jeopardize the claims of the majority Palestinian Arabs. Former CIA analyst Kathleen Christison and her late husband Bill analyzed the post–World War I period and noted that Wilson was under considerable pressure from the nascent Zionist lobby, headed by Wilson's friend Louis Brandeis, as well as from Britain's Lord Arthur Balfour, then serving as the British foreign secretary. Even in this early phase, the Zionists were effectively drafting congressional resolutions and lobbying to support their agenda, and they often managed to obtain favorable treatment in the mainstream media.[5]

In the summer of 1919, the Wilson administration sent a delegation to investigate the situation in Palestine. Known as the King-Crane Commission, it was co-led by theologian Henry Churchill King and businessman Charles Crane. They were charged to investigate the political dynamics in Palestine as well as in Syria, Lebanon, and Anatolia (part of modern Turkey) following the defeat of the Ottoman Empire. The British effectively controlled the commission by setting its daily agenda and providing translators, who at times skewed the messages in favor of British interests. Still, the King-Crane report advised against U.S. support of the Balfour Declaration's proposal for a Jewish homeland in Palestine, but the report was buried under pressure from the Zionists and British. The King-Crane report was completed on August 28, 1919, but not made public until 1922, too late to have any impact on the Treaty of Versailles, which incorporated language from the Balfour Declaration in its text.

Theodor Herzl, the founder of modern political Zionism, had anticipated the need for a major power to give legitimacy to the Zionist cause. Now that Britain had adopted the Balfour language and ensured that it was incorporated into the treaty ending World War I, the initial aspects of Herzl's political vision were fulfilled. Ironically, these achievements came at a time when the majority of Jews opposed Zionism. These political achievements enabled the Zionist colonization of Palestine to expand rapidly during the 1920s and early 1930s, as exclusive Jewish settlements increased under British tutelage.

One cannot help but wonder what motivated President Wilson to facilitate such a one-sided process, particularly after he had argued so strenuously in favor of self-determination for the majority population within a given territory. Whether it was propelled by British or Zionist pressure, a predisposition to Zionism based in his religious upbringing (his father was a Presbyterian pastor), or domestic political concerns, Wilson's support of

5. Christison, *Perceptions of Palestine*, 28–37 and 41–44.

Zionist aspirations set the pattern that all but one of the subsequent U.S. presidents would follow for the next ninety years.

England's Lord Arthur Balfour would later comment on these matters in a revealing statement he made to a gathering of British Zionists:

> . . . in Palestine we do not propose even to go through the form of consulting the wishes of the present inhabitants of the country, though the American Commission has been going through the forms of asking what they are. The four great powers are committed to Zionism, and Zionism, be it right or wrong, good or bad, is rooted in age-long traditions, in present needs, in future hopes, of far profounder import than the desire and prejudices of the 700,000 Arabs who now inhabit the land. In my opinion that is right.[6]

Balfour's commitment to Zionism, "be it right or wrong, good or bad," was not only deep, but it had both religious and political underpinnings. It should be noted that both Balfour and his prime minister David Lloyd-George were predisposed to the Zionists' arguments for at least two reasons. First and foremost was their political goal, which was essentially the expansion of British rule from the Levant to the "Jewel in the Crown" of the empire—India.

However, another motivation was in play, and it is one rarely discussed by historians and political analysts. Both Balfour and Lloyd-George were products of fundamentalist Christian Zionism and as such were predisposed to support Zionism based on their premillennial dispensationalist reading of the Holy Scriptures. Both politicians are examples of how Christian Zionism can orient one to embrace the Zionist narrative for both political and theological reasons. His references to the "age-long traditions" and "future hopes of far profounder import" in the above quotation are evidence of Balfour's blend of evangelical Christian Zionism with his colonialist political vision.[7]

Britain and the United States threw their full support behind the Balfour Declaration, a matter that was challenged in the December 1929 lead editorial in the Protestant journal *The Christian Century*. The editorial raised theological and moral arguments in questioning how the Balfour Declaration could grant nation status to the Jewish people when "it is the conviction of most biblical scholars that the Old Testament contains no anticipation of

6. Igrams, *Palestine Papers*, 73.

7. Young, *Arthur James Balfour*, 25. See also Wagner, *Anxious for Armageddon*, 86–95, and Sizer, *Christian Zionism*, 60–67, for a more complete discussion of the impact of pre-millennial dispensational theology on Balfour and Lloyd George.

the restoration of Israel to its ancient homeland which can apply to the Jew-ish people of the present age."[8] The question remains legitimate to this day.

Zionism was in its infancy in North America in the 1920s and early 1930s and had little support within Judaism or the Protestant churches. Most of the major Jewish movements at that time were resistant to Zion-ism (or practiced benign neglect), for they saw the movement as a fringe group of extremists who were not particularly grounded in Judaic beliefs and practices. Zionists themselves were conflicted over several issues. Many asked whether they should support a single state that honored the rights of the Arab majority and Jews as equal citizens, while others insisted on a sepa-rate "Jewish" state in all or part of historic Palestine. Jewish leaders, such as Hebrew University's first president, Judah Magnes, writer Ahad Ha'Am, Albert Einstein, and philosopher Martin Buber, represented the minority view, arguing for a single state based on equality for all of its citizens or a binational state that honored the political rights of the Palestinians. This view, often called "Humanist Zionism," was eventually eclipsed by the more hard-line Labor Zionism of David Ben-Gurion, which argued for the single Israeli state model. Since the 1970s, Labor Zionism has been effectively sidelined by the more militant Revisionist Zionism of Vladimir Jabotinsky, Menachem Begin, Itzhak Shamir, Ariel Sharon, and Benyamin Netanyahu. Today the "Revisionist" form of Zionism dominates the Israeli political scene as well as most of the Jewish Zionist establishment's organizations in the United States.

Understandably, the rising tide of Nazi anti-Semitism gave impetus to the single Israeli state option, and by the early 1940s it had become the dom-inant view within the Zionist movement. Most Jews believed they would be secure only in a state under their control. As the Nazi threat grew and be-came increasingly genocidal toward Europe's Jewish community, only a few German Christian leaders had the courage to challenge Nazi ideology and the political threat it represented. Even a courageous spokesperson such as theologian Dietrich Bonhoeffer failed to address the Jewish question until the latter part of his career.

The German churches, both Protestant and Roman Catholic, were ef-fectively silenced by various Nazi tactics, such as demanding that church hierarchy, clergy, and academics sign the "Aryan Clause," which pledged their allegiance to the National Socialist Party and its ideology of ethnic superiority. Eventually most university faculty, physicians, clergy, business leaders, members of the media, and local and regional politicians signed the

8. *The Christian Century*, December 1929, quoted in Carenen, *Fervent Embrace*, ch. 1.

clause. Within two years of the Nazis' assuming control of the parliament, the majority of Germany's leadership in multiple sectors of civil society and the political elite were effectively controlled by Nazi ideology and the party. There are many accounts of clergy or university professors receiving visits from Nazi storm troopers who stood over their desks, reminding them of the consequences if they failed to sign the Aryan clause: loss of job, public disgrace, harm to their family, or worse.

3. Profiles in Protestant Support for Zionism: The Influence of Paul Tillich and Reinhold Niebuhr

A case study in Nazi intimidation and control is found in Professor Paul Tillich, an ordained Lutheran clergyman and rising star in the field of philosophical theology at the University of Frankfurt (Goethe University Frankfurt), where he served as dean of the faculty in the early 1930s. The university was an early Nazi target, and a power struggle was underway between pro- and anti-Nazi faculty and students. In early 1933, Nazi storm troopers entered the campus and physically assaulted Jewish students, aided by the pro-Nazi student association. The Jewish students, some beaten severely, took refuge in Dean Tillich's office. Following the incident, Tillich took the case to the university administration and demanded that the students who took part in the beatings be expelled. Tension increased between the faculty and administration, with the pro-Nazi faculty demanding Tillich's dismissal. Within a few weeks, on April 13, 1933, the administration gave Tillich notice that he was suspended as dean. Realizing his academic career in Germany was over, Tillich and his wife departed for the United States, where he accepted a faculty position at one of the leading Protestant theological seminaries in the country, Union Theological Seminary in New York City.

Tillich was welcomed to New York by various Jewish faculty members in nearby universities who had emigrated from Frankfurt University, including the philosopher and political theorist Dr. Herbert Marcuse. Rabbi Abraham Heschel, a native of Poland, who had been part of the sizeable Jewish community in Frankfurt, later joined them. Together with this group of German intellectuals that included faculty members from Union Seminary, Hebrew Union College, and Columbia University, they came to serve as a moral support group and an informal political think tank that was increasingly outspoken against the Nazi regime, demanding U.S. intervention on behalf of European Jewry.[9]

9. Stone, *Politics and Faith*, 199–200.

Tillich found a close ally in fellow Union Seminary Professor Reinhold Niebuhr, still unknown on the national scene but quickly to become a leader in political ethics and an out-spoken advocate for Zionist causes. His influence across generations has been considerable, including with President Barack Obama, who has called Niebuhr "one of my favorite philosophers" and a major influence on his political and ethical thought.[10] Unlike many of their colleagues, Niebuhr and Tillich were not silent about what was occurring in Europe. Tillich, a German native, and Niebuhr, a second-generation American of German descent, began organizing to influence U.S. policy. Their aim was to counter the threat Germany posed to the Jews of Europe and to the unity of Europe and the civilized world.

Tillich and Niebuhr opposed Nazi ideology on theological, political, ethical, and philosophical grounds. Dr. Ronald Stone, professor emeritus at Pittsburgh Theological Seminary, was a student at Union Seminary, arriving just after Tillich retired and when Niebuhr was in his final years. Stone has completed a helpful study of these two theological giants. He comments on the basis for Tillich's critique of Nazi ideology in this way: "Tillich understood his social philosophy to be derived from the spirit of Judaism." According to Stone, Tillich's book *The Socialist Decision* (1933) was his best work on social theory, for in it he "shows the connection between prophetic religion and social criticism."[11]

Tillich dismissed Nazi ideology as "powerful poetry tending toward ecstatic and revolutionary apocalypticism," adding that it was "not a serious school of thought." He condemned Nazism as "a demonic movement in its attempt to make sacred [the] leader, race, party and space [in an] attempt to create a system of meaning and solution by a leap back to myths of origin without critical inquiry."[12] Tillich's critique of Nazi ideology echoes several of the questions raised in this chapter about "founding myths" of the United States and applies equally to Christian and Jewish Zionism. Tillich also noted that Nazi ideology was essentially opposed to the spirit of Judaism, for Judaism was located in the worship of God, who "transcended blood, soil, and communal loyalties and demanded justice."[13]

Tillich called upon all Christians, particularly the churches of the Reformation, to join with Judaism in a prophetic critique of this distorted expression of German nationalism. In a sense, Nazism was a false, secular alternative to prophetic Judaism and Christianity, as it was based on pagan

10. Julian, Hoover Institution, *Policy Review* no. 154.

11. Stone, *Politics and Faith*, 201.

12. Ibid.

13. Ibid.

Teutonic myths of Aryan racial supremacy and was, in essence, a "closed system"[14] with no room for the prophetic critique that the Hebrew prophets and Jesus brought to humanity. Tillich argued for a recovery of the political eschatology that one finds in the Hebrew prophets, claiming that this moral and theological foundation would be necessary for German Christians to oppose Nazism.

Niebuhr challenged the German churches as well as the global church concerning their "quietism" with regard to the "extravagances of Nazi terror."[15] He suspected that the churches in Germany were trapped in "quietism," due in part to the Lutheran theological doctrine of two kingdoms, a distinction Luther had made between the Kingdom of God and the Kingdom of Man (humanity). Tillich claimed this division was inconsistent with the prophetic tradition and was too easily manipulated by political power. He argued that in submitting to the Nazi party the churches were forced into service of the party, and the only space remaining for the churches was within the increasingly narrow religious realm, which under Nazi domination would have no power or relevance in the rest of life.

On November 9, 1938, Nazi storm troopers destroyed seven thousand Jewish businesses and over nine hundred synagogues in coordinated attacks throughout Germany. This became known as *Kristallnacht* (the "night of broken glass"), and it shocked Jews worldwide into recognizing the extreme danger that Jews now faced in Germany, Poland, and much of Europe. Following the event, the *Christian Century,* which had opposed large quotas for Jews settling in Palestine, reversed its position. The pace of events moved quickly as Germany invaded Czechoslovakia in September 1939, and Europe was at war. Many Christian leaders opposed the U.S. joining the war effort, and some, like the *Christian Century*, called for caution and patience and for the U.S. to stay out of the conflict.

Niebuhr lost patience with this position and broke with the *Century*, founding a new liberal journal, *Christianity and Crisis,* in 1941. In 1939 he had described the *Century* as "without question the most vital force in American theology,"[16] but by the early 1940s he came to believe that the *Century* and that portion of the church that stood with it were increasingly irrelevant. While a liberal Protestant himself, Niebuhr differed from traditional liberal Protestant theologians of his day by developing a theology of political realism whereby "evil" was given a more prominent role in human affairs than his liberal peers were claiming. Niebuhr stated that

14. Ibid.

15. Carenen, *Fervent Embrace*, ch. 1.

16. Ibid.

"liberal Protestants who believe that Christianity will shame the enemy into goodness" are fooling themselves.[17] He was convinced that Christians had a moral obligation to fight Nazism and fascism if the Jews of Europe were to be saved. In the first issue of *Christianity and Crisis*, Niebuhr wrote, "I think it is dangerous to allow Christian religious sensitivity about the imperfections of our own society to obscure the fact that Nazi tyranny intends to annihilate the Jewish race."[18] Within ten months of the debut of the new journal, the Japanese bombed Pearl Harbor, and the United States officially entered World War II.

By 1939, if not before, most Zionist leaders were convinced the Nazis were committing genocide against the Jews in Poland and Germany. Zionism began to take a commanding role in the organized Jewish community, and its arguments against Hitler and in favor of a Jewish state in Palestine were gaining attention and sympathy among mainline Protestants. In 1942, Zionist leader Rabbi Stephen Wise brought considerable evidence to the U.S. Department of State demonstrating that the Nazis were exterminating Europe's Jews at unprecedented rates, with the goal of eliminating all the Jews of Poland. He called for the United States to support a Jewish state in Palestine as the only credible response to the genocide. The *Christian Century* continued to challenge the goals of Zionism, but the shift in the media and churches was already turning against this position and in favor of Zionism, and Niebuhr's voice was among the most influential.

As reports confirmed the existence of concentration camps and Nazi genocide, the Zionist movement shifted its operational center from London to New York City and began to concentrate its political efforts on the United States. A Zionist conference held at New York's Biltmore Hotel in May 1942, with its "Biltmore Platform," crystallized the movement's commitment to nothing less than the creation of a Jewish state in Palestine as the answer to Nazi atrocities. As the news from Europe worsened, the hard-line Zionists came to see the binational and single democratic state models as unworkable.

The Biltmore conference united most major Jewish organizations and leadership behind a highly aggressive form of Zionism from that moment forward. Zionist leaders believed it was necessary to demand a Jewish state, utilize all of their political and economic power (in alliance with their Protestant supporters), and take their case to the White House and halls of Congress. They assumed that thousands, if not millions, of Jews would immigrate to the new state after the war and Palestine "should be established as

17. Ibid., ch. 2.
18. Ibid.

a Jewish commonwealth, integrated in the structure of the new democratic world."[19] Membership in the major Zionist organizations grew rapidly as did the donations to underwrite their campaigns.

Also emerging from the Biltmore meetings was a proposal to support two Christian organizations in the political campaign for Jewish statehood: the American Palestine Committee and the Christian Council on Palestine. Both received financial aid from Zionist organizations and recruited political support for Zionism among prominent Christians and members of Congress.[20]

An interesting question concerning Tillich and Niebuhr might be: can they be appropriately labeled "liberal Protestant Christian Zionists?" If one defines Christian Zionism as "Christian support for the Zionist movement," then the answer would be a resounding "yes." Both theologians were strong supporters of Zionism and its goals. Stone notes that Tillich was not initially a supporter of the Zionist cause, questioning the concept of Israel as a nation-state and arguing that the Jewish people should not be limited to an attachment to "space [land] and time."[21] Tillich never believed the creation of Israel was of divine origin but a political necessity, given the threat of Nazism and continuing anti-Semitism. He eventually became a supporter of Zionism once news of the concentration camps and genocide were confirmed.

Niebuhr supported the Zionist movement uncritically, usually with more vigor than did Tillich. Like his colleague, Niebuhr saw the establishment of Israel as the necessary response to the Holocaust and Western anti-Semitism. He insisted that the United States had a primary responsibility to protect Israel and the Jewish people for reasons of morality and national interests, particularly as a dimension of Cold War politics. Niebuhr's support of Zionism was multi-dimensional, including considerations from philosophical ethics, theology, and his theory of "political realism." For Niebuhr, the colossal evils of the Nazis and the Holocaust and the political dynamics of the Cold War and Soviet interests in the Middle East convinced him that the State of Israel was a political and moral necessity, deserving political, military, and financial support from the United States.

Edinburgh University Divinity School Professor Carys Moseley claims that Niebuhr was "the most prominent liberal Protestant theologian to support Zionism in the twentieth century in the United States."[22] He argues

19. Smith, *Palestine and the Arab-Israeli Conflict*, 166.

20. Ibid., 167.

21. Ibid., 204

22. Moseley, "Reinhold Niebuhr's Approach to the State of Israel," 2.

that Niebuhr's Zionism was centered in "his reconstruction of natural law and subjected to his critique of nationalism and religion."[23] According to Moseley, Niebuhr's Christian Zionism was not theologically or biblically grounded, and we might say the same for Tillich's approach. Niebuhr developed a political theology he called "Christian realism" that was shaped by his theological ethics, the Holocaust, and Cold War politics.[24] Niebuhr saw the establishment and funding of Israel as necessary not only to save European Jews but to outflank the Soviet Union. I would add that Niebuhr was aware of the Zionist militias' attacks that forced Palestinians to flee Palestine, and while he opposed the harsh methods, he justified them by supporting the "transfer of the Arabs out of Palestine."[25] It seems clear that there was a moral and ethical gap in Niebuhr's thought with regard to the Palestinians, as he fully ignored, if not justified, their slaughter and expulsion during what Palestinians call the *Nakba* (Catastrophe).

Niebuhr's most revealing writing on Israel and Zionism can be observed in his article "Our Stake in Israel," which appeared in *The New Republic* on February 3, 1957. He states at the outset that one gains an appreciation for Israel by reviewing its beginnings as a state: "The calendar beginning of Israel was the United Nations resolution, which sanctioned the new state, and the heroic battle which the nascent nation waged against the Arab nations, sworn to throttle Israel in its cradle. Thus the state's birth was both a gift from the world community and an achievement of the redoubtable army which the little nation was able to organize."[26] Niebuhr's argument continues in the article as he embraces many of the popular Zionist myths that surrounded the creation of Israel, such as "making the desert bloom" and such as the little Jewish David opposing the Arab nations (Goliath), and as he praises the vision of Theodor Herzl and Chaim Weizmann without challenging their hard-line goals. He adds that Israel became a "melting pot" for Jews without offering a word on Palestinian loss of land and livelihood or noting that half their population was driven into refugee status. He ends the argument on another highly debatable point, claiming the United States had an obligation to support Israel because "Israel is the only democracy in the Middle East."[27]

Thus, there is considerable evidence that Niebuhr was a liberal Protestant Christian Zionist. Others, such as Ronald Stone, argue that we should

23. Ibid.
24. Ibid., 9, 12, 13.
25. Ibid., 7, 8. See Judis, 214.
26. Niebuhr, "Our Stake in Israel."
27. Ibid.

not label him a Zionist because we have to consider the issues of that historical period and the pressures these leaders faced from the Holocaust and World War II.[28] I would argue that the evidence is abundantly clear, and whether people embraced Zionism in the 1940s and 50s or do so today without demonstrating critical analysis or changing their positions, we must judge their stance on the basis of the available evidence. With Niebuhr, there is no evidence that he challenged the Zionist movement or the fractious actions of the State of Israel. On the other hand, it is abundantly clear that he embraced Zionism and consistently held that position until his death.

Regardless of his embrace of Zionism, Niebuhr remains perhaps the most influential mainline American Protestant theologian of the twentieth century, and his legacy continues into the twenty-first. His enduring influence is underscored by the fact that many progressive evangelical theologians and pastors are embracing his social ethics and emphasis on justice and applying them to the social ills of the present era.

The United Nations vote on November 29, 1947, to partition Palestine (General Assembly Resolution 181) was viewed by the Zionist leadership and its supporters as a victory. The division of historic Palestine that granted Israel 54 percent of the land and most of the rich farmland and coastal region was viewed by the Arabs as a serious breach of justice and was bitterly rejected by the Palestinian leadership and Arab governments. Israel declared itself an independent nation on April 15, 1948, and the United States, under President Truman, was the first to recognize Israel.

Various theories have been put forth concerning Truman's motivations, with some arguing that it was purely a political decision, recognizing his need for the Jewish vote on the eve of a presidential election in 1948. Others have argued that his support came because a close Jewish friend from his youth opened the door for significant Zionist pressure on Truman. Still others claim it was a humanitarian and religious motivation, the latter based on his Baptist upbringing and understanding of the Bible. We now know that repeated visits and letters from the Protestant Christian pro-Zionist lobby and the Jewish Zionist leadership were the dominant influences on Truman, by his own admission. We also know that there was strong opposition to Zionism and recognition of the new State of Israel within Truman's own state department and particularly from Secretary of Defense James Forrestal.[29]

---

28. Stone, *Politics and Faith*, 204–5.

29. Carenen, *Fervent Embrace*, ch. 2. Carenen provides a useful survey of the various pressures brought on the Truman administration by both Jewish and Protestant lobbying organizations in the second chapter of her book, including the debate within the Department of State, where there was considerable opposition to the creation of a Jewish state in Palestine.

The fact that Truman overrode his advisors and members of his cabinet by supporting the Zionists' recommendation and thereby becoming the first head of state officially to recognize Israel is sufficient grounds to maintain that Truman held a bias in favor of Zionism.

4. From Statehood to Regional Power: Developments in the 1950s to the War of 1967

Following the turbulent but decisive decade of the 1940s, there was a gradual shift in the Protestant churches toward increased support for Israel. Several pro-Zionist liberal Protestant political and educational organizations put this new sympathy for Israel into action. The primary Protestant organization was the American Christian Palestine Committee (ACPC). With increasing financial support from major Jewish Zionist organizations, it quickly surpassed its competitors in effectiveness and in its sheer volume of effort on behalf of Israel. ACPC worked to control information on Israel, monitoring and challenging any church statements sympathetic to the Palestinians.[30]

ACPC-sponsored study tours of Israel for churches, theological seminaries, and clergy were an extremely effective instrument to advance the Zionist narrative among Christian leaders. Initially, most trips were subsidized by ACPC, but as they grew in popularity, local congregations paid their own way and covered the expenses of their pastors. The trips included visits to sites of biblical and historic interest but also promoted Israel's point of view by including meetings with Israeli officials and showcasing the pioneering spirit and the "miraculous" efforts of the kibbutzim in "making the desert bloom." There was little or no time spent with Palestinians, even with local Palestinian Christian communities, let alone critical reflection on why there were over 750,000 Palestinian refugees living in dire conditions just a few miles from their former homes in West Jerusalem and Israel.

The steady pro-Israel shift of Protestant opinion was noted by the U.S. Department of State. In the early 1950s, the department assessed public opinion on the Israeli-Palestinian conflict and found that approximately 90 percent of the letters and commentary it received concerning the issue were in favor of Israel.[31] It noted that most of the support came from well-

---

30. Ibid., ch. 5. The American Palestine Committee was formed in 1932 to support a Jewish state in Palestine, and by the mid-1940s it merged with the new American Christian Palestine Committee to become a significant political and educational force among clergy and the U.S. Congress.

31. Ibid.

funded and highly organized pro-Israel Jewish organizations but also from the American Christian Palestine Committee. Undoubtedly, the letters and phone calls were often the result of campaigns directed by the pro-Israel lobby organizations, both Christian and Jewish, who were consistently wealthier and better organized than groups sympathetic to Palestinians.

Additional developments that advanced the pro-Israel orientation in Protestantism were the increased interest in Christian-Jewish dialogue and a multiplicity of organizations to facilitate it. The National Conference of Christians and Jews played an important role for many decades, as did the Anti-Defamation League of B'nai B'rith (now known as the Anti-Defamation League, or ADL), and eventually most major Zionist organizations. Both the Jewish and the Protestant Christian communities had serious issues to confront, such as the continuing anti-Jewish discrimination in real estate, private clubs, and universities. Many Christians believed it was time to change this troubled history of anti-Semitism, and dialogue programs seemed to provide a significant instrument to promote healing. One issue that the dialogue groups did not discuss was the question of Palestine.

The Jewish leadership often raised two theological issues in the dialogue groups: Christian efforts to proselytize Jews and the belief in "supersessionism." The latter refers to the traditional Christian contention that the covenant in Christ replaces the Hebrew covenant with the Jews through Abraham, Moses, and David. The two issues are related, as Christians who held the supersessionist theology usually believed that Jews must accept Jesus Christ as their savior or be doomed to hell. Jewish organizations insisted that Christians must accept Jews and Judaism as "complete" with no need to convert to Christianity. These issues would continue to be points of contention and dialogue.

Perhaps the most significant public relations advantage the Zionist movement had with predominantly Christian populations was the decision to call their state "Israel." This single factor provided Israel and the Zionist movement with a "branding" of the new state as a resumption of the ancient Israel mentioned in the Bible. With a population generally acquainted with basic biblical references, there may have been no better public relations mechanism to induce Americans to embrace the new state than this simple choice of a name. Christian references to Israel were familiar in worship, in hymns, and in Bible study, with their many references to the land and geography of ancient Israel. When considered uncritically, this familiarity gave Americans a natural affinity for Jews and the new nation. There was no parallel for Palestinian Arabs, although approximately 20 percent of their population was Christian, with a history dating back to the day of Pentecost. They had absolutely no public relations connection with their fellow

Christians in the West. It would take nearly three decades before a minority of Western Christians would begin to understand the Palestinian narrative and recognize that they had sister and brother Palestinian Christians in the Holy Land.

5. Profile: Dr. Krister Stendahl: Professor, Theologian, Lutheran Bishop, and Liberal Christian Zionist

One of the most influential theologians from the 1950s to the 1990s was the Swedish New Testament scholar and Harvard Divinity School Professor Krister Stendahl. Stendahl was born in Stockholm, Sweden, on April 21, 1921, to a working-class family that was not particularly religious. His wife would later say that Krister's teenage rebellion was to begin attending church. In 1939 Stendahl traveled to a German spa, seeking relief from the pain of his arthritic spine. While in Germany he encountered Swedish missionaries ministering to Jews, a meeting that would change his life, as he learned about Nazi persecution of Jews.

After completing his doctorate at Uppsala University, Stendahl began a long and illustrious ecclesiastical and academic career at Harvard Divinity School, where he gained recognition for his scholarly writings on Pauline theology. Stendahl argued that Paul's letter to the Romans was not primarily a discussion of "justification by faith," thus contradicting the interpretation that had been traditional since St. Augustine and was repeated by Protestant reformers Martin Luther and John Calvin. Instead, Stendahl claimed that Paul's thesis in Romans was a discussion of "God's mysterious plan for the Jews," an argument he found especially in Romans 9–11. In Stendahl's view, Paul argues in Romans that God desires co-existence between Judaism and Christianity, thus paving the way for deeper and more open relationships between Christians and Jews. Christians should not be involved in converting Jews, practicing any form of anti-Semitism, or espousing supersessionism. His exegesis of Romans transformed New Testament scholarship in terms of Christian-Jewish dialogue and interfaith relationships.

In the same volume, Stendahl makes a remarkable statement about Jewish-Christian relationships by claiming not only that Jews are equal to Christians in the eyes of God but also that Christians are "honorary Jews."[32] This claim raises several theological concerns, as Stendahl seems to be suggesting that Christians should adopt a theology of Jewish "chosenness," with implications of Jewish superiority and certain divinely endowed privileges. He also implies that Christians can be called "honorary Jews" because Jews

---

32. Stendahl, *Paul Among Jews and Gentiles*, 37.

are God's first covenant people and, by implication, God's primary "chosen" people. It should be noted that Stendahl's arguments are biblical and theological, not ethical and philosophical, as in the case of Tillich and Niebuhr. However, he too became a strong supporter of Zionism and the State of Israel and embraced the doctrines of exclusivity found in most forms of political Zionism.

It seems to follow from Stendahl's logic that if Christians are "honorary Jews" because Jews are God's "first" and primary "chosen people," then Christians are "secondary," at least theologically. However, this theological position has serious political and ethical consequences, not the least of which is the failure to hold the State of Israel to the same standards of international law and human rights as every other nation

Stendahl, like Niebuhr and Tillich, viewed Israel as the answer to the Holocaust, the state that enables Jews to survive. But Stendahl seems to go beyond the other two theologians, not only in calling Christians "honorary Jews," but also in claiming that the Jewish people are intimately tied to this particular land, the land of Palestine, which he gives a religious value. These claims clearly place Stendahl in the liberal Christian Zionist category, and his writings and public statements supported the Zionist agenda throughout his career.

A new study by Paul Verduin describes Stendahl's relationship with his close friend, the Rabbi David Hartman. As founder and president of the Shalom Hartman Institute in Jerusalem, Hartman distinguished himself as a liberal Jewish defender of Zionism. Hartman and Stendahl became friends during the latter's scholarly career at Harvard and later, when Stendahl moved to Brandeis University. Upon Stendahl's retirement, Hartman offered him an annual appointment to teach at the Shalom Hartman Institute. During his many visits to Jerusalem, Stendahl met several Palestinian Christians, including Lutheran Pastor Rev. Dr. Mitri Raheb, Lutheran Bishop Munib Younan, Sabeel Director the Rev. Dr. Naim Ateek, and others. He also met with the Revs. Susan and Michael Holmes, two American clergy who were serving at the Lutheran Church of the Redeemer in East Jerusalem. Michael had been Stendahl's student at Harvard Divinity School, and Susan had served as a pastor at the Lutheran church in Cambridge, Massachusetts, where the Stendahls worshiped.[33]

On March 3, 2002, Stendahl was at his Cambridge, Massachusetts, home when he received a disturbing email from the Holmeses. As he read down the page, he was directed to an article incorporated in the email that

33. Verduin, "Praiseworthy Intentions," 154–55. Verduin's research located the business cards of these Palestinian Christians and others in the Andover-Harvard Library, Harvard Divinity School, Stendahl Papers, box 7.

had appeared in the *International Herald Tribune* and *The Washington Post* a few days earlier. The article described a Palestinian suicide bombing in Jerusalem and the terrible suffering it brought to Israeli families. As Stendahl came to the end of the article, he saw that his friend Rabbi Hartman was quoted as saying, "What nation in the world would allow itself to be intimidated and terrified as this whole population [Israel] is, where you can't send your kid out for a pizza at night without fear he'll be blown up?" Then came Hartman's conclusion: "Let's really let them understand what the implication of their actions is," he said of the Palestinians. "Very simply, wipe them out. Level them."[34]

Stendahl must have been stunned by his friend's words. He sent, possibly by fax, a handwritten letter to Hartman that is included in the Stendahl papers. Dated March 4, 2002, his message states: "Dear, dear David: How to answer this e-mail we received?" Then Stendahl pasted the text of the interview into the message, followed by an obviously troubled plea for clarity: "If this is true, it puts much stress and pain on one of the most precious friendships I have been given. We will be in Sweden [contact phone number supplied] March 9–13. Then back in C–e [Cambridge]. Yours Krister."[35] Apparently Stendahl never received an answer. How deep was the "precious friendship?" Could it withstand criticism of Israel? It appears that Hartman remained silent and Stendahl went to his grave without an answer.

This experience near the end of his life seems to be the closest Krister Stendahl came to articulating a single criticism or even questioning Israel's intentions, and it remained entirely private. He was obviously stunned by Hartman's phrase, "wipe them out," and chose not to press the case with Hartman. In public he remained silent.

Stendahl stands in a long line of liberal pro-Zionist Protestant, Roman Catholic, and Jewish clergy, theologians, and politicians who influenced several generations of leaders and U.S. policy on behalf of Israel. Most failed to challenge Israel's policies and lacked balance when it came to considering justice and equal rights for Palestinians. Among them are Paul van Buren, James Carroll, Clark Williamson, Karl Barth, John Bright, W. F. Albright (and many scholars in the Albright School of Archeology), and Jewish writers such as Michael Wyschograd, Arthur Hertzberg, Michael Waltzer, Franz Rosenzweig, Irving Greenberg, and—while not a theologian—Elie Wiesel, to name but a few. Regrettably, the *Christian Century* since 2004 would also

34. Ibid., 157.

35. Ibid. Verduin reports that the Krister Stendahl letter to David Hartman was probably faxed on March 4, 2002. It is found among the Stendahl Papers cited in note 33.

be on the list, as its coverage of Israel-Palestine has been muted on justice issues in the Holy Land.

6. The June War of 1967 to Camp David and the Carter Presidency

The question of "who started the June War of 1967" continues to be debated, and I will not attempt to resolve that issue here, but it is indisputable that Israel launched a pre-emptive strike, eliminating the Egyptian air force before the war began. Israel quickly defeated the Egyptian, Syrian, and Jordanian armies in what Israel and much of the West calls "The Six-Day War." The Arabs were humiliated twice as their military forces were crushed and portions of three of their countries were now occupied by Israel—the Sinai, Gaza Strip, East Jerusalem, West Bank, and Golan Heights. Israel was now the undisputed military power in the region, capable of defeating multiple Arab nations at once.

The National Conference of Christians and Jews and the major Jewish organizations celebrated Israel's victory and its control over all of Jerusalem and the Palestinian territories. Sixteen prominent Protestant leaders signed a statement[36] celebrating Israel's victory and gave support to the "unification" of Jerusalem under Israeli control (while showing no concern for the Palestinian residents of the territories now occupied by Israel). Among them were Reinhold Niebuhr, Krister Stendahl, and Martin Luther King, Jr. Niebuhr followed the letter with an editorial in *Christianity and Crisis* that celebrated Israel's victory and noted that Cold War politics demanded that the United States support Israel as a beacon of democracy in the Middle East.[37] This same pro-Israel tendency would continue to dominate mainline Protestant positions on the Middle East for the next two decades.

Israel became the "strategic ally" of the United States, a matter reinforced by Cold War politics and the increasing power and influence of the pro-Israel lobby at the highest levels of U.S. political discourse and policymaking. Led by the America Israel Public Affairs Committee (AIPAC), the lobby began to see remarkable results as Israel became the largest recipient of U.S. foreign and military assistance, beginning in 1968.

An often overlooked dimension of the mainline Protestant interest in the Middle East lies in the Middle East itself. In 1976, the Middle East Council of Churches (MECC) was organized in Beirut, Lebanon, and appointed Gabriel Habib, an Antiochian Orthodox Lebanese layperson, as

36. Carenen, *Fervent Embrace*, ch. 5.

37. Ibid.

its first general secretary. Habib had worked for nearly two decades within various ecumenical venues, including the World Council of Churches and the World Student Christian Federation, where he served as Middle East secretary. Within a decade of its founding, the MECC would become the most inclusive Christian ecumenical body in the world, involving nearly all Protestant, Catholic, and Orthodox Christian church families.

Habib is credited with organizing the first Christian conference on the question of Palestine, held in Beirut, Lebanon, in 1969. It focused on various justice themes related to the Palestinians, including a call for humanitarian relief, the right of return for Palestinian refugees, and the right of Palestinians to self-determination, including an independent state. In addition to the political agenda, the conference included theological reflections on issues of land, justice, and the people of God. Once Habib assumed the leadership position with MECC, member groups, including the World Council of Churches and the National Council of Churches (based in the U.S.), devoted significant attention to the Palestinian question. Most Protestant denominations in the U.S. became better acquainted with the actual situation facing the Palestinians, whether through the relief and development wing of the Church World Service or the educational visits for church leadership arranged by MECC. Moreover, Habib and MECC had planted the seed of theological reflection on Zionism and the Palestinian question.

7. Shifting Sands: Evangelicals and the Mainline Protestants (1970s–1980s)

A discussion of developments in mainline Protestantism regarding Israel, Palestine, and Zionism would be incomplete unless we incorporated a brief assessment of the impact of the fast-growing evangelical and fundamentalist movements. We begin in 1967, which marks the period when evangelicals and fundamentalists became more visible and politically active on behalf of Israel. These communities and their leaders tended to view Israel's success in the War of 1967 as a miracle of biblical proportions. For many, Israel's control of Jerusalem and all of historic Palestine was the fulfillment of biblical prophecy and pointed to the countdown for the Battle of Armageddon and second coming of Jesus. L. Nelson Bell, the father-in-law of evangelist Billy Graham and editor of *Christianity Today,* alluded to this view (premillennial dispensationalist theology) in his lead editorial following the war: "That for the first time in more than two thousand years Jerusalem is now completely in the hands of the Jews gives the student of the Bible a thrill and a renewed faith in the accuracy and validity of the Bible."[38]

After the war of 1967, a vast number of books, journal articles, and even movies exploded on the scene, many invoking the dispensational-ist's end times scenario. Among the most notable was Hal Lindsay's 1970 book, *Late, Great Planet Earth*, which sold over thirty-five million copies and became a full-length feature film. Lindsay painted a doomsday scenario for the coming two decades with selected biblical texts, culminating in the rise of the Antichrist and predicting that the "rapture"[39] would occur in 1988. This would be followed by the Battle of Armageddon and the return of Jesus to establish his one-thousand-year rule on earth. Lindsay spiced up the traditional dispensationalist narrative to make it appear as if it were a current news analysis, a twist that vaulted the book onto the *New York Times* bestseller list. Lindsay's influence on a generation of fundamentalist and evangelical Christians cannot be overestimated and was a significant boost to the revival of fundamentalist Christian Zionism.

In 1976, a self-declared "evangelical" governor of the State of Geor-gia, Jimmy Carter, was elected president of the United States. Carter was a Democrat and had been able to galvanize the conservative evangelical and fundamentalist vote in the "Bible Belt." This was not surprising, as the Democrats had long been the favored party of conservative southern voters, but this was about to change. *Time Magazine* declared 1976 to be "The Year of the Evangelical" in recognition of the growing influence of the evangelical movement and its role in Carter's election. But Jimmy Carter proved to be a different type of evangelical, as the fundamentalist wing of evangelicalism soon discovered.

During the mid- to late 1970s there was a dramatic surge in funda-mentalist Christian political activity, primarily with the establishment of the Moral Majority, led by the Rev. Jerry Falwell, and the growing influence of televangelists such as the Rev. Pat Robertson of the Christian Broadcasting

---

38. Bell, "Unfolding Destiny," 28.

39. "The rapture" is a popular teaching in a theology called pre-millennial dispen-sationalism, according to which Jesus's second coming will occur before he establishes his millennial kingdom. This theology places significant emphasis on certain events in the last days, such as the "rapture," which will occur just prior to Jesus's return. This teaching is based on a controversial and literal interpretation of 1 Thessalonians 4:17. Dispensationalists claim the rapture will be a historical event whereby God will remove "born again" Christians from the earth to meet Jesus in the clouds before they will be transferred to heaven. This view has been on the fringe of Christianity since the early days of the faith but cannot be attributed to the teachings of Jesus, Eastern Orthodox Churches, the Roman Catholic Church, mainline Protestant churches, or the majority of evangelical Christian churches.

Network (CBN). Conservative concerns—including prayer in the public schools, abortion, and Israel—became major issues in the emerging "religious right" agenda, and Carter would soon see his popularity with this constituency plummet.

Carter had affirmed his staunch support for the security of Israel during his presidential election campaign, but he gradually began to adopt the language of human rights and international law, which troubled the major Jewish Zionist establishment and the emerging fundamentalist Christian Zionists. In March 1977 Carter delivered a speech in New Hampshire, in which he stated that the Palestinian people had a right to a "homeland" (he avoided the term "state"). Despite this relatively moderate statement, the pro-Israel lobby and the Christian fundamentalists went into action. Their response may have been the first nationwide political campaign uniting the pro-Israeli Jewish lobby with fundamentalist Christian Zionists.

The campaign featured full-page advertisements in major newspapers from Boston to Los Angeles, including the *New York Times*. Titled "Evangelical Support For Israel," the text of the advertisement stated in part: "The time has come for Evangelical Christians to affirm their belief in biblical prophecy and Israel's divine right to the land. . . . We would view with grave concern any effort to carve out of the Jewish homeland another nation or political entity."[40] Signed by fifteen evangelical and fundamentalist Christian leaders, including the entertainer Pat Boone and the past president of the National Association of Evangelicals, Arnold T. Olson, the ad signaled a significant challenge to the president and his supporters. The campaign was coordinated by Jerry Strober, a former employee of the American Jewish Committee, hired by the pro-Israel lobby for this initiative. Strober told *The Washington Post*: "[The Evangelicals] are Carter's constituency and he had better listen to them. . . . The real source of strength Jews have in this country is from Evangelicals."[41]

The election of Menachem Begin as prime minister of Israel in 1977 accelerated Israel's right turn politically and religiously as the conservative Likud Party assumed power in Israel. Begin and Likud were maximalists in terms of Israeli politics, claiming that Israel must retain sovereignty over the entirety of Palestine, including the West Bank, Gaza Strip, and East Jerusalem (and the Golan Heights). They justified their claims with the "divine right argument": God gave all of historic Palestine to the Jewish people. Begin readily embraced the Christian right in the United States

40. "Evangelicals' Support for Israel," paid advertisement, *Christian Science Monitor*, November 3, 1977.

41. Claibourne, "Israelis Look on U.S. Evangelicals."

and often rolled out the red carpet for the sizeable Bible Land tours led by the Rev. Jerry Falwell, Jimmy Swaggart, Jim and Tammy Baker, and other televangelists. Holy Land tours from the fundamentalist churches increased in remarkable numbers in the 1970s and 1990s, providing a major revenue stream for Israel and adding more members to the ranks of their Christian Zionist political allies. Many analysts mark this era as the period when Israel increasingly employed religious arguments to justify the occupation and its claims to the occupied Palestinian territories, arguments that had considerable appeal to conservative Republican voters and politicians.

After Egyptian President Anwar Sadat's historic visit to Jerusalem in 1977, the Carter administration brought Egypt and Israel together at Camp David, leading to the Camp David Accords of 1978. The negotiations were initially intended to reach an agreement on the Israeli-Palestinian problem, but Begin firmly resisted, and neither Carter nor Sadat demanded that the issues be resolved. Both yielded in the face of Begin's intransigence. This pattern of significant Israeli influence over successive U.S. administrations and Congress in matters related to Palestine has continued until the present day, while the various Arab regimes have consistently refused to challenge either Israel or U.S. officials in any substantive way.

Middle East analyst Rashid Khalidi's 2013 book *Brokers of Deceit* develops a well-documented and carefully reasoned survey of how Israel's dominance over U.S. policy concerning the Palestine issue evolved. He notes that every U.S. president and military leader since Eisenhower has conceded to Israeli directives on this matter. Khalidi traces this pattern to 1975, when Secretary of State Henry Kissinger arranged secret agreements whereby the U.S. would refuse to negotiate with the PLO until it met certain Israeli demands.[42] Begin added further stipulations to the Camp David Peace Accords in 1978 that placed additional constraints on how future U.S. administrations and diplomats could negotiate the Palestinian issue.[43] Khalidi documents the stages of this process and points to a confidential CIA memorandum dated August 24, 1982, that references Begin's interpretation of the Camp David Peace Process. This previously confidential memorandum lays out, as Khalidi puts it, "the extraordinarily restrictive interpretation placed by the Begin government"[44] on what was agreed to at Camp David and how it put a "ceiling" on U.S. diplomatic negotiations.

Among these "restrictive interpretations" that the United States government has submitted to for the past forty-five years are opposition to

---

42. Khalidi, *Brokers of Deceit*, 9
43. Ibid., 15.
44. Ibid., 19.

Palestinian self-determination and an independent Palestinian state; opposition to the Palestinians' right of return; Israel's permanent control over the land and resources of any future Palestinian semi-autonomous area; no restrictions on Israel's confiscation of Palestinian land; and allowances for continued Israeli settlements in the West Bank and East Jerusalem. Khalidi concludes that on these and other points "the United States has acquiesced and effectively supported this radical and uncompromising position."[45] The subtitle of Khalidi's book, *How the U.S. Has Undermined Peace in the Middle East*, captures his understanding of U.S. policy in the Israeli-Palestinian conflict.

In 1980 Ronald Reagan became president of the United States, bringing to the White House the most pro-Israel president in American history to that point. His presidency provides an interesting case study of how a narrowly conceived fundamentalist Christian point of view reinforced Israel's increasingly extreme political positions. Reagan affirmed many of the theological positions of the emerging fundamentalist Christian Zionists, including the dispensationalist end-time theology. He invoked the term "Armageddon" on at least six occasions in public pronouncements. He also convened annual White House briefings on the Middle East for 150 Christian leaders, all of whom were fundamentalists and evangelicals. The mainline Protestant leadership was totally absent from Reagan's White House gatherings, which featured briefings by the ambassador of Israel and Middle East policy advisors, such as Lt. Oliver North, Bud McFarland, and the neo-conservative leader Elliot Abrams. The lines separating the political aspects of the Israeli-Palestinian conflict from the fundamentalist Christian religious interpretations were increasingly blurred, perhaps intentionally.

Not all evangelicals endorsed Christian Zionism. Wes Granberg-Michaelson of *Sojourners Magazine*, for example, rejected the pro-Israeli policies of the Reagan administration and its supporters in the fundamentalist wing of evangelicalism. Granberg-Michaelson challenged both political Zionism and fundamentalist Christian Zionism head-on, explaining that "many evangelicals have unabashedly provided a theological justification for Zionism, granting divine sanction to and even glorifying the violence of modern Israel." He asserted that "Zionism is foreign to the heart of Judaism and the biblical message."[46] None of the mainline Protestant leadership responded as forcefully to this challenge as Granberg-Michaelson, former president of the Reformed Church in America, an evangelical denomination.

45. Ibid., 28.

46. Granberg-Michaelson, *Sojourners Magazine*, quoted in Carenen, *Fervent Embrace*, ch. 7.

8. 1990–Present: Mainline Protestantism at the Crossroads: Can These Bones Live—Again?

Historian Caitlin Carenen's important book, *The Fervent Embrace,* argues that by the late 1980s the evangelical/fundamentalist movement had replaced mainline liberal Protestantism in terms of its influence on U.S. Middle East policies, and perhaps in many other areas of public and political discourse. She writes that the trend began in the 1970s and continued through the 1980s with the so-called "displacement" occurring in the 1990s.[47] The steady numerical growth of evangelicals and fundamentalist Protestants and their growing influence on American politics and culture are beyond dispute.

Actually, the trend began in the late 1950s and 1960s, according to a 1972 study by Dean M. Kelley, *Why Conservative Churches are Growing.* Kelley's study was commissioned by the National Council of Churches in the late 1960s to investigate the reasons for mainline Protestant decline. He concluded that conservative churches were growing because they made more assertive demands on their members in terms of doctrine and personal ethics, and liberal Protestants were declining because they were less strict in personal morality and their belief systems.[48] Moreover, the liberal churches tended to embrace controversial social and political issues (such as gay marriage, racial integration, and anti-war positions) that evangelicals either avoided or opposed.

Some mainline churches have adopted strategies that have allowed them to compete with the growth of the evangelical movement, such as "church growth" (recruiting more members) and an emphasis on individual spirituality and self-help methods. While some of these strategies have been successful, they tend to avoid the significant moral and social issues of our day such as poverty, racial justice, immigration, and international issues. It is ironic that many evangelical churches are discovering social justice and international issues (while maintaining their focus on personal spirituality) even as some of the mainline churches are abandoning their commitment to social justice in an effort to compete with evangelicals.

One of the leading authors of this trend among evangelicals is Brian McLaren, who now consults with mainline Protestant and evangelical churches. In his 2007 best-seller, *Everything Must Change,* McLaren asks, "What do the life and teachings of Jesus have to say about the most critical global problems in our world today?" He cites the increased interest in

---

47. Carenen, *Fervent Embrace,* ch. 7.
48. Kelley, *Why Conservative Churches are Growing,* 13–14.

social and political issues and references the global conversation that he and many others are engaged in, which he calls "being embraced by the prophetic message of the Kingdom of God." McLaren summarizes this development in the following passage:

> . . . more and more of us are realizing something our best theologians have been saying for quite a while: Jesus' message is not actually about escaping this troubled world for heaven's blissful shores, as is popularly assumed, but instead is about God's will being done on this troubled earth as it is in heaven. So people interested in being a new kind of Christian will begin to care more and more about this world, and they'll want to better understand the most significant problems, and they'll want to understand how they can fit in with God's dreams actually coming true down here more often.[49]

His explanation of the prophetic is so obvious that it merits repetition: the prophetic means taking on the difficult, controversial, troublesome issues that involve injustice, violence, and human suffering.

One of the most challenging issues for our time is the long and protracted Israeli-Palestinian conflict that continues to destabilize the Middle East and other regions. Often dismissed as too complicated, controversial, and beyond hope of a just solution, the conflict is currently surprising many observers by capturing the imagination of university students, young Jewish activists, and a new generation of Muslim and Christian youth across Europe and North America, including a new evangelical movement called "Christ at the Checkpoint."[50]

Also below the radar of the mainstream news media are the emerging justice networks of Protestant clergy and laity focused on the Israeli-Palestinian conflict. Some of these networks have called for hearings on Israel's possible violations of international law and U.S. law concerning foreign and military assistance. In the spring and summer of 2012, the Presbyterian Church USA and the United Methodist Church passed resolutions at their general assemblies calling for the boycott of goods manufactured in Israeli settlements. These resolutions and others had the support of Presbyterian and Methodist justice networks. These same churches and several university campuses are considering resolutions calling for divestment from U.S.

49. McLaren, *Everything Must Change*, 4.

50. "Christ at the Checkpoint" is a movement among evangelicals, not only in the United States but globally, that includes conferences under this name held at the evangelically oriented Bethlehem Bible College in Palestine. The conferences are gaining popularity and generating a new discussion of justice for Palestinians and of peace and reconciliation for both Israelis and Palestinians.

corporations doing business with the Israeli military, or in the case of the churches, corporations responsible for the loss of Palestinian lives or livelihood. The campus and church justice networks offer a new wave of activism that was invisible just six to seven years ago. Their focus on the economic dimension of the conflict has drawn hostile reactions from the pro-Israel Zionist organizations.

As the U.S. faces its own economic challenges, particularly in its urban centers, aid to Israel has increasingly been called into question. The U.S. Campaign to End the Israeli Occupation has addressed this issue by noting the amount U.S. taxpayers send to Israel each year:

> From 1949 to 2008, the U.S. government provided Israel more than $103.6 billion of total official aid, making it the largest recipient of U.S. foreign assistance in the post-World War II era. In 2007, the two countries signed a Memorandum of Understanding providing for $30 billion of U.S. military aid from 2009 to 2018. Between FY 2000 and 2009, the United States gave Israel $24.1 billion of military aid. With this taxpayer money, the United States licensed, paid for, and delivered more than 670 million weapons and related equipment to Israel, including almost 500 categories of weapons.[51]

The U.S. Campaign also notes that Israel violates U.S. law by using American weapons in numerous cases of human rights abuses against Palestinians,[52] but it has never been held accountable. With this in mind, in the fall of 2013, fifteen Protestant leaders submitted a letter to ask for congressional hearings. The signatories included most mainline Protestant denominational leaders such as Bishop Mark Hanson (Evangelical Lutheran Church in America), Rev. Gradye Parsons (Stated Clerk of the Presbyterian Church USA), Bishop Rosemarie Wenner (President, Council of Bishops, The United Methodist Church), Rev. Geoffrey A. Black (General Minister and President, United Church of Christ), Rev. Dr. Sharon E. Watkins (General Minister and President, Christian Church [Disciples of Christ]). Notably missing was the Episcopal presiding bishop, Katherine Jefferts-Schori.[53]

In essence, the Protestant leaders were asking their elected representatives to uphold U.S. law and evaluate Israel according to the same standards that apply to all other recipients of U.S. foreign and military aid. The reaction from the conservative pro-Zionist lobby, both Christian and Jewish, was swift and included vitriolic accusations toward the church leaders.

51. "U.S. Military Aid to Israel."
52. "Is U.S. Military Aid to Israel Legal?"
53. Van Marter, "Religious Leaders Ask Congress."

Their initial threat was to break off all dialogue and relationships with denominations whose leaders signed the letter. Then they "summoned" the Protestant leaders to a meeting in the Jewish leadership's headquarters to listen to their complaints. When the church leaders declined that meeting, the charge of "anti-Semitism" was invoked. Ethan Felson, vice president of the Jewish Council for Public Affairs, took the dispute to a new level by threatening to ask the U.S. Congress to charge the leaders with being "delegitimizers of Israel." Rabbi Eric Yoffie, former president of the Union for Reform Judaism, wrote in the Israeli daily *Haaretz:* "Relations between Jews and mainline Protestants in the U.S. have hit a 45-year low, and future relations needed to be reconsidered."[54]

Felson's charge regarding "delegitimizers of Israel" had its source in a relatively new campaign developed in Israel and adopted by these conservative U.S. Zionist organizations. The strategy has been analyzed by Jewish Voice for Peace deputy director and communications specialist Cecilie Surasky, who points to the Reut Institute, an Israeli policy group based in Tel Aviv that advises the Israeli government on its "messaging," or public relations strategies. In 2010, the Institute issued a report to the Israeli Knesset about the growing threat to "Israel's international legitimacy." Citing efforts to "demonize" Israel, to "undermine Israel's right to exist," and to isolate Israel as a pariah state, the report urged the Israeli government to take immediate and aggressive action to combat these "existential" threats.[55] In brief, this new analysis from the Reut Institute was readily adopted by Israel and its major advocacy organizations in Europe and North America to attack the perceived "new anti-Semitism" in the churches, campuses, and various peace and justice movements in civil society. In North America, a well-financed program was organized called "The Israel Action Network" (IAN). IAN charges that criticisms of Israeli policy put forward by those Christian churches and movements that support Palestinian liberation theology (as articulated in the *Kairos Palestine* document and by the Sabeel Ecumenical Center for Palestinian Liberation Theology) are "anti-Jewish":

> Unfortunately, some criticism of Israel is anti-Jewish. There has been a dramatic increase in such anti-Jewish rhetoric from groups promoting anti-Israel boycotts, divestment and sanctions (BDS). The programs, websites, and social media of church groups supporting BDS have been a matter of grave concern. Examples include rhetoric focused on Jews and money, denial of

54. Yoffie, "Heading Toward an Irreparable Rift."

55. Reut Institute, "Eroding Israel's Legitimacy." See also Israel Action Network, "Best Practices."

Jewish national identity, and anti-Jewish theology. The alliance of these groups with pro-BDS extremist groups in the Jewish community does not excuse the use of such anti-Jewish tropes.[56]

This is a clear attack on the *Kairos Palestine* and *Kairos USA* documents, Friends of Sabeel-North America and Sabeel Jerusalem, Jewish Voice for Peace, the Presbyterian Israel Palestine Mission Network, the United Methodist Kairos Response, the Episcopal Palestine Israel Network, United Church of Christ Palestine/Israel Network, and similar Quaker, Mennonite, Church of the Brethren, and other Jewish and Christian organizations. Their political and theological criticisms are directed at Israel's military and political policies toward the Palestinians. To imply that these groups are against "Jews" is erroneous, diversionary, and a sign of desperation on the part of IAN and its supporters. Their attempt to bully and intimidate Christians, Jews, and Muslims into silence over legitimate moral, theological, and human rights violations will in the end be counterproductive. The pendulum is swinging in the direction of justice now.

Mark Braverman paraphrases the IAN message:

> According to IAN and its agencies here in the United States, American Christians, unsuspecting, perhaps, and in good faith, are being lured back into the anti-Semitism of the Christian past, and the Palestinians, who are promoting this toxic, dangerous theology, are responsible. The message to Christians is, therefore: "Don't be taken in by these Palestinian Christians out of sympathy for their plight. Don't listen to them—listen to us."[57]

However, let us consider the fact that the present political and military course of Israel is both dangerous and failing to bring security. The following analysis by former Ambassador Charles Freeman makes the point that Israel's current direction is not sustainable:

> Israel has clearly chosen to stake its future on its ability, with the support of the United States, to maintain perpetual military supremacy in its region. Yet, this is a formula with a convincing record of prior failure in the Middle East. It is preposterous to imagine that American military power can indefinitely offset Israel's lack of diplomatic survival strategy or willingness to accommodate the Arabs who permeate and surround it. . . . The power and influence of the United States, while still great, are declining at least as rapidly as American enthusiasm for following

---

56. Israel Action Network, "Best Practices," 13.

57. Braverman, "Beyond Interfaith Dialogue."

Israel into the endless warfare it sees as necessary to sustain a
Jewish state in the Middle East. . . . The outlook is therefore for
continuing deterioration in Israel's image and moral standing. . .
. Image problems are often symptoms of deeper existential challenges. . . .That is why the question of American enablement
of shortsightedly self-destructive Israeli behavior needs public
debate, not suppression by self-proclaimed defenders of Israel
operating as thought police.[58]

It seems clear from this analysis that the present course of Israel and the
United States regarding the Israeli-Palestinian question is dangerous and
unsustainable. While the pro-Israel lobby, both Jewish and Christian, is
quite skilled in its efforts to silence those who challenge the extreme Zionist
narrative that Israel and its Western advocacy organizations have adopted,
there is now a rising chorus within the churches, campuses, progressive
Jewish organizations, and civil society at large challenging this narrative.
Our concern in this chapter is to encourage mainline Protestant churches
to be numbered among those calling upon Israel and its advocates to return
to their Jewish ethical principles and seek the "things that make for peace"
while there is still time for a solution based on justice.

9. Conclusion: Toward a New Conversation on Justice and Peace in the Holy Land

A passage from the Prophet Jeremiah seems to address the history of mainline Protestants on the issues of Israel and Palestine and the choices that
lie ahead. Jeremiah warned the people of his day: "An appalling and terrible thing has happened in the land: the prophets prophesy falsely, and the
priests rule in their direction; my people love to have it so, but what will you
do when the end comes?" (Jer 5:30–31, NRSV)

Jeremiah, like the other Hebrew prophets, distinguishes between true
and false prophets. The Hebrew prophets repeatedly warned Israel and Judah to change their ways and practice justice, mercy, and compassion lest
they collapse as a nation. The false prophets brought words that sanitized
the injustices and encouraged the people and leadership to continue the
status quo, their behaviors that discriminated against the poor and ignored
injustice. Today we are seeing the same pattern repeat itself in mainline
Protestant, Roman Catholic, and evangelical churches with reference to
the Israeli treatment of Palestinians. What is needed is "tough love," prophetic words that say, "I'm concerned that you are pursuing an ungodly and

58. Freeman, "Israel's Fraying Image."

unsustainable path—and for your sake and those you occupy, it violates the Torah and our Judeo-Christian (and Islamic) traditions."

Those who challenge the status quo will undoubtedly be labeled "anti-Semites" and branded as among those who delegitimize Israel. No one welcomes these smear campaigns that border on libel and defamation, but it is a small price to pay when we consider the suffering of Palestinians and courageous Jews who take stands daily for justice and peace.

We have seen in the above discussion of the mainline liberal Protestants the beginning of a movement for prophetic justice. Many are adopting the basic elements of Palestinian and Jewish liberation theology; some utilize BDS strategies (boycott, divestment, and sanctions) or similar economic leverages. The new movements for justice are found in grass-roots organizations within Protestant denominations such as the Israel-Palestine Mission Network (Presbyterian), Palestine Israel networks (Episcopal Church and United Church of Christ), United Methodist Kairos Response, and many others. We note the new justice movements such as Christ at the Checkpoint among evangelicals and the remarkable growth of justice for Palestine on university campuses (Students for Justice in Palestine), within Jewish Voice for Peace, and among Jews and Muslims under thirty years of age. However, the prophetic tradition is generally absent from most mainline Protestant journals and theological seminaries, and even from the staffs of several denominational offices.

While this chapter has been critical of such iconic Protestant theologians as Reinhold Niebuhr, Paul Tillich, and Krister Stendahl, I have noted that they must be understood within their historical context. I would like to think that if they were alive today they would be far more critical of Israel's present treatment of Palestinians while still being "lovers of Israel." It is this "tough love" that is needed today to achieve peace and justice for both Israel and Palestine.

Our goal must be the pursuit of a seamless ethic that advocates justice for Palestinians and Jews alike, a position that we call prophetic. Such a path will aggressively pursue a just political solution for both peoples, based on guaranteeing political rights for both, with self-determination leading to a fully independent state on contiguous land within secure and internationally recognized borders. The precise nature and parameters of that resolution will need to be negotiated between legitimate representatives of the Israeli and Palestinian people, within an impartial international forum that can hold the two parties accountable until they reach a settlement. Unfortunately, the United States has failed to function as that impartial mediator or forum, as we have noted above.

As we move toward a conclusion, one of my primary goals has been to suggest how a new and urgent conversation must take place now in our places of worship, in academia, and in our culture in order to free us from the myths, barriers, intimidation, and narrowly confined theological and political narratives that have been blind to justice for the Palestinians. For many, what is beyond dispute is that this conversation and the political actions that accompany it must take place in civil society, in the pews, in the classrooms, and at the grass-roots level because there is an imbalance in the upper echelons of power, which are essentially closed to the broader perspective on justice. We in the United States see this imbalance at most levels of the government, both nationally and regionally, as well as in the traditional media, big business, some universities, and sadly, in our churches. There are exceptions, thankfully, but most of them operate below the radar of the mainstream media and public awareness.

What seems clear is that the traditional top-down structures are currently incapable of generating authentic political justice in Israel and Palestine, as they are still wedded to the hard-line Zionist narrative. Until there is a political breakthrough at the upper levels of government, media, big business, and theological centers, we will be in an interim period in which the movements for justice will emerge from the bottom as grass-roots movements. My purpose in raising these issues is to maintain our focus on the core theologies and ideologies that have had so much influence on our narratives, whether in our culture, academia, or religious institutions. Eventually the theological, political, and moral debates will need to take place throughout society and among opinion-makers, but this discussion will evolve in time, just as it evolved with the civil rights movement, the toppling of apartheid in South Africa, and the termination of the Vietnam War. Thankfully, this issue cannot be characterized as Christian-vs.-Jewish, although the pro-Israel Zionist defenders will continue to recast it as such, claiming the "delegitimizing of Israel." At the heart of the issue are justice, peace, equality, and the eventual reconciliation of two peoples on the same land. The path to be followed is found in a rediscovery of the ethics and message of the Torah, Hebrew prophets, Jesus, and the Qur'an.

The *Kairos Palestine* document of December 2009 lays out for us the essential principles of the prophetic conversation and the practical direction we must pursue. While this is a Palestinian Christian document, it has significant value for Muslims and Jews. It is bold in naming the occupation as a sin, but it is also loving in its affirmation of the Jewish and the Muslim people and calls each of them to join us in the conversation and prophetic journey to justice. It is simultaneously realistic in naming the problems—be they the occupation or theologies and ideologies that advocate rights for one religious or ethnic group over others—but it also calls for healing based on confession, forgiveness, justice, and reconciliation. In this regard it follows the model of the *Kairos Document* of South Africa that led largely to healing in the post-apartheid state. Both documents honor the dignity of all people, including the perceived enemy, and call for an honorable conversation and specific actions that lead to a just peace. It is a long, difficult, and courageous journey, but the alternative is what we have now: endless cycles of violence.

We close with the realism and hope that the authors of *Kairos Palestine* cite: that despite the fact that peace negotiations have reached a "dead-end," they will not surrender to despair and hopelessness. They recall the justice traditions that were eventually successful for Gandhi in India, Martin Luther King and others in the civil rights movement in the United States, and the South African struggle to end apartheid. They recall Dr. King's "Letter from a Birmingham Jail" of 1963 and the 1985 *Kairos Document* of South Africa as providing the theological standard of seeking justice and peace in the nonviolent resistance tradition. They cite boycott, divestment, and sanctions as among the instruments of nonviolence that are capable of promoting peaceful change in societies that resist justice. They are well aware that Gandhi, King, Mandela, and Tutu were also told to adopt a slower pace not only by the authorities in power but also by the white, liberal establishment in the churches and synagogues. But Gandhi, King, Mandela, Tutu, and their movements had no choice but to press on.

Near the end of the *Kairos Palestine* document we find this summary:

> Through our love, we will overcome injustices and establish foundations for a new society both for us and for our opponents. Our future and their future are one. Either the cycle of violence that destroys both of us or peace that will benefit both. We call on Israel to give up its injustice toward us, not to twist the truth of reality of the occupation by pretending that it is a battle against terrorism. The roots of "terrorism" are in the human injustice committed and in the evil of the occupation. These must be removed if there be a sincere intention to remove "terrorism." We call on the people of Israel to be our partners in peace and not in the cycle of interminable violence. Let us resist evil together, the evil of occupation and the infernal cycle of violence.[59]

These are indeed prophetic words, offering a way forward to people around the planet, including the mainline and evangelical Christian

---

59. *Kairos Palestine: A Moment of Truth*, 4.3. Those advocating Palestinian liberation theology, the *Kairos Palestine* document, BDS, and the apartheid analogy are among the primary targets of the Zionist watchdog organizations.

communities, pro-Zionist political and religious Jews, and the governments of the United States and Israel. The choice could not be clearer: "Be our partners in peace and not in the cycle of interminable violence." The Prophet Elijah once challenged the people of Israel who had chosen the pagan religion of Baal over the religion of the one true God: "How long will you go limping between two different opinions? If the Lord is God, follow him. But if Baal, then follow him" (1 Kings 18:21, NRSV). The choice is serving either the God of love, justice, repentance, truth, and the renewing community, or the god of unending cycles of violence and injustice. The choice is ours.

Bibliography

Bell, L. Nelson. "Unfolding Destiny." *Christianity Today*, June 1967.

Braverman, Mark. "Beyond Interfaith Dialogue: The *Kairos Palestine* Call and the Challenge to the Church." Plenary address, Friends of Sabeel-North America conference, Albuquerque, NM, September 28–29, 2012. The address can be heard at http://www.youtube.com/watch?v=ni2EUYjYbJM.

Brueggeman, Walter. *The Prophetic Imagination.* Philadelphia: Fortress, 1978.

Carenen, Caitlin. *The Fervent Embrace.* New York: New York University Press, 2012. Kindle edition.

Cavanagh, Edward, and Lorenzo Veracini. "Definition." *Journal of Settler Colonial Studies* blog. Melbourne, Australia: Institute for Social Research, Swinburne University of Technology. http://settlercolonialstudies.org/about-this-blog/.

Chacour, Elias. *We Belong to the Land.* San Francisco: Harper Collins, 1990.

Christison, Kathleen. *Perceptions of Palestine.* Los Angeles: University of California Press, 1999.

Claibourne, William. "Israelis Look on U.S. Evangelicals as Potent Ally." *Washington Post*, March 23, 1981.

Ellis, Marc. *A Jewish Theology of Liberation.* Maryknoll, NY: Orbis, 1988.

Freeman, Charles W. "Israel's Fraying Image and Its Implications." Remarks to a seminar convened to discuss an article by Jacob Heilbrunn. Center for the National Interest, Washington, DC, May 22, 2013. http://chasfreeman.net/israels-fraying-image-and-its-implications/.

Igrams, Doreen. *Palestine Papers, 1917–22: Seeds of Conflict.* London: John Murray, 1972.

"Is U.S. Military Aid to Israel Legal?" U.S. Campaign to End the Israeli Occupation. http://aidtoisrael.org/article.php?id=3180.

Israel Action Network. "Best Practices for Countering the Assault on Israel's Legitimacy." *IAN FACTs* 2, January 2013. Downloadable booklet. http://israelactionnetwork.org/wp-content/uploads/2013/03/JFNA-FACTs2_finallores-.pdf.

Judis, John B. *Genesis: Truman, American Jews, and the Origins of the Arab/Israeli Conflict.* New York: Farrar, Straus and Giroux, 2014.

Julian, Liam. Hoover Institution *Policy Review* no. 154 (April 1, 2009). Stanford University. http://www.hoover.org/publications/policy-review/article/5509.

Kairos Palestine: A Moment of Truth. Portland, OR: Friends of Sabeel-North America, 2009.

Kelley, Dean M. *Why Conservative Churches Are Growing: A Study in Sociology of Religion.* Macon, GA: Mercer University Press, 1972.

Khalidi, Rashid. *Brokers of Deceit.* Boston: Beacon, 2013.

McLaren, Brian. *Everything Must Change: Jesus, Global Crises, and a Revolution of Hope.* Nashville: Thomas Nelson, 2007.

Moseley, Carys. "Reinhold Niebuhr's Approach to the State of Israel." *Electronic Journal of the Center for Christian-Jewish Learning* 4:1 (2009) n.p. http://ejournals.bc.edu/ojs/index.php/scjr/article/view/1517.

Niebuhr, Reinhold. "Our Stake in Israel." *The New Republic,* February 4, 1956.

Prior, Michael. *Zionism and the State of Israel: A Moral Inquiry.* London: Routledge, 1999.

Reut Institute. "Eroding Israel's Legitimacy in the International Arena." *ReViews,* blog of the Reut Institute. January 28, 2010. http://reut-institute.org/Publication.aspx?PublicationId=3766.

Rodinson, Maxime. *Israel: A Colonial-Settler State?* New York: Monad, 1973.

Ruether, Rosemary Radford. *America, Amerikkka.* London: Equinox, 2007.

Sizer, Stephen. *Christian Zionism: Roadmap to Armageddon?* Leicester: InterVarsity, 2004.

Smith, Charles D. *Palestine and the Arab-Israeli Conflict.* 5th ed. New York: Bedford/St. Martin's, 2004.

Smith, Ted A., and Amy-Jill Levine. "Habits of Anti-Judaism: Critiquing a PCUSA Report on Israel/Palestine." *The Christian Century* 127:13 (June 29, 2010) 26–29.

Stendahl, Krister. *Paul Among Jews and Gentiles.* Philadelphia: Fortress, 1976.

Stone, Ronald H. *Politics and Faith: Reinhold Niebuhr and Paul Tillich at Union Seminary in New York.* Macon, GA: Mercer University Press, 2012.

"U.S. Military Aid to Israel: Policy Implications and Options." U.S. Campaign to End the Israeli Occupation. http://www.endtheoccupation.org/militaryaidtoIsrael.executivesummary.

Van Marter, Jerry L. "Religious Leaders Ask Congress to Condition Israel Military Aid on Human Rights Compliance." *Presbyterian News Service,* Oct. 5, 2012. http://www.pcusa.org/news/2012/10/5/religious-leaders-ask-congress-condition-israel-mi/.

Verduin, Paul H. "Praiseworthy Intentions, Unintended Consequences: Why Krister Stendahl's Quest for 'Healthy Relations' between Jews and Christians Ended Tragically." In *Zionism through Christian Lenses,* edited by Carole Monica Burnett, 132–61. Eugene, OR: Wipf & Stock, 2013.

Wagner, Donald E. *Anxious for Armageddon.* Scottsdale, PA: Herald, 1995.

Yoffie, Eric. "Heading Toward an Irreparable Rift Between U.S. Jews and Protestants." *Haaretz,* October 24, 2012.

Young, Kenneth. *Arthur James Balfour.* London: J. Bell, 1963.

Chapter Seven

Evangelicals and Christian Zionism

Gary M. Burge

EVANGELICALISM IS A TWENTIETH-CENTURY expression of Protestant Christianity that began in the United States and has been embraced in a wide number of international settings. It transcends "denominational and confessional boundaries" while "emphasizing conformity to the basic tenets of the faith and a missionary outreach of compassion and urgency."[1] Throughout church history such "reforming" movements have been commonplace, calling the church back to the basics of belief and salvation (hence the term "evangelical" from the Greek *euangelion* or gospel).

For example, in our own era, the European Enlightenment that questioned the centrality of traditional religious faith gave birth to the Methodist revivals of the eighteenth and nineteenth centuries and the Great Awakening in America. And more recently, following the collapse of European optimism and theological liberalism after two world wars, American conservatives tried to forge a new hopeful path that was neither sectarian, separating itself from society as fundamentalists had always done nor liberal, seeing within society true redemptive possibilities. These *evangelical Christians* promoted the centrality of Christ and his saving death on the cross, preached the necessity of conversion and spiritual rebirth ("born again"), defended the authority of scripture, and were *activist*, eager to build social structures that would advance their work. Foreign missionary societies,

---

1. Pierard and Elwell, "Evangelicalism," 405. See also Wheaton College's Institute for the Study of Evangelicals at http://www.wheaton.edu/ISAE/Defining-Evangelicalism/ Defining-the-Term.

Bible colleges and seminaries, evangelistic crusades (most notably Billy Graham's crusades), and publishing programs began in the latter half of the twentieth century. The National Association of Evangelicals was born in 1942, Fuller Theological Seminary, the largest seminary in North America, opened in 1947, and evangelicalism's flagship magazine *Christianity Today* was launched in 1956. From the beginning, Wheaton College, founded in 1860, was evangelicalism's leading college, although today many similar colleges mirror Wheaton's strengths. Today this movement is large and may represent 30–35 percent of the American population or 90 to 100 million adherents.[2]

However, *within* the evangelical community there is tremendous diversity of opinion about many theological and social themes. Some evangelicals are theologically progressive while others are theologically conservative. Some may espouse a Pentecostal/Charismatic theology, others may be indebted to dispensational systems, while still others will find their identity in the Reformed theological world of Calvin. Intense and often incendiary debates are common concerning the inerrancy of scripture, the ordination of women, the preservation of the traditional family, and political activism. Older generations will still see the primary call of the Gospel to be the conversion of the human heart from which social change will evolve. If my Wheaton students are any indication, younger generations disagree. They are fully committed to social change as a faithful obedience to the Gospel. Today they will talk about social justice in ways that their parents never would have done.

That diversity of opinion can be seen with stark clarity when evangelicals discuss the Middle East, Israel, and eschatology. This topic has become a case study in how politics, social justice, and theology can intersect and produces immediate and polarizing opinions among evangelicals.

There is today a wide array of positions about Israel and Zionism. It is an unfortunate confusion when many Christians, particularly in the Middle East, conflate the labels "evangelical" and "Zionist." However, the confusion is understandable. Christian Zionists who hold many classic evangelical theological viewpoints maintain a high profile in Israel/Palestine. In the United States the confusion is even more acute since high profile pastors claim that Christian Zionism is a first-order evangelical commitment. I have had my own evangelical identity as a professor at Wheaton College challenged simply because I have critiqued the Zionist theological and political narrative for the Middle East. Many in the church fail to understand

2. Eskridge, "How Many," para. 5.

that it is fully possible to be evangelical and not Zionist. Zionism is simply one stream, a vocal minority stream, in the evangelical world.

Consider one case study: the Rev. John Hagee of Cornerstone Church in San Antonio, Texas. After attaining two degrees in mechanical engineering, Hagee attended Pentecostal Southwestern Bible School (now Southwestern Assemblies of God University) near Dallas and from there began a ministry that today has become a nineteen thousand member church. Hagee has enormous cultural reach. Many of his books are sold widely in America and can be found on the shelf at Walmart and Target stores. While many see him as "evangelical," his theological positions are deeply controversial. He has published assertions that Jesus never claimed to be the Jewish messiah but only came to save "the Christian church." Additionally, there are political pronouncements embedded in his militant sermons. He has called for pre-emptive bombing strikes on Iran and declares that a primary obligation of Christians everywhere is to support the modern State of Israel.

I am a conservative Protestant working at one of evangelicalism's premier colleges, but I find Hagee's views disturbing and irresponsible. However, a casual observer might think we belong to the same family. To a degree we do, but to a large degree, we do not. We are estranged members of the same extended family, the evangelical movement. How do we clear the fog?

Hagee is a "dispensationalist." I have been shaped by the Reformed theological tradition. He takes his cues from recent (as in one hundred year old) writers such as Darby, Scofield, and Ryrie. I take my cues from older writers such as the sixteenth-century John Calvin, the Anglican and Presbyterian worlds, and from theologians who belong to the "Reformed Tradition" such as John Piper, N. T. Wright, and John Stott. Both of us could be called "evangelicals."

Dispensationalism was born in the late nineteenth century as an attempt to parcel out human history into a series of seven biblical categories (or dispensations) for time. There was the era or covenant of Adam, of Noah, and of others. We live in the era of the church, and it will be followed by the end of time (the millennium). Dispensationalism embraced a pessimistic view of history, believing that the world was coming to its end and that the judgment day was near. As a result, it became sectarian, separating itself from mainstream society, calling sinners to repent and be saved from the inevitable catastrophe of the human story.

Most evangelical theology (especially that shaped by the Reformed tradition) is not so grim. It has generally embraced a hopeful understanding of life, thinking that the Gospel is a call to transform the world (not separate from it) and to participate with society in bringing the good things of God to bear on the things of this world. Note this test: Reformed theology might promote "secular" art and music; dispensationalists will only promote "Christian" art and music. Why? It all depends on whether one thinks the world has anything to offer.

Here is another test. Dispensationalists decided in the twentieth century that the catalyst for the end of time was the reestablishment of the secular State of Israel. Dispensationalists were thrilled in 1948 when Israel announced its nationhood. They saw Israel's various military victories in 1967 and 1973 as confirmations of a divine hand guiding Israel's future. Many dispensationalists are eager to see this age end and the next begin. If prophecies are being fulfilled, if history is at its terminus, then Christians are obligated to join in what God is doing. This expression of faith is nowhere clearer than when one raises the question of Israel. Such Christians who wed politics to this theological framework are called Christian Zionists.

So what would be our differences?

First, some provisional observations: this is not a political question per se centering on Israel's right as a nation to have a place in history, to make a claim for statehood or to enjoy international legitimacy. I would grant each of these. Israel has a right to exist in safety. Nor in my judgment is this topic a moral question concerning the historic treatment of Judaism in Europe. It is true that the Jewish people have suffered beyond imagination, culminating in the Holocaust. Because of this reality, western society indeed bears a moral obligation to guarantee that such horrors do not happen again. I concede this as well. Christians should be vigilant against all forms of anti-Semitism.

The issue of *Christian obligation* invites a *theological* question. It implies that today men and women sitting in the pews of the church ought to support Israel as a first-order commitment because of their Christian faith. The question becomes whether the Christian faith today has a necessary political entailment. Must modern Israel be supported as a religious duty? I recently saw a large banner hanging in front of a major church in Oak Park, Illinois, near Chicago. It said: "We Stand with Israel." Is this a *necessary* announcement for a church?

Christian Zionists will say, "Yes!" They have a passion for Judaism because they easily conflate ancient biblical Israel with the modern State of Israel and see covenant promises in the Old Testament as inherited by modern Israel. They would also be eager to say that the covenant promises given to Abraham are still in effect today and have not been replaced or abolished by the New Testament.

Mainstream evangelical theologians do not abandon the Old Testament covenants, but they see a complex relationship between the Old Testament and New Testament covenants. Christ's coming has affected these covenants, and today believers who belong to Christ also belong to these covenants. They proclaim that the promises of the Old Testament find their fulfillment in the New Testament, and so for them, the people of God share a common life in the Old and New Testaments. Both Christians and Jews are called Abraham's children. In other words, covenant privileges no longer exist *exclusively* to ethnic Judaism outside of Christ. What God has done in Christ takes up and transforms what had been offered in the old covenants, leading to obvious conclusions regarding the modern State of Israel. While Israel has the right to exist, just as does any other nation, it does not enjoy a *theological exceptionalism* that sets it apart from the requirements of behavior expected of other nations.

Christian Zionism Today

Many of us are deeply tired of the subject of Christian Zionism, but when I read material like the transcripts of a meeting that took place in Washington, July 16–18, 2012, I redouble my efforts. This annual conference, hosted by Christians United for Israel [CUFI] draws about five thousand people from every state in the country and culminates with "A Night to Honor Israel." In 2012, unsurprisingly, a list of political aspirants such as Michele Bachmann lined up to speak in support of an American foreign policy that privileges Israel. The aim of the evening was purely political. Its organizers wanted to influence American foreign policy to support any Israeli security or land issue.

Organized by Rev. John Hagee, CUFI works to rally the evangelical Christians of America, who by their count number fifty million, to the support of Israel. With this platform, the leaders hope to show that Christians have a spiritual obligation to stand fully with Israel . As Hagee is fond of saying, "When 50 million evangelical Bible-believing Christians unite with five million American Jews standing together on behalf of Israel, it is a match made in heaven."[3]

This is true or at least partly true, for if these two communities united fully, they would be perhaps the largest voting bloc in America. Hagee continues, "Let us shout it from the housetops that a new day has been born in America. The sleeping giant of Christian Zionism has awakened. If a line has to be drawn, draw the line around Christians and Jews. We are united. We are indivisible. And together we can reshape history."

3. This and all subsequent quotations from Hagee are taken from an interview with Bill Moyers on *Bill Moyers' Journal* (October 5, 2007), at http://www.pbs.org/moyers/journal/10052007/transcript1.html.

This is where Hagee frightens more than he inspires. Not only does he believe that his theological commitments give him biblically defensible views on Israel, but his eschatology has led him to call for America to strike out militarily against Israel's opponents. Using the language of the Book of Revelation, Hagee looks to Iran as the incarnation of evil. "The head of the beast of radical Islam in the Middle East is Iran and its fanatical president Ahmadinejad. Ladies and gentlemen, we are reliving history. It is 1938 all over again. Iran is Germany. Ahmadinejad is Hitler. And Ahmadinejad, just like Hitler, is talking about killing the Jews."

According the Hagee, the answer to this threat is written in the biblical playbook, which he will interpret for us. The answer is to launch a war that will end all war since it will bring the end of human history. He continues, ". . . We want you to recognize that Iran is a clear and present danger to the United States of America and Israel. . . . It's time for our country to consider a military preemptive strike against Iran if they will not yield to diplomacy. And if they continue the pursuit of nuclear weapons we must not allow them to manipulate the economy of the world because they have a nuclear weapon."

Rev. John Hagee, a spokesperson for Jesus Christ, a Texas pastor with no diplomatic credentials, a man with no training in history or political science, a pastor with the most basic theological education, calls for an American military strike against Iran based on what he declares that the Bible teaches, and as a part of this conference, he commissioned his delegates as lobbyists to take his message to Capitol Hill.

I am not the only one who is alarmed. A host of Jewish leaders such as Rabbi Laurie Zimmerman and Rabbi Michael Lerner have spoken out against this "wedding made in heaven." In response to Hagee, Rabbi Zimmerman wrote:

> Other rabbis, including myself, generally support building bridges with other communities. Yet we recognize that there are some groups with whom we should not align ourselves or support in any way. If creating a sustainable peace in the Middle East is important to us, then we cannot support an organization that advocates attacking Iran and launching the region into further chaos. As Pastor John Hagee, stated, "The United States must join Israel in a pre-emptive military strike against Iran to fulfill God's plan for both Israel and the West . . . a biblically prophesied end-time confrontation with Iran, which will lead

to the Rapture, Tribulation . . . and Second Coming of Christ"
(CUFI's Washington, DC inaugural event, July 19, 2006).[4]

Theological Convictions

Christian Zionism is a populist movement led for the most part by pastors, laity, and televangelists who have a wide influence over Christian audiences. Internet blogs and websites are numerous; they are written by surprisingly reactive (and often angry) authors and serve generally to identify and criticize any who would critique Israel. However, rarely does one find theological substance.[5] It is very difficult even to find a scholarly presentation of their views but popular, highly reactionary books are abundant, often written by people with little theological background.

What are the theological convictions of the average Christian Zionist? We can hazard a general outline that is widely embraced by churches throughout America. Most will hold to these points while some will not. Some Christian Zionists are deeply influenced by dispensationalism; others hold some of its elements but do not know their origins. Nevertheless, the widespread opinion in evangelical churches is that the instincts of Christian Zionism are correct and should be defended. In each section of the outline, I will include the objections to these views raised by many of us evangelical leaders.[6]

1. God's Promises to Abraham

In Genesis 12, 15, and 17, God promises the Holy Land to Abraham and his descendants. To Christian Zionists this promise of land inheritance was permanent and unconditional. It is as true today as it was in biblical times.

This means that for Christian Zionists, the covenant of Abraham continues to be in play today. This belief forces Christians to have what we call a "two-covenant" theology. One covenant operates for Jews, and one operates for Christians in the church. In a word, the work of Christ does not replace or supplant the Jewish covenants. In reality, the church and its covenant is an unexpected interruption of what God was doing in Israel,

---

4. Zimmerman, "A Night," para. 5.

5. A good example of this is www.camera.org (Committee for Accuracy in Middle East Reporting in America).

6. For a more thorough theological treatment of these themes, see my *Jesus and the Land*.

thereby explaining in part why these churches have a theology centered so thoroughly in Jewish interests.

However, many evangelicals (like myself) believe that something decisive happened in Christ. His covenant affected not simply the covenant of Moses, creating a new and timeless form of salvation, but also every Jewish covenant, including Abraham's covenant. Christ fulfills the expectations of Jewish covenant life and renews the people of God rooted in the Old Testament and Judaism. Thus Jesus is a new temple, the new Israel; there are twelve tribes and twelve apostles, and so on.

When it comes to the land promises to Abraham—the crux of the matter for dispensationalists—we find in Gal 3:16 (RSV) the Apostle Paul's response: "Now the promises were made to Abraham and to his offspring. It does not say, 'And to offsprings,' referring to many; but, referring to one, 'And to your offspring,' which is Christ." Remarkably Paul argues from the singular noun in Genesis to show that the promises to Abraham, including land, point to Christ. Christ is the locus of the promise of land! The promises to Abraham have been realized in Christ; he holds everything Judaism desired, and knowing Christ gains access to such promises.

Jesus's splendid homily in John 15 reaches the same conclusion. This is the great vine and branches sermon given in the upper room. The Old Testament image of Israel is that of a vineyard filled with many vines rooted in the soil of the Holy Land. This metaphor is outlined beautifully in Isaiah 5, but Jesus upends it. We see a vineyard again, but now we learn that there is one vine, Christ, and the issue is not gaining access to the land but being attached to him.

To think in Christian terms about land and promise is to think differently than Judaism thinks. *In short, the New Testament changes the spiritual geography of God's people.* The Kingdom of God is tied neither to an ethnicity nor to a place. Because the early Christians understood this truth, they carried their missionary efforts to the entire world. At a time when Jews were debating the meaning of Holy Land, Jesus's declaration was quite remarkable: "the meek . . . shall inherit the land" (Matt 5:5),[7] not the aggressor or the conqueror. (I explain this in full in my recent study *Jesus and the Land*.)

The point is this: many evangelical theologians are not convinced that the promises to Abraham, much less those to Moses, are still theologically significant today. The work of Christ is definitive. There is one covenant. And it is with Christ. Thus, we evangelical theologians despair when we

---

7. RSV has "earth," but the Greek word can be translated either way. See Burge, *Jesus and the Land*, 33–35.

hear Rev. Hagee cite the Old Testament again and again without reference to Christ. We are eager to hear him open his Bible again and read it in light of Christ.

2. Israel Has Been Restored to the Land

The next step is crucial. For Christian Zionists, 1948 is not simply a political marker in history; it is a theological marker in which Israel has been restored to the land in fulfillment of prophecy. This modern restoration is no different from the restoration following the Babylonian exile. Therefore, from this perspective, the creation of modern Israel is not simply a politically significant event; it is a theologically ordained event, one that should garner profound Christian respect and awe.

Evangelical theologians do not deny the right of Israel to exist. As I do, they speak against anti-Semitism and claim that Israel has a right to national security. I am among the first to condemn Palestinian acts of terror just as I condemn Israeli acts of terror.

However, while some deny it outright, most evangelical theologians are characteristically agnostic with regard to modern Israel's theological significance. One proposition that we do strongly reject is that to be critical of Israel is the same as being anti-Semitic. Israel began as a secular state, the nation barely reflects the beautiful national aspirations of the scriptures, and it has made choices that would inspire harsh criticisms from any Old Testament prophet such as Amos or Isaiah.

The Israeli writer Avraham Burg has explained the roots of modern Zionism in an article entitled "The End of Zionism" (*The Guardian*, September 30, 2003). In the late nineteenth century, two forms of nationalism were born. First, there was *liberal nationalism,* with its roots in the French Revolution, in which a multi-ethnic state is built and all citizens stand equal under the law. The second model came from German Romanticism and viewed the state as belonging to a particular ethnicity whose members enjoyed privileges that non-members could not have. This German model is what shaped Theodor Herzl, the founder of twentieth-century Zionism and the creator of the World Zionist Organization, and it is this model that shapes Israel today. Therefore, the Zionist idea was not born from the Bible but from an ethnic nationalism that also gave birth to other nations, such as 1930s Germany, with all their attendant problems. Christian Zionists who envision Herzl rebuilding Israel with a Bible under one arm are ignorant of the realities of history.

Many modern Israelis see this model of a state coming to an end. After publication of Burg's very controversial book *Defeating Hitler,* he was interviewed by Avi Shavit for an article entitled "Leaving the Zionist Ghetto" (*Haaretz Magazine,* June 10, 2007). Statements from that interview were subsequently quoted by David Remnick in *The New Yorker:* "The Israeli reality is not exciting. People are not willing to admit it, but Israel has reached the wall. Ask your friends if they are certain their children will live here. How many will say yes? At most fifty percent. In other words, the Israeli elite has already departed this place. And without an elite there is no nation. . . . We are already dead. We haven't received the news yet, but we are dead. It doesn't work anymore. It doesn't work."[8] Avraham Burg is a liberal Jew who sees what is wrong and recognizes—with tears—that Herzl's ethnic state cannot sustain itself without resorting to enormous acts of violence.

For all these reasons, many evangelicals do not see commitment to the State of Israel as a spiritual imperative. They respect Israel but deny Israeli exceptionalism. I personally believe that the protection of political Israel is a moral duty because of what happened to the Jews in European history. But that is a different matter. Christian Zionists want me to know (on the basis of Gen 12:3) that "those who bless Israel" God will bless. And those who "curse Israel" God will curse. They believe that to fail to "Stand with Israel" ultimately will subject us to God's curse. But the vast majority of evangelicals simply see this application of Gen 12:3 as dubious. God was speaking promises of protection to Abraham in his situation but a compelling case cannot be made for applying those promises to a secular state in the Middle East.

3. History is Coming to Its Close

Many Christian Zionists believe that the coming of Israel to the land has started the countdown that will end history. Christian Zionists think that Israel's national life, reborn in 1948, is the key prophetic piece we must watch, but that is not all. According to their view, Israel's return fits with other events occurring in the world: moral values are in decline, an ecological crisis is looming, our oil-based economy is in peril, and, most important, war in the Middle East leads them to widespread agreement that history has reached a cul-de-sac, for all of these have been predicted in prophecy.

Most evangelical theologians remind us that millennial movements that predict the end of the world have been part of Christianity from the

---

8. Remnick, "Apostate," 33.

beginning. But these predictions have not come to pass. So they would have us pause and use sober judgment.

The theologians' chief complaint, however, is the way in which this zeal for the end has shaped the ethics of Christian Zionists. Passion for seeing the Second Coming of Christ now comes before a passion for justice and fairness. For instance, when presented with the remarkable losses of about 4 million Palestinians living under military occupation, Christian Zionists and others typically stand unmoved. Land cannot be returned to them and negotiations are against God's will. During the summer of Hurricane Katrina, Hagee showed us the depth of his opposition to fair play for Palestinians. When the Israeli settlers were removed from Gaza by their own government, he issued a challenge during his interview with Bill Moyers:

> I want to ask Washington a question. Is there a connection between the 9,000 Jewish refugees being forcibly removed from their homes in the Gaza Strip now living in tents and the thousands of Americans who have been expelled from their homes by this tremendous work of nature, the hurricane Katrina? Is there a connection there? If you've got a better answer, I'd like to hear it.[9]

Notice carefully what has just been said. God punished America with Hurricane Katrina because America supported the withdrawal of the Gaza settlers. It is this sort of outrageous interpretation that stuns and embarrasses mainstream evangelicals. They simply cannot understand this interpretation of modern history.

4. Fidelity to Israel

It then follows in the thinking of Christian Zionists that the first obligation of the Christian is to watch the End Times prophecies and to stand guardian over the political decisions of each nation. The first test of righteousness in this dangerous era is to measure oneself by God's litmus test, the rebirth of Israel. One conviction is always held aloft: God blesses those who bless Israel and curses those who curse Israel (Gen 12:2–3). Hence nations will stand or fall on the basis of this one creed.

Most evangelicals observe the zeal of Christian Zionists to bless Israel and wonder if the Gospel has been lost. My first call is fidelity to Christ and his kingdom. I do not believe that two kingdoms of God are at work in the world. There is one and it is found in Christ. Yet this commitment should

---

9. See note 3 above.

inspire in me a deep love for Israel and a desire for its people to become what their scriptures call them to become: a nation of priests, a light to the nations, a people in whom there is such goodness that the nations will see the glory of God and rejoice.

I believe we are called to love the Jews, but love requires that we come alongside, giving reassurances and offering honest truth. Christian Zionists excel in one but fail in the other. They love Israel profoundly, but I await the day when Rev. Hagee exhorts Israel (just once) to pursue a national life of justice and truth.

5. Jesus's Second Coming

This is where everything has been leading. The birth of Israel has now set the stage for the imminent second coming of Jesus Christ. This is the crown jewel in Christian Zionism's worldview. This is why Rev. Hagee is willing to risk throwing the Middle East into war. Any national agenda that would contradict God's plan, any peace overture that would weaken Israel's hold on the land such as the promise of a Palestinian state or the withdrawal of Israeli settlers from Gaza or the West Bank, any decision that stands in the way of this dramatic stage-setting is not a plan that Christian Zionists view as blessed by God.

Mainstream evangelicals believe in the Second Coming as well. We actually stand with Christian Zionists committed to a longing for Christ's return.

The chief difference is that evangelical theologians make profound investments in the world. *We are not sectarian.* We devote ourselves to promoting Christ's commitments here. We do not despair about the course of the world. We have not abandoned it. Dwight Moody, the namesake of the dispensational Moody Bible Institute in Chicago, once asked why anyone would want to polish the brass on a sinking ship. In the question, we can hear the pessimism in pristine simplicity. Christian Zionism with its roots in dispensationalism has a pessimistic view of human history that will be reversed only by Christ's return. Most evangelical theologians, however, are not as convinced that the ship is sinking, and we continue to be committed to polishing its brass, painting its hull, navigating its course, and making its passengers comfortable until we are surprised by Christ's return, just as the Bible tells us we should be.

The technical theological language of this difference is millennialism, from the Latin *mille* (thousand) and *annum* (year). Many Christian Zionists use a literalist reading of the Book of Revelation and apply it to the present time to teach that a series of things will happen in short order: the church will be raptured (or removed) from the world, there will be seven years of dreadful war and tribulation, Christ will return at the height of a climactic war called Armageddon, and then Christ will reign for a literal one thousand (Latin, *mille*) years (Rev 20:4). Most are "pre-millennial," meaning that Christ will return to earth "before" (pre-) his thousand-year rule. In this sense, they are pessimistic about human history: it will sink into disarray and war, and only the coming of Christ will reverse humanity's demise. Jesus alone will stop all wars.

Many evangelicals in the Reformed tradition, on the other hand, are often "a-millennial" (as were Luther, Calvin, and most of the other Protestant reformers). That is, they believe that in the Book of Revelation, the thousand-year reign of Christ is a metaphor and that the present age is a time when Christ is at work restoring the world. Christ will return to end history but not *necessarily* at the end of a catastrophe. In this sense, they tend to be more hopeful about human history—optimistic even—seeing that what Christ is doing now in history will improve it.

This is my ultimate complaint perhaps. Christian Zionists believe in Jesus, but I wonder if they are always thinking like Christians in this matter. They have uncritically inherited the territorial worldview of Judaism and wed it to dubious prophetic predictions that are expected to unfold in the present age. However, it is an eccentric view, one that is peculiar to the present time and unrepresentative of the historic teachings of the church. I predict that it is a view that will embarrass the church in generations to come.

The Problem of Replacement Theology

The chief Christian Zionist complaint against many evangelicals in the Reformed tradition is that they may be "replacement theologians" or "supersessionists." Both terms require some definition. There has been a long tradition in the church that has placed Christian theology at odds with Judaism. For some, the church has "replaced" the Jewish faith and all that remains is for Judaism to be judged for rejecting its messiah and for killing Jesus. Therefore, according to this point of view, the blessings promised to Israel have now been inherited by the church, and the only future for Israel is to be incorporated into the church with Christian faith. (Another way to say this is that the church "supersedes" or supplants Judaism; hence, supersessionism). For many historians this attitude is the historical origin of much anti-Semitism in western culture.

However, it is not *necessarily* the case that a replacement theology always leads to anti-Semitism. It has been an historic teaching of the church and has never been considered a heresy. To some degree, the New Testament is indeed announcing the replacement of one thing with another. Christianity did not arise as a rival religion to Judaism. Christian faith was a religious movement *within Judaism* announcing that what Jewish faith sought had been found in the arrival of the Messiah, Jesus of Nazareth. In other words, the earliest proclamation of how the Messiah affected Judaism was announced by Jews, Messianic Jews like Matthew and Paul, who believed that something had happened in Christ that permanently changed the religious realities of Judaism. The church was not seen as something "Gentile." The church was the community of believers (both Jewish and Gentile) that now represented the people of God.

Nevertheless replacement themes were a part of their understanding of what had happened. Christ was a replacement of the Temple (John 2). Christ's covenant was often contrasted with the covenant of Moses. Those attached to Christ were viewed as having a place with God ordinarily held by Jews in the Old Testament. Peter referred to the church as a chosen priesthood, a holy nation (1 Pet 2:9).

The problem arises when this replacement motif denigrates any valid place for Judaism as a legitimate religious faith. We might express it thus: is Israel's election void and are its promises invalid? When Judaism becomes the target of public opprobrium, only terrible things can result. It is for this reason that today, particularly since the Holocaust, Christians have stepped back from this view.

Some theologians avoid this problem by asserting that the covenants of Israel are still valid. This helpfully provides a secure theological place for Judaism but from a Christian point of view, it offers a "two-covenant" theology that in some manner diminishes the significance of what God has done in Christ. Therefore, if the covenants of Abraham and Moses are still successful bases for a saving relationship with God, then the saving work of Christ is an *option* for Judaism, not something essential. Such theologians have a hard time with verses such as John 14:6: "Jesus said to him, 'I am the way, and the truth, and the life; no one comes to the Father, but by me'" (RSV). Therefore, the vast majority of Christian theologians reject the view that the Old Testament covenants are unaffected by Christ. Simply put, what occurred in Christ was definitive.

However, there is a third view which many including myself find attractive. It rejects replacement theology and its anti-Semitic legacy as well as a two-covenant theology. The first disrespects Judaism; the second diminishes the centrality of Christ. These "third-way" theologians recover a place for Judaism not by affirming Jewish exceptionalism nor by suggesting that Jewish covenants are still saving, but by preserving an *eschatological* (or future) place for Judaism in history. This is the view that springs from Romans 11 and asserts that God's commitment to Judaism is anchored to his promises in history and that despite his new covenant established in Christ, Judaism retains a place of importance and at the end of time will join the church, no doubt at Christ's Second Coming. Here we need to be clear. Anyone who holds an eschatological place for Israel in history cannot be a replacement theologian. Judaism retains an important place of recognition and blessing.

I believe that a thoughtful reading of Romans 11 (particularly because of the biblical history proclaimed in Rom 11:28) affirms that God continues to hold a place for Judaism in history. However this is a "suspended blessing" for they are "branches . . . broken off" (Rom 11:17, RSV) that will be restored at the end of history when Christ returns, when "all Israel will be saved" (Rom 11:26, RSV). This understanding of Romans 11 means that we should not tolerate anti-Semitism and that church and synagogue should share mutual respect.[10]

Bibliography

Ateek, Naim Stifan. *A Palestinian Christian Cry for Reconciliation.* Maryknoll, NY: Orbis, 2008.

Ateek, Naim Stifan, and Rosemary Radford Ruether. *Justice and Only Justice: A Palestinian Theology of Liberation.* Maryknoll, NY: Orbis, 1989.

Braverman, Mark. *Fatal Embrace: Christians, Jews, and the Search for Peace in the Holy Land.* Austin, TX: Synergy, 2010.

Brueggemann, Walter. *The Land: Place as Gift, Promise and Challenge in Biblical Faith.* 2nd ed. Minneapolis: Fortress, 2002.

Burge, Gary M. *Jesus and the Land: The New Testament Challenge to "Holy Land" Theology.* Grand Rapids: Baker Academic, 2010.

————. *Whose Land? Whose Promise? What Christians Are Not Being Told About Israel and the Palestinians.* Second Edition. Cleveland: Pilgrim, 2013.

Carenen, Caitlin. *The Fervent Embrace: Liberal Protestants, Evangelicals, and Israel.* New York: New York University Press, 2012.

Chapman, Colin. *Whose Promised Land? The Continuing Crisis Over Israel and Palestine.* Grand Rapids: Baker, 2002.

Clark, Victoria. *Allies for Armageddon: The Rise of Christian Zionism.* New Haven: Yale University Press, 2007.

10. This essay includes approximately ten pages reprinted from the book *Whose Land? Whose Promise? What Christians Are Not Being Told About Israel and the Palestinians* by Gary M. Burge. All rights reserved. Used by permission.

Davies, W. D. *The Gospel and the Land: Early Christianity and Jewish Territorial Doctrine*. Berkeley: University of California Press, 1974.

———. *The Territorial Dimension of Judaism*. Minneapolis: Fortress, 1992.

Ellis, Marc H. *Toward a Jewish Theology of Liberation*. Waco, TX: Baylor University Press, 2004.

Eskridge, Larry. "How Many Evangelicals Are There?" The Institute for the Study of Evangelicals, Wheaton College. http://www.wheaton.edu/ISAE/Defining-Evangelicalism/How-Many-Are-There.

House, H. Wayne, ed. *Israel: The Land and the People; An Evangelical Affirmation of God's Promise*. Grand Rapids: Kregel, 1998.

Johnston, Philip, and Peter Walker. *The Land of Promise: Biblical, Theological and Contemporary Perspectives*. Downers Grove, IL: InterVarsity, 2000.

Marchadour, A., and D. Neuhous. *The Land, the Bible, and History*. New York: Fordham University Press, 2007.

Pierard, R. V., and W. Elwell. "Evangelicalism." In *The Evangelical Dictionary of Theology*, edited by W. Elwell, 405. Grand Rapids: Baker Academic, 1996.

Raheb, Mitri. *I am a Palestinian Christian*. Minneapolis: Fortress, 1995.

Remnick, David. "The Advocate." *The New Yorker* (July 30, 2007) 32–37. http://archives.newyorker.com/?i2007-07-30# folio = 033.

Sizer, Stephen. *Christian Zionism: Road Map to Armageddon?* Leicester: InterVarsity, 2004.

Wagner, Donald E. *Anxious for Armageddon: A Call to Partnership for Middle Eastern and Western Christians*. Harrisonburg, VA: Herald, 1995.

Walker, P. W. L. *Jesus and the Holy City: New Testament Perspectives on Jerusalem*. Grand Rapids: Eerdmans, 1996.

Weaver, Alain Epp, ed. *Under the Vine and the Fig Tree: Biblical Theologies of Land and the Palestine-Israel Conflict*. Scottsdale, PA: Cascadia, 2007.

Weber, Timothy. *On the Road to Armageddon: How Evangelicals Became Israel's Best Friend*. Grand Rapids: Baker, 2004.

Zimmerman, Laurie. "A Night to Honor Israel? Christian Zionism and Jewish Community." http://www.jewsonfirst.org/Display4.aspx?item=3148.

Chapter Eight

Zionism

A Different Memory

Mustafa Abu Sway

ON THURSDAY, APRIL 18, 2013, I visited in Berlin the Memorial to the Murdered Jews of Europe, also known as the Holocaust Memorial. Even the many concrete stelae commemorating those who died are dwarfed by the magnitude of the memory of the genocide. Such an atrocity should not happen again, either to the Jews or to others, including the Roma and Sinti,[1] who also have a memorial nearby, albeit a modest one.

The history and memories of the Holocaust manifest themselves at different memorials and museums around the world, including Auschwitz, which I hope to visit soon, and Yad Vashem in Jerusalem, which has the largest repository of data on the Holocaust. I delivered two lectures at Yad Vashem reflecting what I describe as an "Islamic Theology of the Holocaust." The essence of the Islamic perspective here is that it is applicable to all human beings who suffer from violence. Our faith calls us to reject not only genocide but also violence against every single human being. The Holy Qur'an, while making reference to an original *biblically* revealed position, considers the unjust killing of one person as tantamount to genocide in terms of cumulative sin:

> Because of that, We decreed upon the Children of Israel that
> whoever kills a soul unless for a soul or for corruption [done] in

---

1. Roma and Sinti are Central European peoples, often referred to as Gypsies, killed during the Holocaust.

the land—it is as if he had slain mankind entirely. And whoever saves one—it is as if he had saved mankind entirely. And Our messengers had certainly come to them with clear proofs. Then indeed many of them, [even] after that, throughout the land, were transgressors (The Holy Qur'an 5:32).[2]

This verse shows that all blood is equal, be it that of a Jew, a Christian, or a Muslim, or others. However, there is no moral equivalency between the perpetrator of an immoral action and its recipient, the victim, between oppressor and oppressed. In today's reality, this means that for the Palestinians, there can be no moral equivalency between occupier and occupied, just as there is no moral equivalency between rapists and rape victims. It is very offensive and unfair to blame the victim or deny her the right to resist the rapist.

As far as the Palestinian narrative is concerned, a rape that took place in 1948 cannot and should not be considered a marriage in 2013 simply because the power structure between occupier and occupied allows this unhealthy relation to continue unabated. Every new Jewish-only colony established in the West Bank, for example, is an act of rape. Israel's *hasbara* ("explanation") initiative is a form of "public diplomacy" aimed at conveying to the international community a positive picture of Israel's policies and actions, even when it is clear that actions such as the continuous confiscation of Palestinian land and the building of exclusive Jewish colonies are devastating and in violation of international law. As part of its propaganda, ironically, the *hasbara* machinery tries to differentiate between "legal settlements" and "illegal outposts," the first being directly planned by the Israeli government and the latter initiated by Jewish settlers without coordination with the Israeli military. However, this is a false distinction because in both cases, settlements are illegal according to international law. The ongoing rape of Palestinian land leaves the West Bank so riddled with colonies that there is no longer any contiguity of land; Palestinian towns are choked, and natural growth prohibited.

The Israeli occupation has negative impact on both societies; it suprahumanizes the Israeli and dehumanizes the Palestinian. Symbolically, even road signs use large font for Hebrew and small font for Arabic! To understand this disparity, it is imperative to address the exclusive Zionist ideology that sets one community above the other and to contrast it with the inclusive view of humanity set forth in The Holy Qur'an, in which the goal is to bring together those who differ, not to separate them further:

2. This quotation and all subsequent quotations from The Holy Qur'an are from the Sahih International English version.

And not equal are the good deed and the bad. Repel [evil] by that [deed] which is better; and thereupon the one whom between you and him is enmity [will become] as though he was a devoted friend (The Holy Qur'an 41:34).

Surprisingly, decades of the ongoing Israeli occupation have failed to destroy the Palestinian moral compass or to make Palestinians accept the notion that one group of humans can be inherently superior to another. In my medical ethics class for Palestinian and Muslim medical students at Al-Quds University, these very bright students uphold universal values vis-à-vis the sanctity of life, even that of the combatant "enemy."

It must be emphasized that the anti-Israeli-occupation, anti-Zionist position is not against Jews or Judaism. It is against injustice and immoral policies. One should recognize that there are many religious and secular Jews who reject the Israeli occupation. Had Palestine been colonized by people who belong to a fourth religion, then Jews, Christians, and Muslims would have joined hands against the occupier. In fact, as an example, one can point to the Jews who were against the apartheid system in South Africa and those Jews who supported the civil rights movement in the U.S. Why not in Israel? In "Israel still failing Martin Luther King's dream," Ze'ev Portner and Amit Oz spoke about honoring the partnership between Martin Luther King and U.S. Jews by "countering the racism that has become politically mainstream in Israel."[3]

Indeed, had the Arab Palestinians, Christian and Muslim, who are indigenous to the Holy Land, belonged to alternative "X" and "Y" religions, they would still have resisted the Israeli occupation. Today's situation has nothing to do with religion *per se*. The original Arab population of the Holy Land belonged to different religions. There were Jebusite Arabs in control of Jerusalem before Prophet David became king; some of their Arab descendants have for the last two thousand years adhered to Christianity, and most of them for the last fourteen hundred years to Islam. The Palestinian people lived ten thousand years ago in Jericho, the oldest known agricultural settlement in the world, seven thousand years before the Jewish sojourn took place, and over time they have practiced various religions. The history of the Holy Land is like a woman who is meant to survive the many husbands she has had over the years, with children from all of them. She grants legitimacy to her newest husband only if he treats all her children from previous marriages equally and with compassion. If not, there will always be one more suitor who pledges to do better.

3. Portner and Oz, "Israel Still Failing."

However, the latest "husband" has failed to meet the expectations of this long history of equality. What this husband did is explained by Shimon Gapso, the Zionist mayor of Upper Nazareth. In his article, "If you think I'm a racist, then Israel is a racist state," he is explicit that racism is the cornerstone of the Zionist project. The following rather lengthy quotation is necessary to give Gapso enough space to make his self-incriminating argument, which reflects a bizarre and exclusivist reading of scripture through Zionist lenses to justify ethnic cleansing:

> Yes—I'm not afraid to say it out loud, to write it and add my signature, or declare it in front of the cameras: Upper Nazareth is a Jewish city and it's important that it remains so. If that makes me a racist, then I'm a proud offshoot of a glorious dynasty of "racists" that started with the "Covenant of the Pieces" [that God made with Abraham, recounted in Gen 15:1–15] and the explicitly racist promise: "To your seed I have given this land" [Gen 15:38].
>
> When the Jewish people were about to return to their homeland after a long journey from slavery in Egypt, where they were enslaved for racist reasons, the God of Israel told Moses how to act upon conquering the land: he must cleanse the land of its current inhabitants. "But if you do not drive out the inhabitants of the land from before you, then those of them whom you allow to remain . . . as I thought to do to them, so will I do to you" [Num 33:55–56].
>
> God gave them an explicit warning. Yes, the racist Joshua conquered the land in a racist manner. More than three thousand years later, the Jewish people stood bruised and bleeding on the threshold of their land, seeking once again to take possession of it from the wild tribes that had seized the land in its absence. And then, an outbreak of racism flooded the country.
>
> The racist Theodor Herzl wrote Der Judenstaat ("The Jewish State," not "The State of All Its Citizens"). Lord Balfour recommended the establishment of a national home for the Jewish people. David Ben-Gurion, Chaim Arlosoroff, Moshe Sharett and other racists established the Jewish Agency, and the racist U.N. decided to establish a Jewish state—in other words, a state for Jews. The racist Ben-Gurion announced the establishment of the Jewish State in the Land of Israel, and during the War of Independence even made sure to bring in hundreds of thousands of Jews and drive out hundreds of thousands of Arabs who had been living here—all to enable it to be founded with the desired racist character.

> Since then, racially pure kibbutzim without a single Arab
> member and an army that protects a certain racial strain have
> been established, as have political parties that proudly bear
> racist names such as "Habayit Hayehudi"—"the Jewish home."
> Even our racist national anthem ignores the existence of the
> Arab minority—in other words, the people Ben-Gurion did not
> manage to expel in the 1948 war. . . .[4]

It should be noted that Gapso's position is not an isolated case; there is
systematic discrimination enshrined in Israeli law. According to Adalah, the
Legal Center for Arab Minority Rights in Israel:

> There are more than 50 Israeli laws that discriminate against
> Palestinian citizens of Israel in all areas of life, including their
> rights to political participation, access to land, education, state
> budget resources, and criminal procedures. Some of the laws
> also violate the rights of Palestinians living in the 1967 OPT
> [Occupied Palestinian Territories] and Palestinian refugees.[5]

The war on Palestinians extends offshore and has been expanded into
a war on Islam. Many pro-Israel Islamophobes in the West, especially in the
U.S., try very hard to spread stereotyped images and false information about
Islam and Muslims, thinking that this helps Israel. Professor of Religion and
International Affairs and of Islamic Studies at Georgetown University John
L. Esposito explained recently that "7 foundations in the US have provided
$42.5 million in support to Islamophobes and their websites over the last
decade." The result is that "[t]oday everyday conversations in mainstream
[American] society express fear about Islam. Their conclusions become so
taken for granted, and become truisms that require no evidence, no substance, they are not challenged in the public square."[6]

It is, therefore, imperative to address some of these misconceptions
and to reflect the true character of Islam. It is hurtful to read false accusations leveled at Islam from people who either have not read The Holy Qur'an
or are blinded by sheer hatred. The inclusive nature of Islam vis-à-vis other
religions and their followers is reflected in many verses in The Holy Qur'an,
including the following:

4. Gapso, "If You Think I'm a Racist."

5. Adalah, "Discriminatory Laws in Israel," at http://adalah.org/eng/
Israeli-Discriminatory-Law-Database.

6. World Bulletin, "Esposito Slams Islamophobia in Egypt," at http://www.world-
bulletin.net/?aType=haber&ArticleID=117743.

> Say, [O believers], "We have believed in God and what has been
> revealed to us and what has been revealed to Abraham and Ish-
> mael and Isaac and Jacob and the Descendants and what was
> given to Moses and Jesus and what was given to the prophets
> from their Lord. We make no distinction between any of them,
> and we are Muslims [in submission] to Him" (The Holy Qur'an
> 2:136).

The prophetic traditions also reflect the same position. In a beautifully
inclusive tradition, Prophet Muhammad explained his relationship with all
other prophets (peace be upon them) who preceded him, when he said:

> My likeness among the prophets is as a man who built a house
> skillfully and beautifully, yet he left one place without a brick in
> one of the corners. People who saw [the house] were fascinated.
> Yet, they would exclaim, "Why is this brick not in its place?"
> He [the Prophet] said: "I am that brick; I am the Seal of the
> Prophets."[7]

Here we have a structure representing the history of revelation. Each prophet forms an integral, organic part, with Prophet Muhammad simply bringing to completion the divine message to humanity. Being part of the same
structure means they all have had the same theological message; it is their
followers who are responsible for post-revelational[8] theological differences,
especially ones that create political structures that systematically discriminate against the other. There is no "Thou shalt establish a nation-state!" It is
anachronistic to think that the Bible or The Holy Qur'an advocates the latter, or that they sanction institutionalized discrimination. Muslims believe
in all the prophets (there are twenty-five names mentioned in the Qur'an
including Abraham, Moses, David, and Jesus) and believe in their original
revealed books. The Qur'an and the Sunnah of the Prophet include direct
verses and traditions that open the door for numerous inclusive religious,
political, social, and business relations.

---

7. Al-Bukhari, *Sahih al-Bukhari*, vol 4, book 56 #735, and Al-Nisaburi, *Sahih Muslim*, book 30, #5673.

8. The Islamic worldview states that all prophets advocated the same theological
message stressing the oneness of God, yet allowing room for some differences, such as
Sabbath being required of the People of the Book, but not of Muslims. Nevertheless,
some of the followers of each prophet, in their attempt to explain revealed scripture,
when available, still ended up creating post-revelational theological and legal constructs
that did not always remain faithful to the original message. This explains not only the
emergence of internal differences that led to the creation of various sects within each
religion, but also the gaps that exist between these religions too.

The following passage from The Holy Qur'an is probably the most theologically inclusive verse found in the world's sacred texts in opening the door for salvation to the followers of previous prophets. Understandably, it is conditioned upon belief in the oneness of God and singling him out for worship; in other articles of faith, including belief in the afterlife in which one is held accountable; and in leading a moral life in line with revelation that shapes the relationship between people, something from which the followers of Prophet Muhammad are not exempt:

> Indeed, those who believed and those who were Jews or Christians or Sabeans [before Prophet Muhammad]—those [among them] who believed in Allah and the Last Day and did righteousness—will have their reward with their Lord, and no fear will there be concerning them, nor will they grieve (The Holy Qur'an 2:62).

This is why I developed an "Islamic Theology of Soft Otherness": The Qur'an prevents the total *othering* of Jews and Christians and names them "People of the Book" because their prophets received revealed books. Islam promotes *conviventia* between Muslims and members of the two other faiths based on sharing commonalities in theology, law, and ethics, despite some serious differences that are mostly post-revelational. In practice, the Jews and Christians enjoy a special status in The Holy Qur'an and the Prophetic traditions, permitting intermarriage with the chaste women of the People of the Book without their conversion, sharing a meal (literally, "the food of the People of the Book is lawful to Muslims"),[9] and doing business transactions and having partnership with them as the Prophet himself did.[10] This leads to a healthy social fabric, where a religious community has a larger place in which it feels at home. A Qur'anic verse requires utmost politeness when addressing the People of the Book:

> And do not argue with the People of the Book except in a way that is best, except for those who commit injustice among them, and say, "We believe in that which has been revealed to us and revealed to you. And our God and your God is one; and we are Muslims [in submission] to Him" (The Holy Qur'an 29:46).

In fact, the People of the Book in the Qur'an are entitled to the good treatment called *birr*, the same Arabic word used to describe being good to parents, as long as the relationship between both sides is peaceful. (Today this includes respect for international law, without precluding the possibility

9. The Holy Qur'an 5:5.
10. Al-Bukhari, *Sahih Al-Bukhari*, # 2366.

of improvement such as making the UN Security Council democratic by removing the "veto rights," a "right" that has helped keep the Palestinians under Israeli occupation for decades, because superpowers, including the U.S., vetoed resolutions that could have helped to bring this conflict to an end.) This call for good treatment of the other is clear:

> Allah does not forbid you from being righteous toward and acting justly toward those who do not fight you because of religion and do not expel you from your homes. Indeed, Allah loves those who act justly (The Holy Qur'an 60:8).

The Qur'an is anything but a self-centered book. Had it been a human creation, it should have an exclusive narrative with Prophet Muhammad being the protagonist. Rather, Prophet Moses is mentioned in The Holy Qur'an about one hundred thirty-nine times while Prophet Muhammad is mentioned only four times. As for Jesus Christ, who is mentioned much more than Prophet Muhammad, suffice it to note the following verse, which reflects an important aspect of his status:

> [Mention] when Allah said, "O Jesus, indeed I will take you and raise you to Myself and purify you from those who disbelieve and make those who follow you superior to those who disbelieve until the Day of Resurrection. Then to Me is your return, and I will judge between you concerning that in which you used to differ" (The Holy Qur'an 3:55).

Yes, this verse appears in The Holy Qur'an, which has an interesting Christology. Muslims love Jesus and Mary, albeit without divinization. In fourteen hundred years of Islamic scholarly literature, not a single negative word is said about either. The Holy Qur'an views Christians as being closer than other communities in amiability:

> . . . and you will find the nearest of them in affection to the believers those who say, "We are Christians." That is because among them are priests and monks and because they are not arrogant (The Holy Qur'an 5:82).

The Qur'anic teachings of acceptance of the People of the Book carry over into practice. The first important inclusive historical covenant, which became known as the "Constitution of Medina," began with the Jewish tribe of Bani 'Awf:

> And the Jews of [the tribe] of Bani 'Awf [establish] one *Ummah* (worldwide community) with the Muslims, to the Jews their religion, and to the Muslims their religion. . . ."[11]

Then the covenant went on to list all the Jewish tribes that existed in and around Medina. They were autonomous, except when there was a general threat to the newly established community, at which time their help was to be enlisted.

As for the Christians, the first major historical event involved a delegation of the Christians of Najran, who came on camels from the southwestern Arabian peninsula near Yemen, covering more than a thousand kilometers, a journey that could take up to two weeks of travel in the harsh weather of the desert. According to Ibn Hisham (d. 218 AH/833 CE), the delegation of the Christians of Najran arrived in the afternoon and entered the mosque when the Prophet was done with afternoon prayer, at which time they needed to pray. Prophet Muhammad permitted them to pray inside the mosque, and they prayed in the direction of the east.[12] By taking Jewish and Christian students and groups to mosques, I am simply following the footsteps of the Prophet.

Shifting the focus from Medina to Jerusalem and from Prophet Muhammad to 'Umar Ibn Al-Khattab, the second caliph, we see that the inclusive spirit continues. Regarding the Christians of Jerusalem, it was 'Umar Ibn Al-Khattab himself who concluded the first interfaith covenant with Patriarch Sophronius to protect churches and the right to free worship. One of the most relevant events for us here comes from the story of the caliph's visit to the Church of the Holy Sepulcher. Patriarch Sophronius invited him to pray inside the church, but 'Umar declined, citing possible future claims by Muslims to the site as a right had he prayed inside.[13]

Regarding the Jews, the Cairo Geniza Jewish manuscripts state that it was 'Umar Ibn Al-Khattab himself who allowed the Jews back into Jerusalem, after they had been deprived of living in the holy city for more than five centuries. A fragment published by S. Assaf in *The Beginnings of the Jewish Community in Jerusalem after the Arab Conquest* includes the following note: "The meeting of the Jews with Caliph 'Umar Ibn Al-Khattab states that the Jews requested and received from him permission to settle in the southern part of the city . . ."[14]

---

11. Ibn Hisham, *Al-Sirah Al-Nabawiyyah*, 2:106.

12. Ibid., 2:199.

13. Al-Aref, *Al-Mufassal fi Tarikh Al-Quds*, 96–99.

14. Gil, "The Jewish Quarters," 262.

Neither the inclusiveness expressed in The Holy Qur'an nor the long history of shared relationships among Muslims, Christians, and Jews has been replicated by Zionists. The first paper I wrote on the topic of Zionism was prepared when I was a student of Professor Hanna Muslih at Bethlehem University. It differentiated among the Hebrews, Israelites, Jews, and Zionists, making clear that the ancient peoples and indeed many contemporary Jews are not Zionists. I still differentiate among these categories; however, my own life has led me to the harsh criticism that is intended as a cry for justice. We Palestinians continue to extend our hands for peace with Jews who desire justice for all people, but we cannot accept a narrative that is alien to us and contradicts our own experience.

Some key events in my life include my time as a student at Bethlehem University during the first *intifada* (uprising) in the 1980s. Even then, some of us commemorated those who had died in the Holocaust although the Israeli occupation forces had shut down Palestinian universities in the West Bank for extended periods of time as collective punishment. Classes took place in the olive groves because faculty and students could not meet inside the campus, and the army searched for these "illegal" classes to prevent them. They also shot students inside the Bethlehem University campus from the rooftop of a building across the street. Yes, the students demonstrated against the Israeli occupation and at times threw stones at armored Israeli military vehicles, perhaps scratching the paint, but we remained mindful of the historical suffering of the Jewish people. Our target was the illegal occupation, not the Jewish people. Ironically, the Palestinian slingshot against the mighty Israeli army was nothing short of a new David confronting the one who had become a nuclear Goliath.

When I became an instructor at Bethlehem University, Abu Srur, a very gentle student of mine from the nearby Aida Palestinian refugee camp, was killed inside our campus. At the time of his death, a paper he had written caused me deep grief because I could never return it. Our Palestinian story reflects these memories of the effects of Zionism, for which we paid and continue to pay a heavy price. While Zionism aimed at establishing a protected national home for the Jews in Palestine, the other side of the coin is that Zionism left Palestinians without protection. Those who could have offered them protection did not. The new State of Israel was granted impunity by the Western powers. The international community and the UN failed to provide protection for the Palestinians in 1948–49, and they were unable to implement UN resolutions in favor of the Palestinians. Over half of the Palestinians were driven from their homes in 1948–49 by the Zionist militias and after April (1948) by the Israeli Defense Forces.

Not much has changed in Zionism's purpose since Israel was born: maximum Palestinian land and minimum Palestinian people. What has changed is the modality: crude brutal force at the beginning continues, now supplemented by laws that make sure the same results are achieved.

The Palestinian narrative is one of ongoing suffering. Hundreds, if not thousands, of Palestinian and other Arab children in places like Qana, Lebanon, have been killed by the Israeli military over the years. I cannot but question the impact of language such as that of Psalm 137:9 addressed to the Edomites ("Happy shall he be who takes your little ones and dashes them against the rock!") and of Joshua 6 (the massacre at Jericho), nor can I accept the words advocating crushing babies against rocks and the genocide in Jericho as divinely revealed or inspired. Today, the same children who are killed across the Middle East and beyond are defined as "collateral damage"! However, children as well as adults in the Middle East and elsewhere are also sometimes killed by Muslims who act in violation of the message of Islam. Islam stresses the dignity of the human being and sanctity of life, but Islam allows self-defense, which should be limited to its defensive purpose. This is a moral imperative. No civilians of any age group or background should be targeted. The Qur'an itself uses indirect speech to permit Muslims to defend themselves in what appears to be a last resort after being persecuted by the people of Mecca for thirteen years, and after the Meccans had followed them all the way to Medina to annihilate the nascent Muslim community. The following verse reflects this permission and contextualizes it:

> Permission [to fight] has been given to those who are being fought, because they were wronged. And indeed, Allah is competent to give them victory. [They are] those who have been evicted from their homes without right—only because they say, "Our Lord is Allah." And were it not that Allah checks the people, some by means of others, there would have been demolished monasteries, churches, synagogues, and mosques in which the name of Allah is much mentioned. And Allah will surely support those who support Him. Indeed, Allah is Powerful and Exalted in Might (The Holy Qur'an 22:39–40).

It should be noted that even when the context warrants self-defense, it does not mean that this self-defense has to be violent.

This limited approval of self-defense in The Holy Qur'an contrasts sharply with the many forms of Zionist repression of Palestinians. Denial of Palestinian life is evident in the fact that many pre-Israel Palestinian villages within Israel are even today considered "unrecognized villages" because if Israel recognizes a village, it must provide basic services and cannot confiscate the village land. The latest attempt by the Israeli lawmakers in the Knesset to remove Palestinians with Israeli citizenship from their own villages is called the Prawer-Begin bill. If it becomes law, nearly thirty thousand Bedouins will be forced to move to communities in the Negev recognized by Israel, and thus they will be relocated, as MK Ahmad Tibi noted, for the second or third time since 1948. It should be noted that the Prawer-Begin bill won a slim Knesset majority in the first reading. This is an important indicator that not all Israelis have the same ideological background and that it might be possible to defeat the bill if there is a strong international outcry protesting these Israeli policies.

Unfortunately, inside the West Bank, the Israeli occupation's hands are even freer in oppression. The Jahalin Bedouin, who live on a land confiscated to create the Maale Adumim string of settlements east of Jerusalem, have been forced to relocate several times. The latest attempt to move them one final time to the Abu Dis dumping site is on hold but not cancelled. There is an Israeli military order to demolish their shacks and tents, as well as their school, which is made out of used tires and mud.[15] Every time I drive behind a Jerusalem municipality dumpster truck on my way to the Al-Quds University campus in Abu Dis, I think of how the Israeli occupation is polluting the West Bank and destroying its environment.

These ongoing dislocations of Palestinians began in 1948 and are typified on the southwestern side of Jerusalem, which witnessed a major demographic shift that left no Palestinian in her home. The mountain in this area where the Israeli Holocaust Museum Yad Vashem is located is called *Har Hazekaron,* which can be translated as "Memory Mountain." But the memory is primarily a memory of a European time and space where the Jews were betrayed by their own countrymen and neighbors. In the valley beneath Yad Vashem, there is a garden dedicated to the "Righteous Among the Nations."[16] It is beautiful to recognize those who put their lives at risk to rescue Jews, yet missing from the picture is that the valley that hosts this garden belongs to a Palestinian village called Ein Karem, which was ethnically cleansed in 1948. This is a different memory, and it is not about Nazi Germany or the larger European context. This is a memory of a Palestinian people who are deeply rooted in history, culture, and land, a land that is pre-biblical.

It is important to remember that the idea of establishing a Jewish state in Palestine arose almost half a century before the Holocaust. Yes, there

15. Hass, "Bedouin Community Wins Reprieve."

16. Yad Vashem, "The Righteous Among the Nations," at http://www.yadvashem.org/yv/en/righteous/.

were pogroms in Russia and the Dreyfus affair in France, but the decision to create a national home for the Jews in Palestine was influenced by the emergence of the nation-state in Europe. Theodore Herzl himself was not ambiguous about what he had achieved in the First Zionist Congress: "In Basel, I founded the Jewish State."[17]

The very idea of nationhood is a problematic social construct that is uniquely complex in Israel because, while indigenous Palestinians are excluded or discriminated against, any Jew in the world is considered a citizen of "the Jewish state." Startling examples include a group of ninety Peruvians, predominantly native South Americans, who were converted to Judaism and became settlers in the West Bank settlement of Alon Shvut: "We are of Indian origin," says Nachshon Ben-Haim, formerly Pedro Mendosa, "but in Peru, in the Andes, there is no Indian culture left. Everyone has become Christian, and before we became Jews, we also were Christians who went to church."[18] The *Guardian* article that recounts their story continues by stating that the "creation of this community of new Jews has to be chalked up wholly and exclusively to the credit—or debit—of the chief rabbinate of Israel. At the order of the Ashkenazi chief rabbi, Israel Meir Lau, a delegation of rabbis travelled to Peru. During their two weeks in the country, they converted ninety people to Judaism, most of them of Indian origin."[19] After a two weeks' conversion process, they "returned" to Palestine!

Another example is more recent. Colombian evangelical Christians converted to Judaism: "For the families of Bello, the journey to Judaism began after the minister of a 3,000-member evangelical church, the Center for Integral Family Therapy, visited Israel in 1998 and 2003 and began to feel the pull of Judaism."[20] While it is time-consuming to convert to Judaism in Israel, it is done. The Colombians join the Peruvians in the feat of "returning" to Palestine.

Historical proselytizing to Judaism was more common. An excellent work on the subject is *The Invention of the Jewish People* by Shlomo Sand. Sand would go as far as arguing that the whole Exile story was an invention. While one could question the notion of "return" based on the logic of the Exile, it is more important to realize what kind of "return" was in the making and how it would impact the indigenous people of the land.

17. Herzl Museum, "First Zionist Congress: Basel 29–31 August 1897," at http://www.herzl.org/english/Article.aspx?Item=544.

18. Livneh, "How 90 Peruvians."

19. Ibid.

20. Ferero, "Colombian Evangelical Christians Convert."

People are free to believe that they form a distinct group, but once this group is privileged at the expense of other groups within the same society, not only is it discriminatory and unfair, but most importantly, it is against God's way. All peoples are equal in the divine plan for humanity, and God's oneness should be reflected in the unity of humanity. To elevate a people unconditionally as the "chosen" one and to use the state apparatus to discriminate against others while crediting God as the source of the injustices is idolatrous in nature. In fact, to put God on the same level as nation and state nullifies the otherness of God and chips away his transcendence. There is a strand of post-Holocaust Jewish theology that addresses God in a way that removes his otherness and reduces him to an actor that can be held accountable for what happened. God ought not and must not be questioned about his plan for humanity, but one can ask him for guidance to understand what is happening, knowing that he is Most Merciful. God does not reward people for what he has given them, nor does he condone injustices done in his name. All humanity goes back to common parents, and no genetic map is special. God loves that which is good and wholesome for humans, he wants them to be saved, and he is equally accessible to all human beings. People, on the other hand, can respond positively to revelation and distinguish themselves morally and ethically. Prophet Muhammad (peace be upon him) said in one of his very last traditions:

> O people! Verily, your God is One. Let it be known that an Arab is not preferable over a non-Arab, or a non-Arab over an Arab, or a red [Caucasian] over a black [person], or a black over a red [person], except in piety. The most distinguished among you in the sight of God, is the most pious.[21]

There is no doubt that Israel was established with the vision of giving preference to Jews in every aspect of life. Israel has complex machinery that privileges Jews and has built-in laws that systematically discriminate against Palestinians. These laws make null and void any claim to Israel's being a democracy. Those who are aware of the extent to which Israel discriminates against its own Arab citizens know that a Jewish democracy is an oxymoron. In its 2012 report, the Coalition Against Racism (CAR) states that Israel will not be a democracy until its laws reflect the equality of its Palestinian citizens and goes on to list thirty-five laws that discriminate against Palestinians with Israeli citizenship. CAR also cites discrimination against

21. Al-Albany, *Ghayat Al-Maram*, 190, Hadith # 313.

Sephardic (Mizrahi) and Ethiopian Jews, indicating white racism against Jewish people of color.[22]

A vivid example of the prohibitions imposed on Palestinian citizens of Israel is the *Nakba* Law. The term *Nakba* (Catastrophe) is widely used to designate the catastrophe experienced by Palestinians at the founding of the State of Israel in 1948. Although it was a seminal event in the life of the country, today it is illegal for Israeli schoolteachers to use the word *Nakba* or to commemorate it in any way. In March 2011, the Israeli Knesset passed amendment no. 40 (2011), which became known publicly as the "*Nakba* Law" and authorizes the finance minister to reduce state funding or support to an institution if it engages in an "activity that is contrary to the principles of the state." Relevantly, these activities include "rejecting the existence of the State of Israel as a Jewish and democratic state" and "commemorating Independence Day or the day of the establishment of the state as a day of mourning."[23] So much for the freedom of expression in Israel!

Hard Ethnic Cleansing

The village of Ein Karem on the western side of Jerusalem was mentioned earlier as one of the Palestinian villages destroyed and its land confiscated in 1948. In what follows, I would like to make it the focal point for understanding the changes that Zionism imposed on Palestine and the negative outcomes that continue to affect the Palestinians more than sixty-five years later. I could use as an example the well-known city of Haifa or the village of Deir Yassin, which is infamous for the massacre that took place there in 1948, but I want to choose an average Palestinian village that lived peacefully with its neighbors until 1948. The story of the ethnic cleansing of the millennia-old indigenous peoples of Ein Karem is a familiar story and is interwoven with that of many villages and cities in 1948. More than five hundred Palestinian villages were totally demolished and their Palestinian inhabitants ethnically cleansed in 1948, their inhabitants fleeing in many directions. Not a single original inhabitant of Ein Karem stayed on, but the buildings of Ein Karem remained intact, without, of course, the rightful owners themselves.[24]

22. The Coalition Against Racism, "The Main Findings," at http://www.fightracism.org/en/Article.asp?aid=241.

23. Abdel-Fattah, "Illegal Mourning."

24. For a complete survey, see Abu Sitta, *The Palestinian Nakba 1948*.

In 1945, three years before the *Nakba*, Ein Karem had a population of 3,180 (2,510 Muslims and 670 Christians).[25] Many Palestinians from Ein Karem fled in 1948 when they learned about the massacre of Deir Yassin, a village less than two miles away. Unlike Auschwitz, Deir Yassin has no explicit memorial to recognize the Palestinian victims. *Remembering Deir Yassin: The Future of Israel and Palestine* promotes the creation of such a memorial:

> Deir Yassin Remembered is an organization of Jews and non-Jews working to build a memorial at Deir Yassin on the west side of Jerusalem within sight of Yad Vashem. It was here in April 1948 that a peaceful Palestinian Arab village was attacked and conquered. After the village fell under Jewish control, more than a hundred were massacred. For Palestinians, this massacre has come to symbolize the destruction of Palestine.[26]

The introductory remarks continue to elaborate the intended aims of the memorial, which are intended to facilitate a change of thinking and to reject the myths that have been promulgated about Israeli and Palestinian history, including "a land without a people" and "the purity of arms."

Today, it is well established that not only was Palestine inhabited at the time of the founding of the State of Israel, but it is still inhabited by a few million Palestinians. Many of the Palestinians who fled their homes within the Green Line still live within a good walking distance or a short ride of their old homes and villages, but they have been accorded by the Israeli occupation a "legal" status that makes it impossible for them to reclaim their property. Gaza Strip and West Bank Palestinian residents can only dream about visiting their original homes.

The original inhabitants of Ein Karem typify this pattern of displacement. Following the massacre in 1948, no one remained in the village and most of the survivors fled to East Jerusalem. Of the original Palestinian inhabitants of Ein Karem who reside in their own ancestral land, only those who have official Jerusalem "residency" cards may visit the village freely, but they may not reclaim their property. The people of Ein Karem are real and remember Ein Karem as their home even now. One of my classmates in high school at the Arab Jordanian Institute in Abu Dis hails from Ein Karem, as does an imam at Al-Aqsa Mosque who helped me acquire a copy of a new edition of *Iyha' 'Ulum Al-Din* (*The Revival of the Islamic Sciences*), a book written by Imam Al-Ghazali (d. 1111) in which he aimed at capturing the original spiritual understanding of Islamic teachings. It is ironic that

25. Al-Khalidi, *All That Remains*, 269–70.

26. Ellis and McGowan, *Remembering Deir Yassin*, v.

another friend of mine in the U.S., who is an expert on Al-Ghazali, is also from Ein Karem.

Ein Karem had several family names before 1948, but there is an interesting trend among Palestinian refugees; many of them have adopted the name of their village or city as their true family name. Therefore, many people that I know from Ein Karem have taken the family name "Eikermawi" for themselves. Two falafel restaurants in East Jerusalem have the "Eikermawi" sign. Even the innocent chickpea, called "falafel," which probably predates the arrival of Palestinian Arabs and the Jews in Palestine, is now being advertised as "Israeli," which we see in the popular postcard of a falafel sandwich with a tiny Israeli flag inserted inside.

The attempt of Palestinian refugees to preserve the memory of their origin, including the use of the name, is not surprising. But what is surprising is that the world quickly forgot or was made to forget about the changes that Zionism has forced on the history and geography of Palestine. Ilan Pappé, after writing in *The Ethnic Cleansing of Palestine* about the systematic ethnic cleansing that took place during the *Nakba* of 1948, exclaimed:

> Imagine that not so long ago, in any given country that you are familiar with, half of the entire population had been forcibly expelled within a year, half of its villages and towns were wiped out, leaving behind rubble and stones. Imagine now the possibility that somehow this act will never make it to the history books and that all diplomatic efforts to solve the conflict that erupted in that country will totally sideline, if not ignore, this catastrophic event.[27]

Pappé considers the ethnic cleansing of Palestine as a "crime against humanity," and he was able to reconstruct the names of those who planned and executed the ethnic cleansing. They were headed by David Ben-Gurion, "in whose private home all early and later chapters in the ethnic cleansing story were discussed and finalized."[28] Pappé provides concrete examples of what happened in 1948, citing a statement in *Haaretz* in 2004 by Yitzhak Pundak, who participated in the ethnic cleansing of Palestinians:

> There were two hundred villages [in the front] and these were gone. We had to destroy them; otherwise we would have had Arabs here [namely, in the southern part of Palestine] as we have in the Galilee. We would have another million Palestinians.[29]

27. Pappé, *Ethnic Cleansing*, 9.
28. Ibid., 5.
29. Ibid., 6.

Moshe Dayan also participated in the ethnic cleansing and saw the rise of Jewish villages in the place of Arab villages. His address to Technion University students in Haifa on March 19, 1969, was reported in *Haaretz*, April 4, 1969:

> You don't even know the names [of the previous Arab villages] and I don't blame you, because those geography books aren't around anymore. Not only the books, the villages aren't around. Nahalal was established in the place of Mahalul, and Gvat was established in the place of Jibta, Sarid in the place of Huneifis and Kfar Yehoshua in the place of Tel Shaman. There isn't any place that was established in an area where there had not at one time been an Arab population.[30]

Even the longer remarks attributed to Dayan, in which he notes that part of the land was bought from the Arabs, do not explain why that purchase would lead to changing the Arab names of all the villages or why the Palestinians cannot return to their land and homes that were not sold. Arab property accounted for close to 94.5 percent of total owned land in Palestine up until 1948, and those landowners still cherish the dream of returning home.

About the year 2000, I visited an ethnically cleansed village within the Green Line. It was surrounded by barbed wire at some point after 1948, with "Military Zone" signs attached to the barbed wire. The village remained as it was, except that the roofs of all houses had collapsed; some of the trees had fruit despite the years of negligence. There was no strategic military significance about the village, except for the sign, the purpose of which was to keep Palestinians, especially its original inhabitants, from returning.

Israel invented the Absentee Property Law to confiscate the land and property of Palestinian refugees or those who were deemed legally to be absent. Now Israel wants to expand the law to include East Jerusalem. The following story of the Ayyad family, in the village of Abu Dis just east of Jerusalem, shows not only the absurdity of the law but also the destructive intentions of the Israeli occupation. Ali Ayyad tells the story:

> In July, 2013, the Israeli Supreme Court discussed whether or not they should consider my family and me absentee owners. I was born in Abu Dis, and I live barely 300 meters from my childhood home there—and yet, under Israel's 1950 Absentee Property Law, I can be considered an absentee owner, and my property can be confiscated by the state.[31]

30. Quoted by Said, *The Question of Palestine*, 14.

31. Ayyad, "Palestinian Property, Absent Justice."

The path of the separation wall, which violates international law and which many call the "apartheid wall," is designed to confiscate and hold the maximum possible land west of the wall and keep the maximum number of Palestinians east of the wall.

Soft Ethnic Cleansing

The problem before us is the fact that the ethnic cleansing of Palestine did not stop after 1948. Laws, not guns this time, are being used to get rid of Palestinians. In *Haaretz*, Akiva Eldar wrote an article entitled "Israel admits it revoked residency rights of a quarter million Palestinians," where he states:

> Israel stripped more than 100,000 residents of Gaza and some 140,000 residents of the West Bank of their residency rights during the 27 years between its conquest of the territories in 1967 and the establishment of the Palestinian Authority in 1994. As a result, close to two hundred fifty thousand Palestinians who left the territories were barred from ever returning . . . . Many of those prevented from returning were students or young professionals, working abroad to support their families.[32]

As for Palestinian Jerusalemites, the revocation of residency continues unabated. The only thing that differs from year to year is the number of Palestinians who lose their IDs and get expelled from the city of their birth simply because their center of life is not Israel anymore. B'Tselem, the respected Israeli human rights watch group, reports the highest number in any given year was 2008, when the Israeli Ministry of the Interior revoked the IDs of 4,577 Palestinians from East Jerusalem.[33] Had this taken place in one day, there would be an outcry all over the world. People and governments around the world would have taken notice, and probably the fate of those East Jerusalemites would be different.

Now, those Palestinian "former" residents of Jerusalem need a tourist visa to visit Jerusalem, the city of their birth, and to see their extended families, who are indigenous to this city. The irony is that the revocation of the ID could take place at the hands of an Israeli immigrant who does not even have a family in Jerusalem.

Translating numbers into real stories reflects the pain that Palestinian families go through. I have Christian and Muslim friends who have lost

---

32. Eldar, "Israel Admits It Revoked."

33. B'Tselem, "Statistics on Revocation of Residency in East Jerusalem," at http://www.btselem.org/jerusalem/revocation_statistics.

their Jerusalem IDs. I have first cousins, too, who were subjected to this tragedy, but I have to admit that the most painful story to us as a family is that of our eldest son, Mahmoud, who lost his Jerusalem ID.

Mahmoud was born in Jerusalem, raised on the slopes of the Mount of Olives, went to the Ivrea Sisters Kindergarten just outside Herod's Gate, and studied in his first year of elementary school at the Collège des Frères in the Old City of Jerusalem just inside New Gate. As do all parents, my wife and I cherished every moment raising Mahmoud, never thinking that our moving to the U.S. as a family when I studied for my M.A. and Ph.D. at Boston College would lead one day to depriving Mahmoud of something that most people on earth take for granted. Mahmoud finished elementary school and went to middle school in Boston. It was only natural for him and his siblings (two of whom were born in Boston) to belong simultaneously to two different geographical places. They were at home in the U.S. and in Palestine. Wearing the black and white Palestinian keffiyeh and the New England Patriots' T-shirt did not feel contradictory. Our children followed the Celtics and the Red Sox games enthusiastically. We simply loved Boston, and we were at home.

I graduated from Boston College, and after my teaching for three years in Malaysia, we returned to Jerusalem. Mahmoud graduated from Bridge Academy, a high school in Jerusalem that was established to cater to American-Palestinian children. Most graduates from this school went back to the U.S. for further education, and so Mahmoud followed suit. After studying in Denver, he returned to Jerusalem to work. For eighteen months he tried very hard, but he could only find odd jobs from time to time, despite being very qualified in management, as the days would prove later on. There is a glass ceiling for the Palestinians. It was heartbreaking to see Mahmoud, who radiates positive energy and who could heal a whole town with his warm smile, slipping into depression!

Then one day he asked for my blessings to return to the U.S. I felt I was being selfish to think only about the possibility of Mahmoud's losing his ID, as he now has done. He was following his dream, but was it necessary for the Israelis to punish him for that by revoking his ID? Why not treat Palestinians from East Jerusalem as the 750,000 Israeli Jews who live overseas are treated without being subjected to this inhumane policy? Why pass these discriminatory laws that cripple our youngsters? What right does Israel have to create these laws in the first place? I am sure of Mahmoud's credentials as a Jerusalemite, but I am not sure of the credentials of those who sit in the Israeli Ministry of the Interior offices in East Jerusalem.

Palestinians from East Jerusalem dread living outside their own city, but many cannot afford to pay the rent or, even worse, to pay the prohibitive fees to get a building permit. They move to nearby West Bank towns and cities such as Bethany, which is only a couple of miles to the east of the Old City, but that is enough grounds ultimately to revoke the Jerusalem ID.

Stealth Ethnic Cleansing

The mountain near Yad Vashem that overlooks Ein Karem is called Mount Herzl, named after one of the most important founders of the political Zionist movement. The only original name of a mountain in that area that I know from the annals of history is Ras El-Tuteh, "Head of the Berry [Tree]," where Hadassah Hospital was built. Theodore Herzl, founder of the World Zionist Organization, for whom the mountain is named, made a very problematic entry in his diary when he spoke about the necessity of removing the indigenous people beyond the border:

> When we occupy the land, we shall bring immediate benefits to the state that receives us. We must expropriate gently the private property on the estates assigned to us. We shall try to spirit the penniless population across the border by procuring employment for it in the transit countries, while denying it any employment in our country. The property owners will come over to our side. *Both the process of expropriation and the removal of the poor must be carried out discreetly and circumspectly* [italics mine]. Let the owners of immovable property believe that they are cheating us, selling us things for more than they are worth. But we are not going to sell them anything back. It goes without saying that we shall respectfully tolerate persons of other faiths and protect their property, their honor, and their freedom with the harshest means of coercion. This is another area in which we shall set the entire old world a wonderful example. . . . Estate owners who are attached to their soil . . . will be offered a complete transplantation—to any place they wish, like our own people. . . . If this offer is not accepted either, no harm will be done. . . . We shall simply leave them there. . . .[34]

This alleged respect for persons of other faiths ("we shall respectfully tolerate persons of other faiths and protect their property, their honor, and their freedom") is an illusion. Christians and Muslims do not have free access to their places of worship in the Old City of Jerusalem. For the Muslims, there is an age restriction; Muslim men must be fifty years of age or older to be able to enter the Al-Aqsa Mosque on occasion. The Israeli police and the

34. Herzl, *Complete Diaries*, June 12, 1895.

Israeli military Border Police check IDs, looking for the year of birth, and calculate the age. For the year 2013, one has to have been born in or before 1963.[35]

The essence of Herzl's plan is to make life for the Palestinians so miserable that they would wish to leave on their own. Did Zionism succeed in making the Palestinians unhappy? The World Happiness Report 2013 ranks the Scandinavian countries in the top ten positions. I understand why these neighbors are all doing well. Then Israel is ranked number eleven, and the Palestinian Territory is ranked 113.[36] Why would two peoples who live on the same very small piece of land, which looks more and more like Swiss cheese because of the settlements, have such a dramatic gap between them on the index of happiness (or misery)?

On Mount Herzl is the site of the Jewish National Cemetery, where the remains of Herzl were brought from Vienna to be re-interred in 1949 in accordance with his will. The Israeli leaders respected Herzl's wish to be buried here, but they disturbed the peace of those who already had been buried nearby, a perverse form of ethnic cleansing. Many Muslim cemeteries have been desecrated over the years within the Green Line. The most striking example that reflects the ethos prevailing in the Israeli Jerusalem municipality, the Israeli government, and the Israeli court system, is that of the Museum of Tolerance, which received a legal permit to be built on top of the historical Muslim cemetery of Mamilla (Ma'manillah) in Jerusalem, a few minutes' walk to the northwest of Jaffa Gate.

Rabbi Hier from the Simon Wiesenthal Center in Los Angeles got the necessary permits to build and broke the ground for a place to be called the "Museum of Tolerance." Of course, breaking the ground at that location yielded bones. Hundreds of boxes were filled with exhumed bones, which were transferred somewhere else. It should be noted that while many rabbis and secular Jews opposed this "Museum of Tolerance," Nir Barakat, the Mayor of Jerusalem, wrote a letter to the Wiesenthal Center, stating:

> The Museum of Tolerance Jerusalem (MOTJ) is set to expand the understanding of tolerance amongst peoples, faiths, and communities from the heart of Jerusalem, a city where people of all religions and backgrounds live together, practicing their

35. Occupied Palestine, "Israeli Police Restrict Entry of Worshipers into Al-Aqsa Mosque," March 22, 2013, at http://occupiedpalestine.wordpress.com/2013/03/22/israeli-police-restrict-entry-of-worshipers-into-al-aqsa-mosque-2/.

36. Helliwell, et al., eds., *World Happiness Report 2013*. Chapter Seven of the *World Happiness Report* provides a detailed description and rationale for the careful methodology employed in its survey and the interpretation of data.

faith freely. The city of Jerusalem is working together with the representatives of the museum in developing the site. . . . The MOTJ is rooted in the enduring Jewish values that advance human dignity and social justice. . . . All friends of Jerusalem should support this great project.[37]

While a mayor might lack good judgment and even make drastic mistakes, those in higher offices have the responsibility to correct significant errors in judgment. However, the top Israeli official, Prime Minister Benjamin Netanyahu, sent a letter on February 20, 2011, including the following paragraphs:

I want to commend all of you at the Simon Wiesenthal Center for your decision to build a Museum of Tolerance in Jerusalem. . . . Recently Rabbi Hier, my good friend, came to visit me. He is absolutely irrepressible; you can't stop him. And I had the opportunity to understand from Rabbi Hier the remarkable vision behind the unique project. What is remarkable is not only the impressive design of the Center, but more importantly what you intend to do inside it. This cultural and education Center which promotes the ideals of universal tolerance and respect will give visitors a better understanding of the history of our people as well as an appreciation of the need to protect the shared values that are so vital to our common future. . . . [T]hese values of tolerance and respect for human rights are so vital to our common future.[38]

Former President Clinton added his support too, and the list of Israeli politicians who had *no problem* with the Museum of Tolerance being built on a cemetery that had been in use until 1948 includes Israeli President Shimon Peres. The Wiesenthal Center website has the following statement by Peres: "The Jerusalem Museum of Tolerance will contribute significantly to this many-faceted city and represent the moral values that guided the people of Zion through the ages."[39] The Wiesenthal Center website's motto for the Museum of Tolerance is "Promoting Jewish Unity, Universal Respect, and Coexistence"! It is for Jews to decide on the validity of the first part as to whether the museum promotes Jewish unity, but to believe that this Museum of Tolerance promotes universal respect and coexistence is virtually impossible.

37. "Letter from Jerusalem Mayor Nir Barakat," Simon Wiesenthal Center, at http://www.wiesenthal.com/site/pp.asp?c=lsKWLbPJLnF&b=5505225#.UiYcXxaMGRZ.

38. "Remarks by Benjamin Netanyahu, Prime Minister," ibid.

39. Ibid.

It should be noted that another part of the Mamilla cemetery was used to establish the Israeli Independence Park. These "moral values" that the Israeli President speaks about have allowed the desecration and misuse of mosques for mundane and offensive purposes since 1948, including mosques that have been transformed into museums, taverns, barns, and a carpentry shop. These actions are examples of subtle but ongoing ethnic cleansing under the umbrella of Zionism.

Theological Conclusions

In The Holy Qur'an, when Abraham is invited to come to the Holy Land, the language used is inclusive: "We delivered him and [his nephew] Lot [and directed them] to the land which We have blessed *for the nations*" (The Holy Qur'an 21:71). This translation of "nations" in the plural is consistent with the original Arabic. In opposition to the Israeli occupation, which is based on a Zionist view that the land is for the exclusive habitation of Jews from anywhere in the world, it establishes an inclusive theology that asserts that it is land for all peoples, certainly including the indigenous inhabitants. At this stage, we need political leaders whose moral values make them sensitive to the needs and rights of the various religious communities. We need political leaders who subscribe to the self-evident truth that all women and men are created equal and who will make sure that this equality is translated into policies, treaties, and laws.

Islamic theology, although it emphasizes the love of God, translates this love into justice for God's creatures. After investing more than twenty-five years in interfaith dialogue, I realize that despite the flow of good intentions in many of these meetings, the major issue should be how to address injustice. It is comfortable to ignore the fact that the Occupation is immoral and to have dialogues to discuss whether Abraham is our common father, but we need to remember that although Adam was the common father of Cain and Abel, this fact did not prevent the siblings from having a conflict, or rather, it did not prevent one brother from killing his own brother.

Am I my brother's keeper? Yes. Abraham never abused his relationship with God to appropriate land or to kill the people of Hebron. When he needed to bury Sarah, he was polite and humble, addressing the Hittites and saying in his plea for a place of burial: "I am a foreigner and stranger among you." He bought the cave and the field of Machpelah from Ephron the Hittite for four hundred silver shekels.[40] Abraham behaved like a civilized person, and

---

40. Gen 23:1–17 (NIV).

his true spiritual progeny are expected to behave in the same way. They do not understand the relationship with God and the Holy Land more than he did.

I was invited to a meeting with the Dalai Lama in Jerusalem on a visit sponsored by a Jewish-American philanthropist. The Dalai Lama was mostly silent during his visit, and not much was achieved, if anything. When the philanthropist asked what could be done about the Israeli-Palestinian conflict, I raised the issue of demolished Palestinian homes as an area where one could make a difference. There are tens of thousands of Palestinians who suffer from this inhumane policy. I suggested rebuilding these homes as a way to reach out to the Palestinians. Of course, no one was willing to consider taking this suggestion and to begin addressing it with concrete actions. It was an exercise only. Hundreds more homes have been demolished since then, and the conflict deepens. One cannot address all the negative impacts that Zionism has left on Palestinian life, but one can assert the key word for the solution: Justice!

Bibliography

Books and Articles

Abdel-Fattah, Randa. "Illegal Mourning: The Nakba Law and the Erasure of Palestine." *ABC*, May 17, 2013. http://www.abc.net.au/religion/articles/2013/05/17/3761661. htm.

Abu Sitta, Salman. *The Palestinian Nakba 1948: The Register of Depopulated Localities in Palestine*. London: Occasional Return Centre Studies, 2000.

Albany, Muhammad Naser Al-Din al-. *Ghayat Al-Maram*. Beirut: Al-Maktab Al-Islami, 1984.

Aref, Aref al-. *Al-Mufassal fi Tarikh Al-Quds*. Jerusalem: Al-Andalus/Fawzi Yusuf, 1999.

Ayyad, Ali. "Palestinian Property, Absent Justice." *Haaretz*, June 12, 2013. http://www. haaretz.com/opinion/.premium-1.529283.

Bayhaqi, Ahmad al-. *Sunan Al-Bayhaqi Al-Kubra*. Edited by Muhammad Ata. Mecca: Maktabat Dar Al-Baz, 1994.

Bukhari, Muhammad Ibn Isma`il al-. *Sahih al-Bukhari*. Damascus: Dar Ibn Kathir, 1993.

Eldar, Akiva. "Israel Admits It Revoked Residency Rights of a Quarter Million Palestinians." *Haaretz*, June 12, 2012. http://www.haaretz.com/news/diplomacy-defense/israel-admits-it-revoked-residency-rights-of-a-quarter-million-palestinians-1.435778.

Ellis, Marc, and Daniel McGowan, eds. *Remembering Deir Yassin: The Future of Israel and Palestine*. New York: Olive Branch, 1998.

Ferero, Juan. "Colombian Evangelical Christians Convert to Judaism, Embracing Hidden Past." *The Washington Post*, November 24, 2012. http://articles.washingtonpost. com/2012-11-24/world/35508360_1_jewish-identity-anusim-jewish-heritage.

Gapso, Shimon. "If You Think I'm a Racist, then Israel Is a Racist State." *Haaretz*, August 7, 2013. http://www.haaretz.com/opinion/1.540278.

Gil, Moshe. "The Jewish Quarters of Jerusalem (A.D. 638–1099) According to Cairo Geniza Documents and Other Sources." *Journal of Near Eastern Studies* 41:4 (October 1982) 261–78.

Hass, Amira. "Bedouin Community Wins Reprieve from Forcible Relocation to Jerusalem Garbage Dump." *Haaretz*, February 6, 2012. http://www.haaretz. com/print-edition/news/bedouin-community-wins-reprieve-from-forcible-relocation-to-jerusalem-garbage-dump-1.411248.

Helliwell, John, et al., eds. *World Happiness Report 2013.* New York: UN Sustainable Development Solutions Network, 2013. http://unsdsn.org/files/2013/09/WorldHappinessReport2013_online.pdf.

Herzl, Theodor. *Complete Diaries of Theodor Herzl.* New York: Herzl, 1960.

The Holy Qur'an. Meaning Translated by Aminah Assami, et al. Jeddah: Sahih International/Abu-Qasim, 1997.

Ibn Hisham, Abdul Malik. *Al-Sirah Al-Nabawiyyah.* Tanta: Dar Al-Sahabah Lit-Turath, 1995.

Khalidi, Walid al-. *All That Remains: The Palestinian Villages Occupied and Depopulated by Israel in 1948.* Washington, DC: Institute for Palestine Studies, 1992.

Livneh, Neri. "How 90 Peruvians Became the Latest Jewish Settlers." *The Guardian*, August 6, 2002. http://www.guardian.co.uk/world/2002/aug/07/israel1.

Nisaburi, Muslim Ibn Al-Hajjaj al-. *Sahih Muslim.* Riyadh: Dar Taybah, 2006.

Pappé, Ilan. *The Ethnic Cleansing of Palestine.* Oxford: Oneworld, 2006.

Portner, Ze'ev, and Amit Oz. "Israel Still Failing Martin Luther King's Dream." *Haaretz*, August 28, 2013. http://www.haaretz.com/opinion/.premium-1.543985.

Said, Edward. *The Question of Palestine.* New York: Vintage, 1992.

Sand, Shlomo. *The Invention of the Jewish People.* Translated by Yael Lotan. New York: Verso, 2009.

Websites

ABC. http://www.abc.news.au.

Adalah: The Legal Center for Arab Minority Rights in Israel. http://adalah.org/eng.

B'Tselem: The Israeli Information Center for Human Rights in the Occupied Territories. http://www.btselem.org.

The Coalition against Racism in Israel. http://www.fightracism.

Haaretz. http://www.haaretz.org.

Herzl Museum. http://www.herzl.org.

Occupied Palestine: Blogging 4 Human Rights and Liberation of Palestine. http://occupiedpalestine.wordpress.com.

Simon Wiesenthal Center. http://www.wiesenthal.com.

World Bulletin. http://www.worldbulletin.net.

Yad Vashem: The Holocaust Martyrs' and Heroes' Remembrance Authority. http://www.yadvashem.org.

Chapter Nine

A Concluding Theological Postscript

Naim S. Ateek

*The Rev. Dr. Naim Stifan Ateek, a Palestinian Anglican priest, is the founder and direc-
tor of the Sabeel Ecumenical Liberation Theology Center in Jerusalem, which has offices
and affiliates in many locations around the world. He is the author of* A Palestinian
Christian Cry for Reconciliation *(Orbis, 2008) and* Justice and Only Justice: A Palestinian Theology of Liberation *(Orbis, 1989).*

WE IN SABEEL WELCOME this study of Zionism because we agree with its
fundamental premise: Zionism *is* the problem. Zionism is a doctrine that
provides the State of Israel with a firm—even dogmatic—religio-national
identity justified by an appeal to God's will, to historical memory, and to
mythical racial ancestry. It provides many Jews in Israel and worldwide
with a deep-seated, emotionally powerful, personal and social identity. As
such, Zionism is a theologically infused ideology of Jewish identity that has
changed the course of Jewish life in the twentieth and twenty-first centuries.

Chapter Two of this book declares that there is a positive side to the
Zionist dream of creating "A New Jew." At the same time it also recognizes
what Palestinians uniformly claim: Zionism with its creation of "A New
Jew" has a dark side that has resulted in almost a century of Palestinian
humiliation, dispossession, and death.

The recent creation of a new Israeli government bureau entitled the
"Jewish Identity Administration" appears to be an attempt to strengthen the
dark side of Zionism at a time when Zionism is once again under attack

by the international human rights community and by thousands of Jews of conscience.[1]

For Palestinians and a growing number of internationals around the world it is clear that Zionism is *false theology* that drives our ongoing humiliation and dispossession by the Israeli government, with the active co-operation of the U.S. government and American Jewish communal organizations. Israel simply could not continue to do this without the support, encouragement, or silent acquiescence of the majority of Jewish Israelis and their Zionist supporters abroad.

In its evangelical Protestant manifestation, Zionism functions to justify and support this ongoing humiliation and dispossession, not primarily for the sake of Jews, but to hasten the return of Christ and the apocalyptic "End Times," in which Jews will be given their last opportunity to convert to Christ and be saved or to be condemned to Hell.

In its liberal Christian manifestations, Zionism serves as a "price-tag" theology providing Christians with a vehicle of repentance for the guilt accrued during centuries of European Christian anti-Semitism, which culminated in the Holocaust.

Kairos Palestine: A Moment of Truth,[2] is a document issued by Palestinian Christians in 2009. As a statement of faith and a call to action, it proclaims, "We . . . declare that the Israeli occupation of Palestinian land is a sin against God and humanity because it deprives the Palestinians of their basic human rights, bestowed by God. It distorts the image of God in the Israeli who has become an occupier just as it distorts this image in the Palestinian living under occupation." (*Kairos Palestine*, section 2.5).[3]

This word of faith is unique among Christian confessions in that its central theme, from start to finish, is Christ's command to love our enemies even while resisting the evil they visit upon us.

The tone of this document is simple, direct, and uncompromising. It declares the truth in stark terms, just as Palestinians experience it in our daily lives. We know how constant humiliation and deprivation distort the image of God in us, and with equal certainty, we see daily how the image of God is distorted in our oppressors, who often express pleasure and even humor in their cruelty.

---

1. Or Kashi, "Israel's new Jewish identity initiative based on fascist values, consultant warns," *Haaretz*, July 10, 2013, at http://www.haaretz.com/news/national/. premium-1.534791.

2. The document is reprinted as the appendix to this book. It is also available at http://www.kairospalestine.ps/sites/default/Documents/English.pdf.

3. Subsequent citations from *Kairos Palestine* in this chapter will list only the section and paragraph.

Kairos Palestine does not stop with the declaration of the Israeli occupation as a sin against God and humanity. It raises the stakes by proclaiming, "We declare that any theology, seemingly based on the Bible or on faith or on history, that legitimizes the occupation, is far from Christian teachings, because it calls for violence and holy war in the name of God Almighty, subordinating God to temporary human interests, and distorting the divine image in the human beings living under both political and theological injustice." (2.5)

Zionism commits *theological* injustice by its appeal to God, history, and race. Zionism claims the right to *Eretz Yisrael* on the basis of *Yahweh's* promises to the ancient Hebrew tribes in the Torah; the age-long dreams of religious Jews to return to Zion; and the erroneous claim that all Jews are racial descendants of the Israelites of biblical times. Thus, Zionism is considered "far from Christian teachings." The document states, "Therefore, we declare that any use of the Bible to legitimize or support political options and positions that are based upon injustice, imposed by one person on another, or by one people on another, transform religion into human ideology and strip the Word of God of its holiness, its universality and truth." (2.4)

The casual reader may miss the severity of these charges. It is the equivalent of declaring Zionism heretical, a doctrine that fosters both political and *theological* injustice. This is the strongest condemnation that a Christian confession can make against any doctrine that promotes death rather than life.

Of course, Christian theological statements have little merit in the eyes of non-Christians, Jews included, but such theological statements, made in the context of a confession of faith, commit the Christian churches to oppose the ideology in question as a matter of faithfulness to the Gospel. In the Christian church such condemnations carry the weight of a charge of heresy. When fellow Christians fall prey to theological injustice, churches have the right to punish the perpetrators with exclusion. This was the case with the Dutch Reformed Church in South Africa during the 1980s and 1990s.[4] When those of other religions fall prey to similar theological injustice, opposition, such as boycotts and divestment, is warranted. (4.2.6)

The implications of this condemnation are clear in the major sections dealing with faith, hope, and love. In *Kairos Palestine* these cardinal Christian virtues are regarded as both personal and social, *requiring* Christians to

---

4. In 1982 the World Alliance of Reformed Churches (WARC) excluded the white Dutch Reformed Church of South Africa until it ended its support for apartheid. It was only readmitted to WARC in 1998 after it repudiated this racist doctrine. See http://www.sahistory.org.za/dated-event/dutch-reformed-church-rejoins-world-alliance-reformed-churches.

oppose that which is evil and to carry out that opposition in a spirit of faith, hope, and love. *Faith* in God means that "it is our duty to liberate [this land] from the evil of injustice and war. It is God's land, and therefore it must be a land of reconciliation, peace, and love." (2.3.1) "*Hope* means not giving in to evil but rather standing up to it and continuing to resist it." (3.2) "*Love* is the commandment of Christ our Lord to us and it includes both friends and enemies. . . . Resistance is a right and duty for the Christian. But it is resistance with love as its logic. It is thus a creative resistance for it must find human ways that engage the humanity of the enemy. . . . Christ our Lord has left us an example we must imitate. We must resist evil, but he has taught us that we cannot resist evil with evil." (4.2; 4.2.3; 4.2.4)

This, therefore, is the challenge at hand. It is a challenge addressed directly to Christians around the world, to their churches and denominations, as well as to people of all faiths or no faith. It is a challenge that should confront all those who are concerned about a just peace in Israel-Palestine. It is a call for courage and action in taking a clear and uncompromising stand for justice by using all the nonviolent means available to stop the injustice and oppression perpetrated by the government of Israel against the Palestinian people. It is a call to do everything we can to end Israel's occupation of Palestine and to implement the requirements of international law so that their God-given human dignity can be restored to the Palestinian people and justice will be done. The words of the prophet Isaiah of long ago can then assume new meaning and relevance: ". . . and justice will produce lasting peace and security" (Isa 32:17 CEV).[5]

---

5. Scripture taken from the Contemporary English Version © 1991, 1992, 1995 by American Bible Society, Used by Permission.

Appendix One

Kairos Palestine

A Word of Faith, Hope, and Love from the Heart of Palestinian Suffering

2009

Patriarchs and Heads of Churches
Jerusalem
We hear the cry of our children

We, the Patriarchs and Heads of Churches in Jerusalem, hear the cry of hope that our children have launched in these difficult times that we still experience in this Holy Land. We support them and stand by them in their faith, their hope, their love and their vision for the future. We also support the call to all our faithful as well as to the Israeli and Palestinian Leaders, to the International Community and to the World Churches, in order to accelerate the achievement of justice, peace and reconciliation in this Holy Land. We ask God to bless all our children by giving them more power in order to contribute effectively in establishing and developing their community, while making it a community of love, trust, justice and peace.

His Beatitude Patriarch Theophilos III, Greek Orthodox
His Beatitude Patriarch Fouad Twal, Latin Church
His Beatitude Patriarch Torkom Manougian, Armenian Orthodox
Very Revd Father Pierbattista Pizzaballa, Custody of the Holy Land
H.E. Archbishop Dr Anba Abraham, Coptic

H.E. Archbishop Mar Swerios Malki Murad, Syrian Orthodox
H.E. Archbishop Paul Nabil Sayah, Maronite
H.E. Archbishop Abba Mathaious, Ethiopian
H.E. Archbishop Joseph-Jules Zerey, Greek Catholic
Bishop Gregor Peter Malki, Syrian Catholic
Bishop Munib A. Younan, Lutheran
Bishop Suheil Dawani, Anglican
Bishop Raphael Minassian, Armenian Catholic

Jerusalem, December 15, 2009

Kairos Palestine

This document is the Christian Palestinians' word to the world about what is happening in Palestine. It is written at this time when we wanted to see the Glory of the grace of God in this land and in the sufferings of its people. In this spirit the document requests the international community to stand by the Palestinian people who have faced oppression, displacement, suffering and clear apartheid for more than six decades. The suffering continues while the international community silently looks on at the occupying State, Israel. Our word is a cry of hope, with love, prayer and faith in God. We address it first of all to ourselves and then to all the churches and Christians in the world, asking them to stand against injustice and apartheid, urging them to work for a just peace in our region, calling on them to revisit theologies that justify crimes perpetrated against our people and the dispossession of the land.

In this historic document, we Palestinian Christians declare that the military occupation of our land is a sin against God and humanity, and that any theology that legitimizes the occupation is far from Christian teachings because true Christian theology is a theology of love and solidarity with the oppressed, a call to justice and equality among peoples.

This document did not come about spontaneously, and it is not the result of a coincidence. It is not a theoretical theological study or a policy paper, but is rather a document of faith and work. Its importance stems from the sincere expression of the concerns of the people and their view of this moment in history we are living through. It seeks to be prophetic in addressing things as they are without equivocation and with boldness, in addition it puts forward ending the Israeli occupation of Palestinian land and all forms of discrimination as the solution that will lead to a just and lasting peace with the establishment of an independent Palestinian state with Al-Quds as its capital. The document also demands that all peoples, political leaders and decision-makers put pressure on Israel and take legal measures in order to oblige its government to put an end to its oppression and disregard for the international law. The document also holds a clear position that non-violent resistance to this injustice is a right and duty for all Palestinians including Christians.

The initiators of this document have been working on it for more than a year, in prayer and discussion, guided by their faith in God and their love for their people, accepting advice from many friends: Palestinians, Arabs and those from the wider international community. We are grateful to our friends for their solidarity with us.

As Palestinian Christians we hope that this document will provide the turning point to focus the efforts of all peace-loving peoples in the world, especially our Christian sisters and brothers. We hope also that it will be welcomed positively and will receive strong support, as was the South Africa Kairos document launched in 1985, which, at that time proved to be a tool in the struggle against oppression and occupation. We believe that liberation from occupation is in the interest of all peoples in the region because the problem is not just a political one, but one in which human beings are destroyed.

We pray God to inspire us all, particularly our leaders and policy-makers, to find the way of justice and equality, and to realize that it is the only way that leads to the genuine peace we are seeking.

With thanks

- His Beatitude Patriarch Michel Sabbah

- His Eminence Archbishop Atallah Hanna

- Rev. Dr. Jamal Khader

- Rev. Dr. Rafiq Khoury

- Rev. Dr. Mitri Raheb

- Rev. Dr. Naim Ateek

- Rev. Dr. Yohana Katanacho

- Rev. Fadi Diab

- Dr. Jiries Khoury

- Ms. Cedar Duaybis

- Ms. Nora Kort

- Ms. Lucy Thaljieh

- Mr. Nidal Abu El Zuluf

- Mr. Yusef Daher

- Mr. Rifat Kassis—Coordinator

Note: You can review the list of Palestinian Christian institutions and personalities signed the document and copies in other languages on the following website: www.kairospalestine.ps

A Moment of Truth

*A Word of Faith, Hope, and Love from the Heart of
Palestinian Suffering*

Introduction

WE, A GROUP OF Christian Palestinians, after prayer, reflection and an exchange of opinion, cry out from within the suffering in our country, under the Israeli occupation, with a cry of hope in the absence of all hope, a cry full of prayer and faith in a God ever vigilant, in God's divine providence for all the inhabitants of this land. Inspired by the mystery of God's love for all, the mystery of God's divine presence in the history of all peoples and, in a particular way, in the history of our country, we proclaim our word based on our Christian faith and our sense of Palestinian belonging—a word of faith, hope and love.

Why now? Because today we have reached a dead end in the tragedy of the Palestinian people. The decision-makers content themselves with managing the crisis rather than committing themselves to the serious task of finding a way to resolve it. The hearts of the faithful are filled with pain and with questioning: What is the international community doing? What are the political leaders in Palestine, in Israel and in the Arab world doing? What is the Church doing? The problem is not just a political one. It is a policy in which human beings are destroyed, and this must be of concern to the Church.

We address ourselves to our brothers and sisters, members of our Churches in this land. We call out as Christians and as Palestinians to our religious and political leaders, to our Palestinian society and to the Israeli society, to the international community, and to our Christian brothers and sisters in the Churches around the world.

1. The reality on the ground

1.1 *"They say: 'Peace, peace' when there is no peace"* (Jer. 6:14). These days, everyone is speaking about peace in the Middle East and the peace process. So far, however, these are simply words; the reality is one of Israeli occupation of Palestinian territories, deprivation of our freedom and all that results from this situation:

1.1.1 The separation wall erected on Palestinian territory, a large part of which has been confiscated for this purpose, has turned our towns and villages into prisons, separating them from one another, making them dispersed and divided cantons. Gaza, especially after the cruel war Israel launched against it during December 2008 and January 2009, continues to live in inhuman conditions, under permanent blockade and cut off from the other Palestinian territories.

1.1.2 Israeli settlements ravage our land in the name of God and in the name of force, controlling our natural resources, including water and agricultural land, thus depriving hundreds of thousands of Palestinians, and constituting an obstacle to any political solution.

1.1.3 Reality is the daily humiliation to which we are subjected at the military checkpoints, as we make our way to jobs, schools or hospitals.

1.1.4 Reality is the separation between members of the same family, making family life impossible for thousands of Palestinians, especially where one of the spouses does not have an Israeli identity card.

1.1.5 Religious liberty is severely restricted; the freedom of access to the holy places is denied under the pretext of security. Jerusalem and its holy places are out of bounds for many Christians and Muslims from the West Bank and the Gaza strip. Even Jerusalemites face restrictions during the religious feasts. Some of our Arab clergy are regularly barred from entering Jerusalem.

1.1.6 Refugees are also part of our reality. Most of them are still living in camps under difficult circumstances. They have been waiting for their right of return, generation after generation. What will be their fate?

1.1.7 And the prisoners? The thousands of prisoners languishing in Israeli prisons are part of our reality. The Israelis move heaven and earth to gain the release of one prisoner, and those thousands of Palestinian prisoners, when will they have their freedom?

1.1.8 Jerusalem is the heart of our reality. It is, at the same time, symbol of peace and sign of conflict. While the separation wall divides Palestinian neighbourhoods, Jerusalem continues to be emptied of its Palestinian citizens, Christians and Muslims. Their identity cards are confiscated, which means the loss of their right to reside in Jerusalem. Their homes are demolished or expropriated. Jerusalem, city of reconciliation, has become a city of discrimination and exclusion, a source of struggle rather than peace.

1.2 Also part of this reality is the Israeli disregard of international law and international resolutions, as well as the paralysis of the Arab world and the international community in the face of this contempt. Human rights are violated and despite the various reports of local and international human rights' organizations, the injustice continues.

1.2.1 Palestinians within the State of Israel, who have also suffered a historical injustice, although they are citizens and have the rights and obligations of citizenship, still suffer from discriminatory policies. They too are waiting to enjoy full rights and equality like all other citizens in the state.

1.3 Emigration is another element in our reality. The absence of any vision or spark of hope for peace and freedom pushes young people, both Muslim and Christian, to emigrate. Thus the land is deprived of its most important and richest resource—educated youth. The shrinking number of Christians, particularly in Palestine, is one of the dangerous consequences, both of this conflict, and of the local and international paralysis and failure to find a comprehensive solution to the problem.

1.4 In the face of this reality, Israel justifies its actions as self-defence, including occupation, collective punishment and all other forms of reprisals against the Palestinians. In our opinion, this vision is a reversal of reality. Yes, there is Palestinian resistance to the occupation. However, if there were no occupation, there would be no resistance, no fear and no insecurity. This is our understanding of the situation. Therefore, we call on the Israelis to end the occupation. Then they will see a new world in which there is no fear, no threat but rather security, justice and peace.

1.5 The Palestinian response to this reality was diverse. Some responded through negotiations: that was the official position of the Palestinian Authority, but it did not advance the peace process. Some political parties followed the way of armed resistance. Israel used this as a pretext to accuse the Palestinians of being terrorists and was able to distort the real nature of the conflict, presenting it as an Israeli war against terror, rather than an Israeli occupation faced by Palestinian legal resistance aiming at ending it.

1.5.1 The tragedy worsened with the internal conflict among Palestinians themselves, and with the separation of Gaza from the rest of the Palestinian territory. It is noteworthy that, even though the division is among Palestinians themselves, the international community bears an important responsibility for it since it refused to deal positively with the will of the Palestinian people expressed in the outcome of democratic and legal elections in 2006.

Again, we repeat and proclaim that our Christian word in the midst of all this, in the midst of our catastrophe, is a word of faith, hope and love.

2. A word of faith

We believe in one God, a good and just God

2.1 We believe in God, one God, Creator of the universe and of humanity. We believe in a good and just God, who loves each one of his creatures. We believe that every human being is created in God's image and likeness and that every one's dignity is derived from the dignity of the Almighty One. We believe that this dignity is one and the same in each and all of us. This means for us, here and now, in this land in particular, that God created us not so that we might engage in strife and conflict but rather that we might come and know and love one another, and together build up the land in love and mutual respect.

2.1.1 We also believe in God's eternal Word, His only Son, our Lord Jesus Christ, whom God sent as the Saviour of the world.

2.1.2 We believe in the Holy Spirit, who accompanies the Church and all humanity on its journey. It is the Spirit that helps us to understand Holy Scripture, both Old and New Testaments, showing their unity, here and now. The Spirit makes manifest the revelation of God to humanity, past, present and future.

How do we understand the word of God?

2.2 We believe that God has spoken to humanity, here in our country: *"Long ago God spoke to our ancestors in many and various ways by the prophets, but in these last days God has spoken to us by a Son, whom God appointed heir of all things, through whom he also created the worlds"* (Heb. 1:1–2).

2.2.1 We, Christian Palestinians, believe, like all Christians throughout the world, that Jesus Christ came in order to fulfil the Law and the Prophets. He is the Alpha and the Omega, the beginning and the end, and in his light and with the guidance of the Holy Spirit, we read the Holy Scriptures. We meditate upon and interpret Scripture just as Jesus Christ did with the two disciples on their way to Emmaus. As it is written in the Gospel according to Saint Luke: *"Then beginning with Moses and all the prophets, he interpreted to them the things about himself in all the scriptures"* (Lk. 24:27).

2.2.2 Our Lord Jesus Christ came, proclaiming that the Kingdom of God was near. He provoked a revolution in the life and faith of all humanity.

He came with *"a new teaching"* (Mk. 1:27), casting a new light on the Old Testament, on the themes that relate to our Christian faith and our daily lives, themes such as the promises, the election, the people of God and the land. We believe that the Word of God is a living Word, casting a particular light on each period of history, manifesting to Christian believers what God is saying to us here and now. For this reason, it is unacceptable to transform the Word of God into letters of stone that pervert the love of God and His providence in the life of both peoples and individuals. This is precisely the error in fundamentalist Biblical interpretation that brings us death and destruction when the word of God is petrified and transmitted from generation to generation as a dead letter. This dead letter is used as a weapon in our present history in order to deprive us of our rights in our own land.

Our land has a universal mission

2.3 We believe that our land has a universal mission. In this universality, the meaning of the promises, of the land, of the election, of the people of God open up to include all of humanity, starting from all the peoples of this land. In light of the teachings of the Holy Bible, the promise of the land has never been a political programme, but rather the prelude to complete universal salvation. It was the initiation of the fulfilment of the Kingdom of God on earth.

2.3.1 God sent the patriarchs, the prophets and the apostles to this land so that they might carry forth a universal mission to the world. Today we constitute three religions in this land, Judaism, Christianity and Islam. Our land is God's land, as is the case with all countries in the world. It is holy inasmuch as God is present in it, for God alone is holy and sanctifier. It is the duty of those of us who live here, to respect the will of God for this land. It is our duty to liberate it from the evil of injustice and war. It is God's land and therefore it must be a land of reconciliation, peace and love. This is indeed possible. God has put us here as two peoples, and God gives us the capacity, if we have the will, to live together and establish in it justice and peace, making it in reality God's land: *"The earth is the Lord's and all that is in it, the world, and those who live in it"* (Ps. 24:1).

2.3.2 Our presence in this land, as Christian and Muslim Palestinians, is not accidental but rather deeply rooted in the history and geography of this land, resonant with the connectedness of any other people to the land it lives in. It was an injustice when we were driven out. The West sought to make amends for what Jews had endured in the countries of Europe, but it made amends on our account and in our land. They tried to correct an injustice and the result was a new injustice.

2.3.3 Furthermore, we know that certain theologians in the West try to attach a biblical and theological legitimacy to the infringement of our rights. Thus, the promises, according to their interpretation, have become a menace to our very existence. The "good news" in the Gospel itself has become "a harbinger of death" for us. We call on these theologians to deepen their reflection on the Word of God and to rectify their interpretations so that they might see in the Word of God a source of life for all peoples.

2.3.4 Our connectedness to this land is a natural right. It is not an ideological or a theological question only. It is a matter of life and death. There are those who do not agree with us, even defining us as enemies only because we declare that we want to live as free people in our land. We suffer from the occupation of our land because we are Palestinians. And as Christian Palestinians we suffer from the wrong interpretation of some theologians. Faced with this, our task is to safeguard the Word of God as a source of life and not of death, so that "the good news" remains what it is, "good news" for us and for all. In face of those who use the Bible to threaten our existence as Christian and Muslim Palestinians, we renew our faith in God because we know that the word of God can not be the source of our destruction.

2.4 Therefore, we declare that any use of the Bible to legitimize or support political options and positions that are based upon injustice, imposed by one person on another, or by one people on another, transform religion into human ideology and strip the Word of God of its holiness, its universality and truth.

2.5 We also declare that the Israeli occupation of Palestinian land is a sin against God and humanity because it deprives the Palestinians of their basic human rights, bestowed by God. It distorts the image of God in the Israeli who has become an occupier just as it distorts this image in the Palestinian living under occupation. We declare that any theology, seemingly based on the Bible or on faith or on history, that legitimizes the occupation, is far from Christian teachings, because it calls for violence and holy war in the name of God Almighty, subordinating God to temporary human interests, and distorting the divine image in the human beings living under both political and theological injustice.

3. Hope

3.1 Despite the lack of even a glimmer of positive expectation, our hope remains strong. The present situation does not promise any quick solution or the end of the occupation that is imposed on us. Yes, the initiatives, the conferences, visits and negotiations have multiplied, but they have not been followed up by any change in our situation and suffering. Even the new US position that has been announced by President Obama, with a manifest desire to put an end to the tragedy, has not been able to make a change in our reality. The clear Israeli response, refusing any solution, leaves no room for positive expectation. Despite this, our hope remains strong, because it is from God. God alone is good, almighty and loving and His goodness will one day be victorious over the evil in which we find ourselves. As Saint Paul said: *"If God is for us, who is against us? (. . .) Who will separate us from the love of Christ? Will hardship, or distress, or persecution, or famine, or nakedness, or peril, or sword? As it is written, "For your sake we are being killed all day long" (. . .) For I am convinced that (nothing) in all creation, will be able to separate us from the love of God"* (Rom. 8:31, 35, 36, 39).

What is the meaning of hope?

3.2 Hope within us means first and foremost our faith in God and secondly our expectation, despite everything, for a better future. Thirdly, it means not chasing after illusions—we realize that release is not close at hand. Hope is the capacity to see God in the midst of trouble, and to be co-workers with the Holy Spirit who is dwelling in us. From this vision derives the strength to be steadfast, remain firm and work to change the reality in which we find ourselves. Hope means not giving in to evil but rather standing up to it and continuing to resist it. We see nothing in the present or future except ruin and destruction. We see the upper hand of the strong, the growing orientation towards racist separation and the imposition of laws that deny our existence and our dignity. We see confusion and division in the Palestinian position. If, despite all this, we do resist this reality today and work hard, perhaps the destruction that looms on the horizon may not come upon us.

Signs of hope

3.3 The Church in our land, her leaders and her faithful, despite her weakness and her divisions, does show certain signs of hope. Our parish communities are vibrant and most of our young people are active apostles for justice and peace. In addition to the individual commitment, our various Church institutions make our faith active and present in service, love and prayer.

3.3.1 Among the signs of hope are the local centres of theology, with a religious and social character. They are numerous in our different Churches. The ecumenical spirit, even if still hesitant, shows itself more and more in the meetings of our different Church families.

3.3.2 We can add to this the numerous meetings for inter-religious dialogue, Christian–Muslim dialogue, which includes the religious leaders and a part of the people. Admittedly, dialogue is a long process and is perfected through a daily effort as we undergo the same sufferings and have the same expectations. There is also dialogue among the three religions, Judaism, Christianity and Islam, as well as different dialogue meetings on the academic or social level. They all try to breach the walls imposed by the occupation and oppose the distorted perception of human beings in the heart of their brothers or sisters.

3.3.3 One of the most important signs of hope is the steadfastness of the generations, the belief in the justice of their cause and the continuity of memory, which does not forget the "Nakba" (catastrophe) and its significance. Likewise significant is the developing awareness among many Churches throughout the world and their desire to know the truth about what is going on here.

3.3.4 In addition to that, we see a determination among many to overcome the resentments of the past and to be ready for reconciliation once justice has been restored. Public awareness of the need to restore political rights to the Palestinians is increasing, and Jewish and Israeli voices, advocating peace and justice, are raised in support of this with the approval of the international community. True, these forces for justice and reconciliation have not yet been able to transform the situation of injustice, but they have their influence and may shorten the time of suffering and hasten the time of reconciliation.

The mission of the Church

3.4 Our Church is a Church of people who pray and serve. This prayer and service is prophetic, bearing the voice of God in the present and future. Everything that happens in our land, everyone who lives there, all the pains and hopes, all the injustice and all the efforts to stop this injustice, are part and parcel of the prayer of our Church and the service of all her institutions. Thanks be to God that our Church raises her voice against injustice despite the fact that some desire her to remain silent, closed in her religious devotions.

3.4.1 The mission of the Church is prophetic, to speak the Word of God courageously, honestly and lovingly in the local context and in the midst of daily events. If she does take sides, it is with the oppressed, to stand alongside them, just as Christ our Lord stood by the side of each poor person and each sinner, calling them to repentance, life, and the restoration of the dignity bestowed on them by God and that no one has the right to strip away.

3.4.2 The mission of the Church is to proclaim the Kingdom of God, a kingdom of justice, peace and dignity. Our vocation as a living Church is to bear witness to the goodness of God and the dignity of human beings. We are called to pray and to make our voice heard when we announce a new society where human beings believe in their own dignity and the dignity of their adversaries.

3.4.3 Our Church points to the Kingdom, which cannot be tied to any earthly kingdom. Jesus said before Pilate that he was indeed a king but *"my kingdom is not from this world"* (Jn. 18:36). Saint Paul says: *"The Kingdom of God is not food and drink but righteousness and peace and joy in the Holy Spirit"* (Rom.14:17). Therefore, religion cannot favour or support any unjust political regime, but must rather promote justice, truth and human dignity. It must exert every effort to purify regimes where human beings suffer injustice and human dignity is violated. The Kingdom of God on earth is not dependent on any political orientation, for it is greater and more inclusive than any particular political system.

3.4.4 Jesus Christ said: *"The Kingdom of God is among you"* (Luke 17:21). This Kingdom that is present among us and in us is the extension of the mystery of salvation. It is the presence of God among us and our sense of that presence in everything we do and say. It is in this divine presence that we shall do what we can until justice is achieved in this land.

3.4.5 The cruel circumstances in which the Palestinian Church has lived and continues to live have required the Church to clarify her faith and to identify her vocation better. We have studied our vocation and have come to know it better in the midst of suffering and pain: today, we bear the strength of love rather than that of revenge, a culture of life rather than a culture of death. This is a source of hope for us, for the Church and for the world.

3.5 The Resurrection is the source of our hope. Just as Christ rose in victory over death and evil, so too we are able, as each inhabitant of this land is able, to vanquish the evil of war. We will remain a witnessing, steadfast and active Church in the land of the Resurrection.

4. Love

The commandment of love

4.1 Christ our Lord said: *"Just as I have loved you, you also should love one another"* (Jn 13:34). He has already showed us how to love and how to treat our enemies. He said: *"You have heard that it was said, 'You shall love your neighbour and hate your enemy.' But I say to you, Love your enemies and pray for those who persecute you, so that you may be children of your Father in heaven; for he makes his sun rise on the evil and on the good, and sends rain on the righteous and on the unrighteous (. . .) Be perfect, therefore, as your heavenly Father is perfect"* (Matt. 5:45–47).

Saint Paul also said: *"Do not repay anyone evil for evil"* (Rom. 12:17). And Saint Peter said: *"Do not repay evil for evil or abuse for abuse; but on the contrary, repay with a blessing. It is for this that you were called"* (1 Pet. 3:9).

Resistance

4.2 This word is clear. Love is the commandment of Christ our Lord to us and it includes both friends and enemies. This must be clear when we find ourselves in circumstances where we must resist evil of whatever kind.

4.2.1 Love is seeing the face of God in every human being. Every person is my brother or my sister. However, seeing the face of God in everyone does not mean accepting evil or aggression on their part. Rather, this love seeks to correct the evil and stop the aggression.

The aggression against the Palestinian people which is the Israeli occupation, is an evil that must be resisted. It is an evil and a sin that must be resisted and removed. Primary responsibility for this rests with the Palestinians themselves suffering occupation. Christian love invites us to resist it. However, love puts an end to evil by walking in the ways of justice. Responsibility lies also with the international community, because international law regulates relations between peoples today. Finally responsibility lies with the perpetrators of the injustice; they must liberate themselves from the evil that is in them and the injustice they have imposed on others.

4.2.2 When we review the history of the nations, we see many wars and much resistance to war by war, to violence by violence. The Palestinian people has gone the way of the peoples, particularly in the first stages of its struggle with the Israeli occupation. However, it also engaged in peaceful struggle, especially during the first Intifada. We recognize that all peoples must find a new way in their relations with each other and the resolution of their conflicts. The ways of force must give way to the ways of justice. This applies above all to the peoples that are militarily strong, mighty enough to impose their injustice on the weaker.

4.2.3 We say that our option as Christians in the face of the Israeli occupation is to resist. Resistance is a right and a duty for the Christian. But it is resistance with love as its logic. It is thus a creative resistance for it must find human ways that engage the humanity of the enemy. Seeing the image of God in the face of the enemy means taking up positions in the light of this vision of active resistance to stop the injustice and oblige the perpetrator to end his aggression and thus achieve the desired goal, which is getting back the land, freedom, dignity and independence.

4.2.4 Christ our Lord has left us an example we must imitate. We must resist evil but he taught us that we cannot resist evil with evil. This is a difficult commandment, particularly when the enemy is determined to impose himself and deny our right to remain here in our land. It is a difficult commandment yet it alone can stand firm in the face of the clear declarations of the occupation authorities that refuse our existence and the many excuses these authorities use to continue imposing occupation upon us.

4.2.5 Resistance to the evil of occupation is integrated, then, within this Christian love that refuses evil and corrects it. It resists evil in all its forms with methods that enter into the logic of love and draw on all energies to make peace. We can resist through civil disobedience. We do not resist with death but rather through respect of life. We respect and have a high esteem for all those who have given their life for our nation. And we affirm that every citizen must be ready to defend his or her life, freedom and land.

4.2.6 Palestinian civil organizations, as well as international organizations, NGOs and certain religious institutions call on individuals, companies and states to engage in divestment and in an economic and commercial boycott of everything produced by the occupation. We understand this to integrate the logic of peaceful resistance. These advocacy campaigns must be carried out with courage, openly sincerely proclaiming that their object is not revenge but rather to put an end to the existing evil, liberating both the perpetrators and the victims of injustice. The aim is to free both peoples from extremist positions of the different Israeli governments, bringing both to justice and reconciliation. In this spirit and with this dedication we will eventually reach the longed-for resolution to our problems, as indeed happened in South Africa and with many other liberation movements in the world.

4.3 Through our love, we will overcome injustices and establish foundations for a new society both for us and for our opponents. Our future and their future are one. Either the cycle of violence that destroys both of us or peace that will benefit both. We call on Israel to give up its injustice towards us, not to twist the truth of reality of the occupation by pretending that it is a battle against terrorism. The roots of "terrorism" are in the human injustice committed and in the evil of the occupation. These must be removed if there be a sincere intention to remove "terrorism." We call on the people of Israel to be our partners in peace and not in the cycle of interminable violence. Let us resist evil together, the evil of occupation and the infernal cycle of violence.

5. Our word to our brothers and sisters

5.1 We all face, today, a way that is blocked and a future that promises only woe. Our word to all our Christian brothers and sisters is a word of hope, patience, steadfastness and new action for a better future. Our word is that we, as Christians we carry a message, and we will continue to carry it despite the thorns, despite blood and daily difficulties. We place our hope in God, who will grant us relief in His own time. At the same time, we continue to act in concord with God and God's will, building, resisting evil and bringing closer the day of justice and peace.

5.2 We say to our Christian brothers and sisters: This is a time for repentance. Repentance brings us back into the communion of love with everyone who suffers, the prisoners, the wounded, those afflicted with temporary or permanent handicaps, the children who cannot live their childhood and each one who mourns a dear one. The communion of love says to every believer in spirit and in truth: if my brother is a prisoner I am a prisoner; if his home is destroyed, my home is destroyed; when my brother is killed, then I too am killed. We face the same challenges and share in all that has happened and will happen. Perhaps, as individuals or as heads of Churches, we were silent when we should have raised our voices to condemn the injustice and share in the suffering. This is a time of repentance for our silence, indifference, lack of communion, either because we did not persevere in our mission in this land and abandoned it, or because we did not think and do enough to reach a new and integrated vision and remained divided, contradicting our witness and weakening our word. Repentance for our concern with our institutions, sometimes at the expense of our mission, thus silencing the prophetic voice given by the Spirit to the Churches.

5.3 We call on Christians to remain steadfast in this time of trial, just as we have throughout the centuries, through the changing succession of states and governments. Be patient, steadfast and full of hope so that you might fill the heart of every one of your brothers or sisters who shares in this same trial with hope. *"Always be ready to make your defence to anyone who demands from you an accounting for the hope that is in you"* (1 Pet. 3:15). Be active and, provided this conforms to love, participate in any sacrifice that resistance asks of you to overcome our present travail.

5.4 Our numbers are few but our message is great and important. Our land is in urgent need of love. Our love is a message to the Muslim and to the Jew, as well as to the world.

5.4.1 Our message to the Muslims is a message of love and of living together and a call to reject fanaticism and extremism. It is also a message to the world that Muslims are neither to be stereotyped as the enemy nor caricatured as terrorists but rather to be lived with in peace and engaged with in dialogue.

5.4.2 Our message to the Jews tells them: Even though we have fought one another in the recent past and still struggle today, we are able to love and live together. We can organize our political life, with all its complexity, according to the logic of this love and its power, after ending the occupation and establishing justice.

5.4.3 The word of faith says to anyone engaged in political activity: human beings were not made for hatred. It is not permitted to hate, neither is it permitted to kill or to be killed. The culture of love is the culture of accepting the other. Through it we perfect ourselves and the foundations of society are established.

6. Our word to the Churches of the world

6.1 Our word to the Churches of the world is firstly a word of gratitude for the solidarity you have shown toward us in word, deed and presence among us. It is a word of praise for the many Churches and Christians who support the right of the Palestinian people for self determination. It is a message of solidarity with those Christians and Churches who have suffered because of their advocacy for law and justice.

However, it is also a call to repentance; to revisit fundamentalist theological positions that support certain unjust political options with regard to the Palestinian people. It is a call to stand alongside the oppressed and preserve the word of God as good news for all rather than to turn it into a weapon with which to slay the oppressed. The word of God is a word of love for all His creation. God is not the ally of one against the other, nor the opponent of one in the face of the other. God is the Lord of all and loves all, demanding justice from all and issuing to all of us the same commandments. We ask our sister Churches not to offer a theological cover-up for the injustice we suffer, for the sin of the occupation imposed upon us. Our question to our brothers and sisters in the Churches today is: Are you able to help us get our freedom back, for this is the only way you can help the two peoples attain justice, peace, security and love?

6.2 In order to understand our reality, we say to the Churches: Come and see. We will fulfil our role to make known to you the truth of our reality, receiving you as pilgrims coming to us to pray, carrying a message of peace, love and reconciliation. You will know the facts and the people of this land, Palestinians and Israelis alike.

6.3 We condemn all forms of racism, whether religious or ethnic, including anti-Semitism and Islamophobia, and we call on you to condemn it and oppose it in all its manifestations. At the same time we call on you to say a word of truth and to take a position of truth with regard to Israel's occupation of Palestinian land. As we have already said, we see boycott and disinvestment as tools of non violence for justice, peace and security for all.

7. Our word to the international community

7. Our word to the international community is to stop the principle of "double standards" and insist on the international resolutions regarding the Palestinian problem with regard to all parties. Selective application of international law threatens to leave us vulnerable to a law of the jungle. It legitimizes the claims by certain armed groups and states that the international community only understands the logic of force. Therefore, we call for a response to what the civil and religious institutions have proposed, as mentioned earlier: the beginning of a system of economic sanctions and boycott to be applied against Israel. We repeat once again that this is not revenge but rather a serious action in order to reach a just and definitive peace that will put an end to Israeli occupation of Palestinian and other Arab territories and will guarantee security and peace for all.

8. Jewish and Muslim religious leaders

8. Finally, we address an appeal to the religious and spiritual leaders, Jewish and Muslim, with whom we share the same vision that every human being is created by God and has been given equal dignity. Hence the obligation for each of us to defend the oppressed and the dignity God has bestowed on them. Let us together try to rise up above the political positions that have failed so far and continue to lead us on the path of failure and suffering.

9. A call to our Palestinian people and to the Israelis

9.1 This is a call to see the face of God in each one of God's creatures and overcome the barriers of fear or race in order to establish a constructive dialogue and not remain within the cycle of never-ending manoeuvres that aim to keep the situation as it is. Our appeal is to reach a common vision, built on equality and sharing, not on superiority, negation of the other or aggression, using the pretext of fear and security. We say that love is possible and mutual trust is possible. Thus, peace is possible and definitive reconciliation also. Thus, justice and security will be attained for all.

9.2 Education is important. Educational programs must help us to get to know the other as he or she is rather than through the prism of conflict, hostility or religious fanaticism. The educational programs in place today are infected with this hostility. The time has come to begin a new education that allows one to see the face of God in the other and declares that we are capable of loving each other and building our future together in peace and security.

9.3 Trying to make the state a religious state, Jewish or Islamic, suffocates the state, confines it within narrow limits, and transforms it into a state that practices discrimination and exclusion, preferring one citizen over another. We appeal to both religious Jews and Muslims: let the state be a state for all its citizens, with a vision constructed on respect for religion but also equality, justice, liberty and respect for pluralism and not on domination by a religion or a numerical majority.

9.4 To the leaders of Palestine we say that current divisions weaken all of us and cause more sufferings. Nothing can justify these divisions. For the good of the people, which must outweigh that of the political parties, an end must be put to division. We appeal to the international community to lend its support towards this union and to respect the will of the Palestinian people as expressed freely.

9.5 Jerusalem is the foundation of our vision and our entire life. She is the city to which God gave a particular importance in the history of humanity. She is the city towards which all people are in movement—and where they will meet in friendship and love in the presence of the One Unique God, according to the vision of the prophet Isaiah: *"In days to come the mountain of the Lord's house shall be established as the highest of the mountains, and shall be raised above the hills; all the nations shall stream to it (. . .) He shall judge between the nations, and shall arbitrate for many peoples; they shall beat their swords into ploughshares, and their spears into pruning hooks; nation shall not lift up sword against nation, neither shall they learn war any more"* (Is. 2: 2–5). Today, the city is inhabited by two peoples of three religions; and it is on this prophetic vision and on the international resolutions concerning the totality of Jerusalem that any political solution must be based. This is the first issue that should be negotiated because the recognition of Jerusalem's sanctity and its message will be a source of inspiration towards finding a solution to the entire problem, which is largely a problem of mutual trust and ability to set in place a new land in this land of God.

10. Hope and faith in God

10. In the absence of all hope, we cry out our cry of hope. We believe in God, good and just. We believe that God's goodness will finally triumph over the evil of hate and of death that still persist in our land. We will see here "a new land" and "a new human being," capable of rising up in the spirit to love each one of his or her brothers and sisters.

Appendix Two

After Zionism

Claiming the Heart of the Church

Mark Braverman

Mark Braverman serves on the Advisory Board of Friends of Sabeel North America and is National Program Director for Kairos USA. He is the author of A Wall in Jerusalem: Hope, Healing, and the Struggle for Justice in Israel and Palestine *(Jericho Books, 2013) and* Fatal Embrace: Christians, Jews, and the Search for Peace in the Holy Land *(New York: Beaufort Books, 2011).*

In conversations about the conflict between the State of Israel and the Palestinians, I often find myself pointing out that this is not a religious conflict. Rather, it is a human rights struggle—about land, water, freedom of movement, and self-determination. I make the point because the narratives asserting an age-old (and by implication everlasting) enmity between Jews and Arabs (and here we must note the common conflation of "Arab" with "Muslim") are brought forward to obscure the fact that the current struggle is not about religion but is the inevitable result of the oppression of one group by another—in this case the dispossession of the indigenous Palestinians by the State of Israel beginning in 1948 and continuing to this day. It is also the case, however, that because of the upheaval in Christian theology that took place in the aftermath of the near-extermination of the Jews of

Europe in the mid-twentieth century and the equally intense theological and identity issues raised for Jews in the post-Nazi era, it can be said that historic Palestine today is the place where religion and politics meet. The present volume demonstrates this vividly.

As Canon Naim Ateek writes in his postscript, "Zionism *is* the problem," not only politically but theologically—in his words "a doctrine that fosters both political and *theological* injustice."[1] As the ideological and political basis for an ethnic nationalist state, Zionism has become the source of the most longstanding and systematic violation of human rights in the world today, and, many would claim, the epicenter of world conflict. Rabbi Brant Rosen makes the case in this volume that the actions of the State of Israel present an ethical and spiritual crisis for Jews, requiring nothing short of a fundamental reevaluation of the relationship of God to the Jewish people and of the nature of Jewish identity.[2] It is equally true that the institutional church on a global basis must reevaluate its relationship to the State of Israel, the Jewish people, and the Palestinians. Because of the nature of the interfaith discourse and the theological challenge presented by the Israel-Palestine conflict, the plight of the Palestinians presents us not only with an urgent human rights situation but also with a struggle for the heart of the Gospel and the true nature of the church. What we are seeing with the publication of the *Kairos Palestine* document in 2009[3] and the global church-based *kairos* movement that has emerged in response is a call to the church to realize its potential as a force for justice, societal transformation, and political change. That is why this volume is so timely.

An Interfaith Conundrum

Dominating the current discourse on Israel and Palestine is the attitude of Christians, on individual and institutional levels, about their relationship with the Jewish community. As Don Wagner points out, for Paul Tillich, Krister Stendahl, Reinhold Niebuhr, and the American-born theologians who followed them, notably Paul van Buren and Franklin Littell, the State of Israel was the answer to the Nazi Holocaust.[4] The deep and wide-ranging philojudaism that arose among Christian scholars and writers in the aftermath of World War II served as both a renunciation of and atonement

1. Ateek, "A Concluding Theological Postscript," pp. 218 and 220 in the present volume.

2. Rosen, Chapter Three in the present volume.

3. The *Kairos Palestine* document is reproduced as Appendix One in this book.

4. Wagner, Chapter Six in the present volume.

for historic Christian anti-Semitism. This movement, which began in the German Protestant church in the postwar years and soon spread to North America, involved a fundamental revision in Christian theology, with respect to how the Jewish people and Judaism were viewed, as well as a powerful impulse toward reconciliation with the Jewish people.[5]

A key outcome of this revisionist movement was a conflation of Zionism with Judaism. In the theological realm, a wholesale rejection of supersessionism, also known as replacement theology, brought with it an endorsement of Zionism in what might be termed a "soft eschatology" that asserted that the creation of the State of Israel and the "return" of the Jewish people to their homeland were proof of God's love for the Jewish people. Continuing to the present day, this project of penitence and reconciliation has morphed into an interfaith industry that supports not only a compelling form of Jewish exceptionalism but, ironically, the very same Christian triumphalism that fueled the anti-Jewish sins of the church from its earliest history. What we have in the current support of the institutional church for the State of Israel as the Jewish state and in the varied forms of Christian Zionism to be found across the theological spectrum is a potent Judeo-Christian triumphalism, and its language is Zionism.

This embrace of Zionism as inextricably linked to Judaism and Jewish identity and as necessary for Jewish survival is a key component of the unwritten rules now governing the Jewish-Christian interfaith conversation. The effect of supersessionism having been now turned on its head is that Christians' hands are tied when it comes to witness and activism with respect to Israel and the Palestinians. This holds true in the seminaries, from the pulpits, in Christian media, and in the headquarters of the major denominations. It also provides a theological platform for Jewish defenders of Israel, not only those in the employ of Jewish organizations but those holding prominent positions in seminaries and other institutions of higher learning.

The Gospels at Stake

Amy-Jill Levine is Professor of New Testament Studies at Vanderbilt Divinity School. As a Jewish scholar at a Protestant seminary, her authority in the area of Christian-Jewish relations is unchallenged. Levine presents her views on Christian-Jewish relations in her 2006 book, *The Misunderstood Jew: The Church and the Scandal of the Jewish Jesus*. The stated purpose of the book is to challenge the depiction of Jesus as one who stood in opposition to the

---

5. See Braverman, *Fatal Embrace*.

priestly and monarchical leadership in Jerusalem. Levine argues that this is a Christian view that erases Jesus's Jewishness and promotes the distorted picture of Judaism that became the basis for Christian anti-Semitism. Levine thus views Jesus through the lens of the painful history of Christian-Jewish relations. She is committed to rehabilitating first-century Judaism by presenting the picture of "a quite observant Jesus" in tune with the Judaism of his time.[6] This argument has important implications for interfaith discourse today. In asking us to look at the Jesus who was used as a way to persecute Jews through the centuries rather than the Jesus who stood up to the Jewish power structure's betrayal of Jewish values, Levine has changed the subject from Jewish responsibility to Jewish suffering. Her bid to recover what she characterizes as Jesus's Jewishness in the service of continuing the fight against anti-Semitism—and her significant influence in interfaith circles as well as in the education of Christian clergy—is an important example of how one particular Jewish perspective, presenting itself as the *only* legitimate Jewish perspective, has come to dominate the interfaith conversation.

The publication of the 2009 *Kairos Palestine* document, with its appeal from Palestinian Christians to American Christians to "come and see" their plight, helped mobilize the "anti-delegitimization" campaign discussed by Don Wagner in this volume, specifically the formation of the Israel Action Network (IAN), a well-financed organization dedicated to neutralizing negative attitudes about Israel among Americans.[7] Jewish scholars, working closely with Jewish denominations and advocacy groups, have lent their voices to this effort, in particular by charging Palestinian Christian theologians with anti-Semitism. As the voice of Palestinian Christians becomes more prominent in the United States, through study of the *Kairos Palestine* document, the publication in 2012 of the U.S. Kairos document "Call to Action, a U.S. Response to the *Kairos Palestine* Document," and the work of Friends of Sabeel North America as well as denominational and church-linked grassroots organizations throughout the United States, the efforts of the IAN and similar groups have intensified, their message becoming more pointedly targeted at Palestinian Christian theology. Christians are being warned, through websites, website telecasts, and public education events, that *Kairos Palestine* is not only anti-Semitic but *is in error theologically*, because of what is claimed falsely to be its anti-Jewish theology and anti-Israel bias. In this view, the Palestinian Christians, pursuing their own, clearly anti-Israel and thus anti-Semitic agenda, are to be disqualified as fellow Christians in need, crying out for unity with the body of Christ outside

6. Levine, *The Misunderstood Jew*, 181.

7. Wagner, Chapter Six in the present volume.

Palestine. What is notable here is that these Jewish scholars are not simply articulating a point of view, but they are presuming to instruct Christians on *their (Christians') own theology.* In this, they have been assisted by prominent Christian theologians and church leaders who have acceded to the unwritten rule that Jewish sensibilities and the Jewish perspective (as defined by some Jews for all Jews) trump all other considerations with respect to Zionism and the State of Israel. Krister Stendahl exemplified this dramatically in his caution to Christians against coming between the Jews and their national homeland project in a 1981 interview in the *Christian Science Monitor* in which he urged Christians never to "break the first rule of dialogue: Listen to how the other party defines itself."[8]

There is much more at stake, therefore, than the church's support for Palestinian human rights. South African theologian Allen Boesak put it this way in a recent essay entitled "Kairos Consciousness":

> There are those Christians, and sometimes whole hierarchies of churches, who seek to use the Bible, the tradition and theology to serve and protect to the detriment of the poor, the weak and the vulnerable. On the other side of the conflict are those with a Kairos consciousness—who understand God's call as a call to commit themselves to justice and the liberation of the oppressed. . . . Much more than only the liberation of the oppressed is at stake here . . . the integrity of the Gospel, and the credibility of the witness of the church are at stake here. The moment of truth is a moment to act for the sake of justice and humanity, but also *for the sake of the integrity of the Gospel.*"[9]

Beyond Interfaith Dialogue: Toward a Prophetic Theology

Boesak's point is central to the present volume's call for "a new conversation on justice and peace in Palestine and Israel."[10] The urgent issue confronting us today is not anti-Semitism. It is, rather, whether we will commit our efforts to the expansion of empire or to the building of community, to tolerating and even supporting tyranny or to committing ourselves to equality on a global level. The Christians and Jews who attack the *Kairos Palestine* document and the global movement of discipleship that it has spawned are more interested in detecting evidence of replacement theology and anything that

8. Verduin, "Praiseworthy Intentions," 148.

9. Boesak, "Kairos Consciousness"; emphasis added.

10. Wagner and Davis, "Introduction: A Call for a New Conversation on Justice and Peace in Palestine and Israel," pp. xvii–xxiii in the present volume.

might be connected to the history of Christian anti-Semitism than in confronting the way theology is being used today to justify the dispossession of the Palestinians. This is why efforts such as that of this volume to develop a theology for our times are so urgently needed. As the voices calling for justice—secular as well as from the faith community—increase, the forces gathering to oppose this movement will also gain in force. And much of this battle will be fought on theological grounds.

The work to forge bonds of trust and reconciliation between the faith communities is important and must continue. Anti-Semitism still exists, and Islamophobia is pervasive and may in fact be on the increase. But the struggle for justice for Palestine is not an interfaith issue. The Christian and Jewish communities are each presented with important, indeed critical, opportunities. For Jews, as so powerfully articulated by Brant Rosen in this volume, the challenge is to let go of our preoccupation with our own suffering and, leaving behind our fear and our focus on self-protection, in Rosen's words "understand Jewish values as universal values and connect Jewish liberation with the liberation of all nations."[11] For Christians it is to claim the heart of the Gospels as expressed in Matthew 25, putting compassion for the most vulnerable above other considerations, even when this priority puts treasured relationships at risk. Christians must learn to withstand the accusations that they have betrayed their commitment to interfaith reconciliation and even outright charges of anti-Semitism. Do we really believe that the deeply felt Christian penitence over anti-Semitism is now being replaced by a resurgence of anti-Jewish feeling? Far from it. Indeed, Christian awareness of historic sins has never been more acute. What is being swept aside, rather, is sinful inaction and muzzling in the face of actions that violate not only the Palestinians' dignity and ties to their own homeland but the humanity and the dreams of freedom for which the original Jewish settlers of what is now Israel sacrificed with such courage and idealism.

This commitment to justice on the part of Christians on local, denominational, and national levels, in concert with Jewish, Muslim, and secular partners, is being carried out in many forms of nonviolent direct action, including political advocacy, divestment of church funds from companies profiting from the occupation of Palestinian lands, and increasingly, in countering the theology that is being used to justify the oppression of one people by another. This has begun on all five continents—in the academy and in the global network of *kairos* organizations that is arising in response to the Palestinian call.[12] Alongside the global and grassroots efforts of local

11. Rosen, chapter 3, p. 71 in this volume.

12. For a listing of national *kairos* organizations and statements, see http://www.

and congregation-based education is the recent appearance of *kairos* studies in seminaries, graduate studies departments, and symposia and conferences, most recently in South Africa, Palestine, the United Kingdom, the United States, Germany, the Netherlands, and South Korea. This is a highly significant development and must be energetically supported. The success of a global movement for justice in Israel and Palestine requires an academy no longer captive to invisible "red lines" that block the development of a prophetic theology to take us into a new era of coexistence.

Bibliography

Boesak, Allan. "Kairos Consciousness." *Kairos Southern Africa* (March 25, 2011) n.p. http://kairossouthernafrica.wordpress.com/kairos-consciousness/.

Braverman, Mark. *Fatal Embrace: Christians, Jews, and the Search for Peace in the Holy Land.* New York: Beaufort, 2011.

Levine, Amy-Jill. *The Misunderstood Jew: The Church and the Scandal of the Jewish Jesus.* New York: HarperCollins, 2006.

Verduin, Paul. "Praiseworthy Intentions, Unintended Consequences: Why Krister Stendahl's Quest for 'Healthy Relations' between Jews and Christians Ended Tragically." In *Zionism through Christian Lenses,* edited by Carole Monica Burnett, 132–61. Eugene, OR: Wipf & Stock, 2013.

kairospalestine.ps/?q=content/news-global-kairos.

Permissions

Permissions for Quotations
from Sacred Texts

The Scripture quotation in Chapter Two, by Walter T. Davis and Pauline Coffman, is from the New King James Version®. Copyright © 1982 by Thomas Nelson, Inc. Used by permission. All rights reserved.

Scripture quotations in Brant Rosen's essay, Chapter Three, are reprinted from the *Tanakh: The Holy Scriptures* by permission of the University of Nebraska Press. Copyright 1985, 1999 by the Jewish Publication Society.

Scripture quotations in Chapters Four, Five, and Seven, that is, in the essays by Carole Monica Burnett, Rosemary and Herman Ruether, and Gary M. Burge, are taken from Revised Standard Version of the Bible, copyright 1952 [2nd edition, 1971] by the Division of Christian Education of the National Council of the Churches of Christ in the United States of America. Used by permission. All rights reserved.

Scripture quotations in Chapter Six, by Donald E. Wagner, are taken from the New Revised Standard Version Bible, copyright 1989, Division of Christian Education of the National Council of the Churches of Christ in the United States of America. Used by permission. All rights reserved.

Quotations from The Holy Qur'an in Mustafa Abu Sway's essay (Chapter Eight) are from The Holy Qur'an, Meaning Translated by Aminah Assami, *et al.* Jeddah: Sahih International/Abu-Qasim Publishing, 1997.

In Chapter Eight, by Mustafa Abu Sway, the Scripture quotation comes from the HOLY BIBLE, NEW INTERNATIONAL VERSION©. Copyright © 1973, 1978, 1984 by International Bible Society. Used by permission of Zondervan. All rights reserved.

The Scripture quotation in Naim S. Ateek's postscript is taken from the Contemporary English Version © 1991, 1992, 1995 by American Bible Society. Used by Permission.

Other Permission

Approximately ten pages have been reprinted from the book *Whose Land? Whose Promise? What Christians Are Not Being Told About Israel and the Palestinians,* by Gary M. Burge (Cleveland: Pilgrim, 2004). All rights reserved. Used by permission.

Printed in Great Britain
by Amazon